Latin@s in the World-System

LATIN@S IN THE WORLD-SYSTEM
Decolonization Struggles in the Twenty-First Century U.S. Empire

edited by
Ramón Grosfoguel, Nelson Maldonado-Torres, and
José David Saldívar

Political Economy of the World-System Annuals, Volume XXVIII
Immanuel Wallerstein, Series Editor

Paradigm Publishers
Boulder • London

Copyright © 2005 by Paradigm Publishers

Published in the United States by Paradigm Publishers, 3360 Mitchell Lane, Suite C, Boulder, Colorado 80301 USA.

Paradigm Publishers is the trade name of Birkenkamp & Company, LLC, Dean Birkenkamp, President and Publisher.

Library of Congress Cataloging-in-Publication Data

Latin@s in the world-system : decolonization struggles in the twenty-first
century U.S. empire / edited by Ramón Grosfoguel, Nelson Maldonado-Torres,
and José David Saldívar.
p. cm. — (Political economy of the world-system annuals ; v. 28)
Includes bibliographical references and index.
ISBN 978-1-59451-135-6 (hardcover : alk. paper)   ISBN 978-1-59451-136-3 (pbk.)
1. United States—Civilization—Hispanic influences. 2. Hispanic
Americans. 3. Decolonization—United States. I. Grosfoguel, Ramón. II.
Maldonado Torres, Nelson. III. Saldívar, José David. IV. Series.
E169.12.L347 2005
305.868'073'09051—dc22

2005008327

Printed and bound in the United States of America on acid-free paper that meets the standards of the American National Standard for Permanence of Paper for Printed Library Materials.

Designed and Typeset by Straight Creek Bookmakers.

11 10 09 08
2 3 4 5

Contents

PART V Decolonizing Spiritualities

PART VI Latinization and Decolonization

PART I

Introduction

Latin@s and the "Euro-American Menace"

The Decolonization of the U.S. Empire in the Twenty-First Century

*Ramón Grosfoguel, Nelson Maldonado-Torres, and
José David Saldívar*

Immanuel Wallerstein (1991; 1998) characterizes the beginning of the twenty-first century as a transitional moment, a bifurcation toward the end not only of U.S. hegemony but also of the present historical system. According to Wallerstein, during the twenty-first century we will witness the demise of the U.S. empire and of capitalism as a world-system. Both are in terminal crisis (Wallerstein 1991; 2003). This historical system has lasted for more than 500 years. Moreover, according to Wallerstein (1991), we will witness a bifurcation toward a new historical system. Depending on our social agencies and interventions in this moment of bifurcation, the transition toward a new historical system could lead either to a better or to a worse system than the present one. Nothing is predetermined nor guaranteed about the future. There could be a fairer, just and egalitarian historical system or a more exploitative and coercive one. If Wallerstein (1998) is correct in this assessment, then we need to urgently rethink our utopias in order to create alternative worlds.

As Immanuel Wallerstein has shown in his historical sociology, the transition from feudalism to the modern/colonial world in Europe was not as the Marxist and liberal narratives have represented it: a bourgeois class that emerged in the cities and displaced through reforms or revolutions the feudal aristocracy (Wallerstein 1974, 1979). Rather, it was the same feudal aristocracy that in looking for a solution to the crisis of the old system created a new historical system; namely, the "European modern/colonial capitalist/patriarchal world-system" (Grosfoguel 2004). Wallerstein's provocative thesis is that the new historical system that emerged in the late fifteenth century was worse; that is, less egalitarian, more destructive of nature and more discriminatory than the old system it replaced (Wallerstein 1991). Can this scenario repeat itself? In recent work, Wallerstein suggests that similar to the transition between the previous historical system and the modern/colonial world in the late fifteenth century, today we are facing a moment of bifurcation. And like before, such a moment opens up new historical possibilities. Among those possibilities, one cannot rule out that the twenty-first-century-transnational capitalist elites will follow a strategy similar to the feudal aristocracy of the late fifteenth century and may create a new historical system worse than the one in which we live, in order to maintain their privileges. Another possible scenario is that subaltern groups around the globe—those to whom Fanon referred as the *condemned of the earth*—effectively mobilize and help to create a new and/or diverse historical system better than the one in which we live now. To be sure, there are many other possible scenarios on the horizon of historical possibility. The power of political and religious fundamentalisms, as they are clearly manifested today in the actions of Western state leaders and "sworn enemies of the West," cannot be underestimated. The "clash of fundamentalism," as Tariq Ali has referred to them (2002), gives new impulse to old colonial legacies and not so old racist configurations of society. Subjects who find themselves in the interior of states or regions under the power or strong influence of such ideologies sometime comply, sometime oppose, but many times simply do whatever is necessary to survive. Just like one cannot underestimate the strength and influence of the fabrication of new ideologies of war by the world's new fundamentalists and their allies, one cannot lose from view the decolonizing potential of multiple projects and demographic changes in many parts of the globe, including the very metropolitan centers that have taken the lead in designing a twenty-first-century ideology of war. Transformations in the metropolitan centers of the capitalist world-system are crucial for future transformations, including any possible bifurcation. One of these transformations is the significant growth and political/cultural impact of Latin@ populations within the United States, the most powerful core country in the capitalist world-system today. We will examine here the topic of the growth of the Latin@ population in the United States in light of the global context of world-systemic changes as well as in relation to the continuous efforts to decolonize the U.S. nation and empire.

Latin@s and the Decolonization of the U.S. Empire

In the year 2000, non-Hispanic whites were a demographic minority in 70 percent of the U.S. cities while Latin@s were the fastest growing population. Latin@ populations increased 50 percent between 1990 and 2000. The majority are working class and racialized subjects (Chican@s, Salvadoreans, Puerto Ricans, Dominicans, indigenous People, Afro-Latin@s, etc.) coming from colonial and neocolonial experiences in the periphery of the world-economy. They are among the groups with the worst poverty rates in the country (see Table 1). Today the Latin@

Table 1. Poverty Status of People in 2001 by Household Relationship, Race, and Hispanic Origin (numbers in thousands)

	All Races	White, not of Hispanic Origin	Blacks	Hispanics
Total Individuals	281,475	194,538	35,871	37,312
-% below poverty	11.7	7.8	22.7	21.4
-% above poverty	88.3	92.2	77.3	78.6
Married Couple	182,212	133,990	1,234	23,544
-% below poverty	5.7	3.6	8.2	15.3
-% above poverty	94.3	96.4	91.8	84.7
Female Householder, no spouse present	39,261	18,365	4,694	6,830
-% below poverty	28.7	19.9	37.4	37.8
-% above poverty	71.3	81.1	62.6	62.2
Male Householder, no spouse present	12,438	6,823	461	2,736
-% below poverty	13.6	9.9	20.8	17.6
-% above poverty	86.4	90.1	79.2	82.4

Source: U.S. Census Bureau, Current Population Survey, March 2002. Web Page:
http://ferret.bls.census.gov/macro/032002/pov/new04_001.htm

population constitutes the largest minority in the United States: they represent around 12.8 percent of the total population. Conservative estimates made by the U.S. Census of Population in 1998 and based on the 1990 U.S. Census, project that by the year 2060 non-Hispanic whites will be a demographic minority in the U. S. (see Table 2) and Latin@s will be the largest minority in the country (25 percent of the total population). Recent estimates based on the 2000 Census, project that non-Hispanic whites will be half of the U.S. population in 2050 (see Table 3). Alternative estimates suggest that if the Latin@ population continues growing at the same rate of the 1990s, they will represent at least half, if not the majority, of the total population of the United States sometime in the twenty-first century.

These processes posit important challenges that are at the heart of the contemporary debates about the political transformations inside the U.S. empire and the future transformation of the world-system toward a new historical system. A struggle for the decolonization of the U.S. empire is at the center of the agenda for the twenty-first century. Decolonization has been traditionally used to characterize the transition from colonial administrations to the formation of independent states in peripheral regions of the world-economy. Part of the Eurocentric myth is that we live in a so-called postcolonial era and that the world and, in particular, metropolitan centers, are in no need of decolonization. In this conventional story, coloniality is reduced to the presence of colonial administrations. However, as the work of Peruvian sociologist Aníbal Quijano (1993, 1998, 2000) has shown with his "coloniality of power" perspective, we still live in a colonial world and we need to break away from the narrow ways of thinking about colonial relations, in order to accomplish the unfinished and incomplete twentieth-century dream of decolonization (Grosfoguel 2005).

The Coloniality of Power and Latin@ Migrants' Incorporation

Latin@s are by no means a homogeneous group. They come from different regions and countries. Some of them did not have to move anywhere in order to suddenly find themselves within the entrails of the United States. One must not assume any kind of allegiance or common perspective among Spanish-speaking peoples and descendents of Spanish-speaking peoples in this country. Some of them identify themselves in relation to their country, others highlight the specificity of their history and situation within the United States (e.g., some Puerto Ricans, Cubans, and Chican@s), while others like Afro-Latin@s and Indo-Latin@s continually find themselves excluded from discourses that identify Latinoness with brownness, a notion that tends to privilege whiteness

Table 2. Projections of the Resident Population by Race, Hispanic Origin and Nativity: Middle Series, 2000 to 2070 (numbers in thousands consistent with the 1990 estimates base)

	2000	2050	2055	2060	2070
USA	275,306	403,686	417,477	432,010	463,639
Non-Hispanic Whites	71.4%	52.8%	51.1%	49.6%	46.8%
Hispanics	11.8%	24.3%	25.5%	26.6%	28.6%
Non-Hispanic Blacks	12.2%	13.2%	13.3%	13.3%	13.2%
Non-Hispanic Asian and Pacific Islanders	3.9%	8.9%	9.3%	9.8%	10.6%
Non-Hispanic American Indians	0.7%	0.8%	0.8%	0.8%	0.8%

Source: National Population Projections, I. Summary Files, Total Population by Race, Hispanic Origin, and Nativity: (NP-T5) Projections of the Resident Population by Race, Hispanic Origin, and Nativity: Middle Series, 1999 to 2100. Population Projections Program, Population Division, U.S. Census Bureau. 1998. Web page: http://www.census.gov/population/www/projections/natsum-T5.html Internet Release Date: January 13, 2000.

Table 3. Projected Population of the United States, by Race and Hispanic Origin:
2000 to 2050 (in thousands as of July 1 Resident Population)

	2000	2050
USA Total Population	282,125	419,854
Non-Hispanic Whites	69.4%	50.1%
Hispanics	12.8%	24.4%

Source: U.S. Census Bureau, 2004, "U.S. Interim Projections by Age, Sex, Race, and Hispanic Origin," http://www.census.gov/ipc/www/usinterimproj/. Internet Release Date: March 18, 2004.

over indigeneity and blackness. These groups either consciously resist or simply find it very difficult to be recognized as "Hispanic" or even "Latin@." At the same time, there are also those who adopt the "Latin@" label to highlight historical experiences and a social situation that connect and can potentially mobilize politically Spanish-speaking peoples and descendents of Spanish-speaking peoples in this country. For us, any critique or recuperation of the notion of "Latin@" needs to consider the complex ways in which race and ethnicity combine with colonization and migration to produce a neocolonial situation within the United States that affect Spanish-speaking peoples and descendents of Spanish-speaking peoples in this country. One important and often neglected factor is the differential mode of incorporation of migrants and minorities in metropolitan societies.

In order to understand the transnational processes of migrant and minority incorporation into the metropolitan societies, it is important to make some conceptual distinctions among diverse migration experiences. The application of the "coloniality of power" perspective to migration studies would allow us to come up with a different conceptualization from the rest of the literature. Migrants do not arrive to an empty or neutral space. Rather, migrants arrive to metropolitan spaces that are already "polluted" by a colonial history, a colonial imaginary, colonial knowledges, a racial/ethnic hierarchy linked to a history of empire. That is, migrants arrive to a space of power relations that is already informed and constituted by coloniality. There is no neutral space of migrant incorporation. If we apply the coloniality perspective to the history of U.S. migration studies we would need to distinguish between three types of transnational migrants: "colonial/racial subjects of empire," "colonial immigrants" and "immigrants" (Grosfoguel 2003). Latin@s are no exception to this history. Within the Latin@ category there are multiple experiences of incorporation inside the United States.

"Colonial/racial subjects of empire" are those subjects that are inside the empire as part of a long colonial history that included racial slavery such as African Americans, Native Americans, Chicanos, Puerto Ricans, Pacific Islanders, Filipinos, Chinese Americans, etc. The metropolitan colonial imaginary, racial/ethnic hierarchy and racist discourses are frequently constructed in relation to these colonial subjects. They arrived to the United States or the United States "arrived" to them as part of a colonization process that gave wealth and privileges to Euro-Americans. There is a long history of racialization and inferiorization toward "colonial/racial subjects of the empire" that informs the present power relations of the U.S. empire. The "coloniality of power" of the metropolitan country is organized around and against these colonial subjects with a long history inside the empire. Colonial subjects are frequently at the bottom of the racial/ethnic hierarchy.

In the conceptualization used here, "immigrants" are those migrants that are racialized as "white" (other European migrants such as British, Dutch, Germans, French, Italians, Polish, Jewish, Irish, etc., or migrants coming from other regions of the world but from European origin such as Euro-Australians, Euro-Latin@s, Euro-Africans, etc.) and that experience upward social mobility in the first, second or third generation. These are migrants who, once they adopt the metropolitan language, accent, demeanors and manners, are assimilated, within the public domain, to the dominant metropolitan populations. They pass as "whites" or are constructed as "honorary whites." These migrants are composed of the following: European migrants that after one or two generations become incorporated into the mainstream as "white"; Japanese executives that are invited as "honorary whites"; or the 1960s cohort of Cuban anti-communist refugees who, through a combination of U.S. foreign policy and federal government policies, were transformed into a Cold War showcase and incorporated as "honorary whites" in Miami (Grosfoguel 2003).

"Colonial immigrants" are those migrants coming from peripheral neo-colonial locations in the capitalist world-economy that, although they were never directly colonized by the metropolitan country to which they migrate, at the time of arrival were "racialized" in similar ways to the "colonial/racial subjects of empire" that were already there for a longer time. We refer here to the "Puertoricanization" of Dominicans in New York City, the "Chicanoization" of Salvadoreans in Los Angeles, the "Africanamericanization" of Haitians and Afro-Cuban marielitos in Miami, the "Algerianization" of Turks in Paris, the "Antillanization" of Dominicans in Amsterdam, the "Arabenization" of Dominicans in Madrid, the "Antillanization" of Moroccans in Amsterdam, the "Afrocaribbeanization" of Africans in London and so on. When racist discourses constructed toward the "colonial/racial subjects of empire" are transferred to the recently arrived migrants from the periphery, we have the reproduction of the experience of "colonial immigrants." Thus, many migrants from the formally "independent" Caribbean, Central American and South American countries become "colonial immigrants" in the United States, even though they are not directly colonized by the metropolis to which they migrate and they have class backgrounds that are higher than the "colonial migrants" that are part of the colonial/racial subjects of empire. However, it is important to mention that many of these migrants arrived to the United States as part of direct U.S.

military interventions, such as Dominicans, or as part of U.S. indirect military interventions in support of military dictators such as Guatemalans and Salvadoreans (Grosfoguel 2003). During the Cold War, the U.S. government fostered mass migration in those countries where U.S. military support or direct interventions was needed to support or to establish a "friendly" anticommunist pro-U.S. dictatorship. These served two purposes: to use migration as a safety valve for political stability inside those countries and to provide the U.S. labor market with a pool of non-European cheap labor from the South.

The conceptualization provided here is a response to the "immigrant analogy" that informs many migration studies. The "immigrant analogy" takes as a point of reference the successful European migration experience and extrapolates this experience to the rest of the migrant groups. Consequently, if a migrant group is not as successful as the European migrants, it is accounted for by a "cultural" problem inside the migrant community (Glazer and Moynihan 1963). By flattening down the diverse modes of incorporation and experiences of migrant groups with a cultural reductionist argument, the hegemonic population in the racial/ethnic hierarchy avoids confronting their own racist discrimination and colonial legacies.

Something similar could happen with the recent migration theories such as the transnationalist approach (Basch et. al. 1993). Although in the transnationalist literature, the "immigrant analogy" based on the early European migration to the United States is avoided and has a more complex understanding of the dynamics of race, class and gender, it still falls into a form of "immigrant analogy from the South." In this case, the "immigrant analogy" is that of a Third World migrant who circulates between two nation-states and whose political, cultural and identity allegiances are divided between two nations. This is not a rejection of the transnationalist approach but a call for a more sophisticated understanding of the transnationalist migratory experience in relation to colonial legacies. The transnationalist literature has challenged the most static models of migration that kept thinking in terms of a unidirectional mobility from the sending to the host society. In the transnationalist literature there is a more complex and multidirectional immigrant interaction between country of origin and country of arrival. Migrants do not only circulate themselves but they also circulate money, commodities, and resources across borders. This has important implications in terms of the migrants' identification processes, political strategies, and economic survival. The old way of thinking about migration is obsolete today given the compression in time and space. However, despite its important insights, the lack of a notion of "coloniality" and the multiple migrant distinctions that it implies could lead the transnationalist literature to a kind of "immigrant analogy" from a Third World migration experience. It is not an accident that most transnationalist studies of international migration are based on the Caribbean migration experience. The Haitian, Grenadian, and St. Vincentean migration experiences to the United

States were the first case studies used to sustain the new transnationalist paradigm. By not making distinctions between different types of transmigrants in relation to the coloniality of power of the metropolitan center, this literature has the danger of reproducing an "immigrant analogy from the South" as opposed to the "immigrant analogy from the North" of the old migration literature. It could flatten out the diverse experiences and be unable to account for the different processes of migrants' success and failure if it does not incorporate the "coloniality of power" perspective into its approach.

Moreover, a more nuanced distinction among transnational migrants would offset the celebratory transnationalist approach to international migration. The celebratory approach as articulated by Alejandro Portes (1996) looks at transnational migration as a successful strategy of upward mobility. It takes the few success stories of transnational entrepreneurs and makes them a model for transnational migration. It underestimates the "coloniality of power" in the host society as well as in the home countries. Despite the fact that the majority of the transnational migrants from the periphery end up as "colonial immigrants" in the core (Grosfoguel 2003), the celebratory approach to transnational migration overlooks the complex and difficult reality that these migrants confront.

The diverse distinctions of migrant incorporation provided by the "coloniality" perspective are crucial in order to avoid culturalist explanations about the failure or success of migrant groups. These culturalist explanations are complicit with the transnational hegemonic ideology that is very popular in the new forms of "antiracist racisms" in the core of the capitalist world-economy (United States, France, The Netherlands, United Kingdom, Spain, Germany, etc.). This is linked to what has been called "new racism" or "cultural racism."

From Biological Racism to Cultural Racism

A crucial Eurocentric myth in today's world is the argument that colonial structures and racist ideologies are a "problem" of peripheral regions but not of core zones. However, what we see today is the reproduction and consolidation of the old colonial/racial hierarchies of Europeans/Euro-Americans versus non-Europeans and the hegemony of racist ideologies inside each metropolitan center. In order to understand this process we need to link the present racial/ethnic hierarchy to the colonial history of each empire. Otherwise, it makes no sense to question why people coming from colonial or neocolonial experiences keep being at the bottom of the social structures and the targets of metropolitan racism. It is not an accident that in London, Amsterdam, Paris and New York, colonial Caribbean minorities share the bottom of the city's racial/ethnic hierarchy with other colonial/racial subjects of these respective empires. In London, West Indians are together with Pakistanis and Bangladeshis at the bottom of the racial/ethnic hierarchy. In Amsterdam, Dutch Antilleans and

Surinamers share with Moroccans and Turkish the experience of racist oppression. In Paris, French Caribbeans share with Algerians and Senegalese the racial discrimination produced by French colonial racism. In New York's racial/ethnic hierarchy, Mexicans, Dominicans, Puerto Ricans and African Americans share the bottom of the hierarchy while Euro-Americans are at the top. A constant feature of coloniality is that white European/Euro-American groups are always at the top of the racial/ethnic hierarchy despite the changes over time of racist discourses, racial dynamics and the groups that share the bottom of the hierarchy. The same could be said of Latin@s in Los Angeles, Chicago or Philadelphia. Those groups coming from colonial or neocolonial experiences are the ones with the highest poverty rates. Chicano, Puerto Rican, Salvadoran, Guatemalan, and Mexican migrants share the bottom of the racial/ethnic hierarchy of these cities together with African Americans, Native Americans, Filipinos and Pacific Islanders.

There are other migrant groups that, due to their particular class origin, a process of favorable state policies or dominant groups political strategies of "divide and rule," experience upward social mobility very similar to the "immigrant experience" of early century European immigrants. These groups are usually portrayed in the mainstream press as "model minorities." This is the case of migrants coming from Korea, Cuba, Hong Kong and Taiwan. By creating a middle strata of "successful" minority groups (model minorities), the dominant white Euro-American groups can create racial/ethnic symbolic showcases to escape criticism about racial discrimination coming from colonial immigrants and colonial/racial subjects of empire. This contributes to the invisibility of the still persistent racial discrimination in America.

For metropolitan populations racism is invisible. The denial of racism is a common feature of metropolitan discussions about racial minorities. The prevalent ideology is that racism and colonial relations ended after the 1964 Civil Rights Act and are a thing of the past. This invisibility and denial is linked to the transformation of racist discourses from biological racist discourses to cultural racist discourses (Balibar 1991, Gilroy 1993, Essed 1996, Grosfoguel 2003, Fanon 1988).

A major transformation in racist discourses was experienced after the Second World War. We need to make a distinction between those metropolitan countries occupied by the Nazis and those that were not. Metropolitan core powers like France and The Netherlands were directly occupied by the Nazis. Therefore, after the war, biological racist discourses were so associated with the Nazi occupation in the mainstream of these core countries that it was legally forbidden from public discourse. Freedom of speech in France and The Netherlands, for example, does not justify or make legal racist discourses in the public domain against anybody. Nevertheless, racism did not simply disappear. Racism shifted meaning from biological to cultural forms of racism. Cultural racism is a pervasive form of racist discourse in which the word "race" is not even used. Cultural racist discourse uses "culture" as a marker of inferiority and superiority, reinstalling again the same colonial/racial hierarchy of the European/Euro-American colonial expansion. However, cultural racism is indirectly linked to biological racism in that the former naturalizes/essentializes the culture of the "Other" racial/colonial subject.

In Great Britain and the United States, this is a different story. Due to their victory in the Second World War over the Nazis, after the war biological racist discourses continued with "business as usual." The victorious forces were not forced to change their own racist discourses. It took another twenty years for this to happen in both the United States and Great Britain. As a result of the civil rights struggles of the colonial/racial subjects of these empires, laws against racist discrimination were passed in both metropolises: the Civil Rights Act in the United States in 1964 and the Race Relations Act in Britain in 1965. Overt discrimination based on a biological racist discourse was forbidden in both Britain and the United States since the mid-1960s. Like in France and The Netherlands before, this forced a shift in racist discourses from biological racism to cultural racism. Thus, racist discourses did not end there but acquired new forms. Cultural racism became the hegemonic racist discourse in the core of the capitalist world-economy.

The difficulty in the struggle against the new cultural racist discourses is its denial about its own racism. By not using the word "race" in its discourse, cultural racism claims to be nonracist. So, if colonial/racial subjects experience higher unemployment rates, higher poverty rates, higher dropout rates, less quality of education at schools, are paid less for the same jobs as white workers or are always hired in the "dirty" jobs, it is because they are "lazy," "unassimilated," "uneducated," have "bad habits," "bad attitudes," or "unadapted/inadequate culture." By internalizing the "causes" inside the discriminated communities and explaining their social situation in terms of their own cultural features, cultural racist discourses conceal the reproduction of racism and the old colonial/racial hierarchies inside the metropolis. By essentializing and naturalizing cultural features or habits, cultural racism reproduces indirectly a form of biological racist reduction. "Meritocratic" discourses in public spaces and "culture of poverty" discourses in academia contribute to the invisibility and perpetuation of the problem. Metropolitan centers do not have a "minority problem" as it is defined in The Netherlands and Great Britain or an "immigration problem" as it is defined in France and the United States, but a "racist/colonial problem" that needs to be addressed in order to make reality the decolonial claim of equal opportunities for all and to transform into more egalitarian decolonial societies. In other words, the problem is not one of the "unassimilated features" or the cultural differences/deficiencies of non-European migrants as Huntington (2004a, 2004b) would claim nor the unfinished and incomplete project of modernity that metropolitan thinkers such as Jürgen Habermas would claim (Habermas 1987, 1997), but a problem of fulfilling the incomplete and unfinished project of decolonization

(Grosfoguel 2005, Maldonado forthcoming). This project has cultural, socio-logical, and philosophical dimensions that are necessary to explore in detail. Here we concentrate on a set of issues that relate to the question of decolonization in the United States.

U.S. Coloniality of Power

The U.S. coloniality of power is constituted by the supremacy of white males, which is premised first and foremost on the erasure of the significance of indigenous peoples and on the continuous existence of what Franz Fanon called "negrophobia." The founding fathers of the country were all white plantation owners that wrote in the U.S. Constitution an ambiguous and sometimes contradictory set of ideals and norms that merged ideas of freedom and liberty, as lived and desired by the majority of the white settlers, who were themselves the majority in the new independent states (a majority achieved, to be sure, partly through segregation and cleansing), with conceptions of self and society that safeguarded racial and sexual discrimination, exclusion and hatred toward women and minorities. It is true that the ambiguous ideas about freedom and liberty of the white settlers were to some extent in contradiction with the reality of slavery and serfdom, but they were also to some extent consistent with it, which makes any present or future project of decolonization not only one of appropriation of ideas but also one of conceptual creation. The process of decolonization that took place in the Americas in the late eighteenth and early nineteenth centuries was, in this light, an incomplete project. Like many other countries after it, but with the important difference that the "majority" of the population was white, the United States achieved "independence without decolonization"; that is, a "colonial independence" in 1776 with white male elites in ruling positions. These paradoxical terms, used by Quijano to describe the independences of the Americas, refer to the fact that the old colonial/racial hierarchies put in place during several centuries of colonial administrations were left intact after independence. That the majority of the population in the new independent states was white guaranteed the acceleration of capitalistic forms of relations, which depended on salaried labor—historically associated with whiteness. It is to such a relation between race and labor roles that developed in the heat of the colonial enterprise in the sixteenth century that the coloniality of power refers (Quijano 2000). In this configuration most whites could become salaried workers, while most blacks and indigenous peoples were confined to roles as slaves and serfs. Countries where the majority of the population was white thus "developed" differently than those composed in their majority or to a large extent by black or indigenous peoples. According to Quijano, difference in "development" cannot be attributed solely or primarily to racial or cultural differences. Underdevelopment is neither something imposed on a "nation-state" or region from without, as the classical theory of dependency had it, nor an innate feature of a people's culture—a "state of mind" as some have put it. As we have commented already, arguments that essentialize cultural differences tend to reflect the racist structure of power rather than explain it. They themselves are part and parcel of the coloniality of power, which is tied not only with labor but with knowledge as well.

The coloniality of power is therefore not a reality of the past or simply an event, but a very powerful matrix with global reach that shapes intersubjective viewpoints and structures relations of power. Its presence in the United States is very obvious. It helps to explain why the 1964 Civil Rights Act and the 1965 Voting Rights Act did not eradicate the racial and gender inequalities of the country. As Table 1 shows, poverty in America is still constituted along racial and gender lines. Blacks and Latin@s have over one-fifth of their total population living under poverty while whites of non-Hispanic origin have less than 8 percent of people living under poverty. Female-headed households are in the worst conditions. Around 20 percent of the total individuals in households headed by white females of non-Hispanic origin live in poverty. For people living in African American or Latina female-headed households, 37 percent of the total population live under poverty. In sum, poverty is racialized and gendered in America. One gets similar results when one considers the prison complex. As Angela Davis (1998) notes, of the 1.8 million people who were in jails and prisons in 1997, approximately half were black. Based on the findings of Mauer and Huling (1995), Davis also reports that "almost one-third of all young black males are either incarcerated or directly under criminal justice surveillance. "Although women constitute a statistically small percentage of the overall prison population (7.4 percent), the rate of increase in the incarceration of black women surpasses that of their male counterparts" (Davis 1998, 75). These disturbing statistics show the persistence of the ideological link between blackness and criminality (Davis 1998, 75), which clearly shows another way in which the coloniality of power works. Blacks are liminal subjects who not only are deprived of salaried jobs, but who are also imprisoned. The prison complex can indeed be considered, as Davis and others have pointed out, slavery by a different means. The persistence of slavery beyond the political economy in which it is formed partly suggests that the basis of slavery and antiblack racism is much more complex than what a classical historical materialist analysis would show. Antiblack racism is therefore strong in the United States, which gives a particular accent to the also persistent unequal colonial relations between Euro-Americans and non-European peoples, males and females. Ideological and institutional forms of racism and sexism define the fate of human beings with certain features or histories in this country. Most discourses around the nation perceive these inequalities as exceptions, rather than well-defined patterns, or as vestiges of old institutions that have been formally transcended by legal decrees and measures. That the majority of the U.S. population is white, and can therefore claim all the benefits of citizenship while also feeling that it is being adequately represented in the political structure, has helped to deny the presence of antiblack racism and coloniality. However, given the forthcoming demographic transformations of the United States in this century, if the legacy of white supremacy in the United States continues, we will move very rapidly within a few decades to a near-apartheid form of democracy where the demographic majorities are politically excluded and disempowered and with a demographic minority ruling the country. Euro-Americans would continue to dominate the minorities as it has always been for the last four centuries, but with the aggravated fact that now non-Hispanic whites will be the demographic minority not just in a few states but in the whole country.

So far, the U.S. elites have managed to legitimize the characterization of the country as democratic due to a one-to-one correspondence between the demographic majority and the political majority as represented in the state structures. The correspondence between the Euro-American origin of the political, economic and cultural elites and the Euro-American demographic majority in the country has been the main argument used to justify the characterization of the United States as democratic. Even though minorities have always been second-class citizens and their participation in the democratic process of the country has always been constrained due to white supremacy and institutional forms of racism (the most recent example being the disappearance of thousands of African American voters lost in cyberspace in Florida, giving the victory of the 2000 presidential election to George W. Bush), still the large Euro-American demographic majority have always been represented in the structures of power. It is with this rhetorical argument that white Anglo-Saxon Protestant (WASP) elites make a claim that despite all the problems of discrimination existing in the country, the U.S. is a democracy. This is a questionable premise that could be challenged, but conceding to this argument the benefit of the doubt, we believe that there are several questions that need to be raised. What will happen when the social majority, that is, WASP America, no longer remains the demographic majority? What will happen when the economic, political, and cultural structures keep being dominated by WASPs while the demographic majority are nonwhite groups? Can this still be called a democracy? This scenario for the near future of the country is already a reality in many cities across the country and in California.

Right-Wing's California Dreams

Since the 1990s, California has been a laboratory for the right-wing hegemony of the United States (Saldívar 1997). It is the first state facing what is coming to the rest of the country in the twenty-first century: a large growth of non-European populations replacing WASPs as the demographic majority. Most of the propositions in California for the last ten years have been directed at how to contain the power of the new nonwhite demographic majority. These propositions served as a model for the rest of the country. The idea behind the Republican Right was, from the beginning, to make of California a showcase for the rest of the country. States where WASPs become a demographic minority can look at the California model as an answer to the challenge of how to keep controlling power structures within the new demographic shifts in the country. Mainstream intellectuals such as Harvard University's Professor Samuel Huntington are building their own WASPish utopias for the future of U.S. empire (Huntington 1996; 2004a; 2004b). Samuel Huntington is to the twenty-first century what Alfred Mahan was for the twentieth century; that is, a geopolitical strategist for the U.S. empire (Grosfoguel 2002). The main difference is that Mahan was the strategist of an ascending and growing empire, while Huntington is the ideologue of an empire that is declining.

Huntington's most recent book, entitled *Who Are We?* (2004b), for example, attempts the most amazing feat in revisionist historiography: after three hundred years during which WASPs in the United States have enslaved, colonized, and conquered indigenous peoples, blacks, Mexicans, Puerto Ricans, Filipinos and other "minority" groups, as well as helped maintain a global structure of power that is fundamentally unfair, the book wants to make it appear that so-called Hispanics are a threat to its national security (Maldonado-Torres 2005). *Who Are We?* brings Huntington's *The Clash of Civilizations* home and provides a neoliberal response to the challenges we have been describing so far. "Clash of Civilizations" is the ideological strategy for the U.S. empire in the international arena to keep Euro-American global domination abroad, while the so-called Hispanic Challenge is the ideological strategy to keep white supremacy in the domestic arena.

The "challenge" that lurks on the horizon of Huntington's efforts is this: If white America's demographic majority in the United States is not going to last long and Latin@s are becoming the largest growing population, how can white America justify an exclusive and exclusionary leadership of the country? Samuel Huntington provides a culturalist, racist, xenophobic response to this white Anglo-Euro-American challenge. In his view, Latin@s are foreigners who do not speak English and who are not willing to assimilate. But assimilate to what? Who decides what are the racial and cultural features that define an "estadounidense"? In Huntington's argument, cultural and linguistic assimilation should privilege Northwestern Europeans and in particular the English language. Huntington provides the political discourse to the current and future WASP elites of the country on how to respond to the twenty-first century challenge that they will no longer be the demographic majority. For Huntington, if white Americans cannot claim to be a demographic majority, they can at least claim to be the most apt and capable population to represent the national values and culture of the country by privileging white Anglo-Protestant Northwestern European culture and identity as the defining criteria for national identity. Huntington's future utopia represents continuity with the present

WASP-centric construction of U.S. national identity, within a new demographic context. In sum, according to Huntington's logic the main claim that WASP Americans could make to continue being in a position of power domestically and to lead the country in a context where they are no longer the demographic majority is to foster an Eurocentric cultural racist argument. The political consequences of Huntington's WASP identity politics are to build more frontier walls, more border patrols and to pursue a cultural and linguistic imperial assimilationist policy. The agenda here is not that far from that of right-wing xenophobic and racist politicians and journalists such as Pat Buchanan.

Who Are We? subverts the tables of any rigorous account of history and accountability. Doesn't Huntington's revisionist effort obey the racist logic to which indigenous peoples, blacks, and so many others have been exposed from the very birth of modernity in the Americas? The temptation for so-called Hispanics, of course, is to attempt to achieve recognition in the face of subjects who adhere to this ethnic WASP view of the world. The temptation would be to prove to bigots like Huntington that they have what it takes to be Americans. Instead of legitimating the terms of assimilation, the challenge for Latin@s is to redefine the terms of the debate, to bring accountability to the national scene, to help in rescuing the memory of displaced peoples, and to attempt to understand the claims of indigenous peoples and descendents of slaves in this country. The challenge to Latin@s consists of resisting the temptation to reproduce mainstream standards and cultural values uncritically. Latin@s risk wanting to assimilate to ethnic WASP culture at the cost of becoming a real "challenge" to everyone else but ethnic WASPs elites in this country (Maldonado-Torres 2005). Would they attempt to join others in the consistent decolonization of space, knowledge, and consciousness in this nation and other parts of the world? Only time will tell.

While the right wing of the United States is building their utopian scenarios, the left has been reacting against them without offering any positive proposal to the country. In this context, there are several questions that we think are crucial for the threat that white Euro-Americans, right-wing Latin@s and others pose for a future nonracist, nonsexist, radical and diverse democracy in the United States. Can identity politics provide an answer to the present challenges or is it part of the problem? What forms of democracy can provide a solution to these dilemmas? How can equality be reconciled with fraternity given our epistemic, class, gender, racial and colonial inequalities? Fortunately, we count ourselves with a long history of survival, struggle, and creativity represented not only in the Civil Rights Movement but also in the Chican@ Movement (Haney-López 2003) and in the work of feminists of color (Anzaldúa 1987; Christian 1985; Kaplan, Alarcón, and Moallem 1999; Lorde 1984; Moraga and Anzaldúa 1983; Sandoval 2000), among other movements, groups of peoples, and individuals who have maintain alive the dream and hopes for decolonization.

The increased representation of minorities in government structures is important but not sufficient, as the recent examples of General Colin Powell,

General Ricardo Sanchez and Dr. Condoleezza Rice demonstrate, to challenge the ideological and political hegemony of non-Hispanic white males and U.S. imperial power around the world. So the challenge that we face in the twenty-first century is in our perspective the following: either people living in the United States decolonize the country by transforming, deracializing, demasculinizing and radicalizing its democracy or we risk moving rapidly to a near-apartheid form of democracy with a white demographic minority leading the country and a non-white majority excluded from the structures of power, resources and decision making. The latter scenario could be articulated together with the creation and co-optation of model minorities as "honorary whites." This is already happening with Japanese, Koreans and Cubans. This strategy of divide and rule could be successful if white supremacy in the United States is not challenged and if the prejudices/stereotypes within the minority communities are not confronted.

Following the notion of transmodernity, developed by Latin American philosopher of liberation Enrique Dussel (2002), we need to think of "alternative" forms of democracy in the United States that could contribute to decolonizing the power structures of the country. For Dussel, an alternative to the present Eurocentered modernity might be the building of a transmodern world. Transmodernity is not a project to fulfill the incomplete project of modernity (a la Habermas), but rather, an attempt to strengthen and fulfill the twentieth century's unfinished and incomplete project of decolonization (Grosfoguel 2005, Maldonado forthcoming). The unfinished project of decolonization refers to the most consistent attempts to act maturely and responsibly in the face of modernity and coloniality. That is, it is a way not simply to react, or try to "catch up," but to redefine the terms of the struggle. Eurocentered modernity defines a unilateral and unidimensional form of democracy, citizenship, liberty, human rights, authority, and economy. A transmodern world—a world beyond modernity—is open to a diversity of definitions of democracy, citizenship, liberty, human rights, authority, and economy from the ethical-epistemological perspectives/historical projects (Maldonado-Torres 2004) of the silenced, subalternized and dominated side of the "colonial difference" (Mignolo, 2000). In this sense, the unfinished project of decolonization refers to the legacies of critical responses to coloniality by colonized subjects and others from the very inception of modernity and coloniality to our days (Grosfoguel, Maldonado-Torres, and Saldívar 2005). So far, Euro-American white supremacy operates by taking one single form of democracy, that is, the European liberal form, and imposing it domestically and internationally as a global design on the rest of the non-European peoples. From the white conquest of Native American territories in the North American West, to the U.S. annexation of North Mexican territories, to the recent war in Iraq, the Euro-American project of democracy has always been one of imperial/colonial global designs. During the last 500 years of the "European/Euro-American Capitalist/Patriarchal Modern/Colonial World-System," we went from the sixteenth century "Christianize or I shoot you," to the nineteenth century "civilize or I shoot you," to the twentieth century "develop or I shoot you," to the late twentieth century "neoliberalize or I shoot you" and to the early twenty-first century "democratize or I shoot you." No respect or recognition for indigenous, African, Islamic or other non-European forms of democracy. The liberal form of democracy is the only one accepted and legitimated. Forms of democratic alterity are rejected. If the non-European population does not accept the Euro-American terms of liberal democracy, then it is imposed by force in the name of civilization and progress. Democracy needs to be reconceptualized in a transmodern form in order to be decolonized from the white supremacy form of racialized democracy in the United States. For example, Native Americans cannot continue to be ruled by the federal government's colonial Bureau of Indian Affairs. Native Americans have their own forms of indigenous democracy and should have the right to self-determination. African American and Latin@ communities cannot continue to be ruled under the coloniality of power of urban regimes. They should have the right to organize alternative forms of democracy in their own communities and in the whole country that are not only inclusive of non-European peoples but also of a qualitative different nature. However, how can all these diverse alternative projects build their own political coalitions? The common agenda is one of anticapitalist, anti-imperial, antipatriarchal and antiracist forms of social equality. This leads to one of the main goals of this volume that links to our initial point about the urgency of discussions about utopias and collective agencies in this moment of bifurcation: What does decolonization mean in the twenty-first century? How can we think about the decolonization of the U.S. empire? How can Latin@s contribute to developing a qualitatively different relationship from the tradition of white supremacy between the different ethnic/racial groups of the United States and contribute to a different qualitative relationship with the world from that of traditional imperial relations that the U.S. empire developed with the rest of the world?

Decolonization and Latin@ Legacies

Decolonization in the nineteenth and twentieth century was limited to the juridical-political decolonization of a country. Given the persistent international division of labor, where core powers continue to exploit peripheral regions and its entanglement with a racial/ethnic hierarchy of Europeans/Euro-Americans and non-European peoples and with a gender hierarchy of male and female, we need to think of decolonization in a broader sense in the twenty-first century. This is what Quijano (2000) calls the global coloniality of power. The twentieth-century juridical-political decolonization did not decolonize the global economy, the gender/sexual hierarchies, the racial/ethnic hierarchies, the epistemic hierarchies or the religious hierarchies (Grosfoguel 2004). Our conception of decolonization is broader and more complex than what is commonly held (Grosfoguel 2004; Maldonado-Torres 2004). In our perspective, the project of decolonization remains unfinished and incomplete. Thus, to decolonize the U.S. empire would require an intervention in many spaces of power relations that have been historically colonized by European/Euro-American conceptions of gender, sexual, racial, epistemic, religious, economic, and political power relations. Latin@s are not exempted from these practices and conceptions.

Although Latin@s cultural legacies include a diversity of world cultures (Arab, Jewish, European, indigenous peoples, African, Asian, etc.), Afro-Latin@s and Indo-Latin@s are often discriminated by Euro-Latin@s. This points to a larger reality of antiblack racism and anti-indigenous discrimination that runs very deep in the histories and memories of Euro-"estadounidenses," Latin Americans, as well as U.S. Latin@s. Latin@s within their own communities have an enormous variety of the world's sacred spiritualities and cultures. Which traditions, imaginaries, identities and utopias prevail within the Latin@ population in the twenty-first century will be a crucial factor in the future of the U.S. empire and the future of the capitalist world-system given their demographic growth and their strategic location at the center of the U.S. empire.

This leads to another major issue of this book: How can Latin@s build a different relationship within themselves (in racial, gender, sexual and class terms) and with other groups (Asian Americans, Euro-Americans, African Americans, Native Americans, and different oppressed people in other parts of the world) that could begin breaking away from the legacies of white supremacy, patriarchy and coloniality domestically and abroad? As we very well know, neoliberalism, racism, sexism and homophobia are not a white Euro-American disease, they are global ideologies of which Latin@s are not exempted. In order to be part of the solution and not part of the problem, Latin@s need to deal with our own colonialities, sexisms, and racisms. The larger challenge may consist of the project of redefining the very idea of "human" (Wynter 2003).

If Latin@s affirm only their European culture or adopt a Eurocentric attitude, they will be part of the problem rather than part of the solution. However, if Latin@s affirm in a critical and decolonial way their diverse European and non-European epistemic and cultural backgrounds (we should not limit ourselves to whatever virtues a culture can have), they could become a positive bridge between different groups and help to provide nonracist ideas needed for consistent emancipation and for decolonization. A prime example of this is the work of Cheríe Moraga, Gloria Anzaldúa, and Analouise Keating, who, along with other women of color, proposed a vision of decolonization as bridging (Moraga and Anzaldúa 1983; Anzaldúa and Keating 2002). Also of high importance for a reconceptualization of self, space and knowledge are theorizations of border consciousness (Anzaldúa 1987) and border thinking (Mignolo 2000), along with elaborations of the relevance of border experience in culture, art, and literature (Saldívar 1997). Forms of scholarship that recognize the exchanges and dialogues among subaltern subjects in the Americas

(Saldívar 1991), open up new ways of thinking about space and tradition beyond what Lisa Lowe refers to as national ontologies (Lowe 2001). Neither patriotism nor cosmopolitanism, but a critical cosmopolitanism (Saldívar 1991, Mignolo 2000), grounded on the histories of migration, displacement, slavery, and oppression of peoples in the Americas provides a critical decolonial response that is familiar to Latin@s and other racialized subjects in the United States and elsewhere in the Americas.

One area where there are very interesting and important processes and conceptualizations of decolonization is spirituality. As the works of Anzaldúa, Moraga, and other women of color testify, spirituality is central to the decolonizing projects of women of color (Anzaldúa 2000, Moraga and Anzaldúa 1983, Maldonado-Torres 2003). Laura Pérez provides in this volume an incisive account of decolonizing spiritualities in visual art. Also of relevance are Latin@ youth spiritual movements. They critically relate and reactivate African traditions in the East Coast and indigenous roots in the West Coast. Since most East Coast Latin@s are from Afro-Caribbean origin and most West Coast Latin@s are from indigenous and mestizo origins in Mesoamerica, they have alternative resources and spiritualities to rely on that could become an alternative to the mainstream Euro-American and Euro-Latin American cosmologies. These Latin@ youth spiritual movements are decolonizing in practice the hegemonic Eurocentric culture and epistemology that prevail not only in the country but also among Latin@ populations. They are already involved in a process of decolonization that is challenging hegemonic cosmologies, epistemologies, and historical narratives. Theirs is not a romantic return to some pure and idyllic identity in the past, but a re-creation and reimagining of the present from indigenous and African cosmologies in a process of decolonization of the U.S. empire in the transmodern sense of Dussel (2002). They are directly involved in oppositional struggles against the war in Iraq and Afghanistan, police brutality, neoliberalism, and destruction of the environment. These Latin@ youth spiritual movements are providing an "alternative" ethics to the Eurocentric world. They are fighting for a transmodern decolonial diverse future beyond Eurocentered modernity.

Final Remarks

The capitalist world-system today is in crisis. Responses to it include neofundamentalist and neoconservative postures, new patriotisms, new discourses on development, and a vigorous oppositional discourse that continues to find voice in the works and activities of critical subaltern peoples and their allies all around the globe. This anthology aims to re-state the decolonizing potential of Latin@s in the United States. What role does this new emergent (economical and cultural and thus also to some extent political) force have in a country that faces its own crisis by deploying new ideologies of war? Will Latin@s political postures simply continue the legacies of antiblack racism in this country? Will the Latin@ label lead to one-sided affirmation of European Latin legacies, or will it provide the occasion for critical investigations into the workings of race and ethnicity as well as an exploration of the multiple knowledges and viewpoints found in the "Latin@" standpoint?

Immanuel Wallerstein has commented that we stand today between the "spirit of Davos" and the "spirit of Porto Alegre." The essays presented here are all inspired by the "spirit of Porto Alegre." But they also continue a tradition of what might be thought of as an older spirit, the "spirit of Berkeley." With the "spirit of Berkeley" we refer to the institutional and intellectual legacy of the struggle of blacks, indigenous peoples, Asian Americans, Chican@s, and others at Berkeley in the late 1960s. This book quite literally is an expression of the "spirit of Berkeley." Not only do the coeditors form part of a department that owes its existence to the struggles in the late sixties and early seventies at the University of California, Berkeley, but also all the essays in this volume were presented in a conference at such institutions, where there was also discussion and debate around the topics of the essays. The conference "Latin@s in the World-System" at Berkeley began to be organized in April 2003 and took place a year after in April 2004, just a month after Harvard University professor Samuel P. Huntington published his infamous essay, "The Hispanic Challenge" (Huntington 2004a). Huntington's patriotic intervention was very interesting to us, given that we were also trying to address a Latin@ challenge of sorts. Contrary to Huntington, for us any possible Latin@ challenge was not the challenge to the mainstream traditions and cultures of the nation-state, but the challenge to other racialized people in the United States, including Latin@ subjects who are racialized by the mainstream "brown" Latin@s. But rather than a Latin@ challenge our preferred formulation is that of a challenge to colonized/racialized subjects, colonial immigrants, and others, which we formulate in terms of decolonization and emancipation.

The primacy of decolonization in this work testifies first and foremost to our inspiration in the "spirit of Berkeley." Does Huntington's patriotic, culturalist, and protectionist scholarship also owe inspiration to a similar spirit? Perhaps it won't be too far-fetched to consider that Huntington, a prestigious professor at Harvard and a native son of New England, may indeed owe inspiration to what could be referred to as the "spirit of Harvard." Certainly Harvard has given birth to more than patriotic scholarship, yet it is at the same time the first university of the nation and it can trace its roots to times before independence. Huntington's investigation of national identity thus seems to fit very well his own locus of enunciation. Berkeley, on the other hand, is first and foremost known around the world for its radical politics and critical scholarship. If there is any basis to compare and oppose the "spirit of Berkeley" with a similar "spirit of Harvard" then perhaps Huntington's most recent book and this volume represent the clearer instantiations of these respective "spirits" and their difference today.

The "spirit of Berkeley" is decisively connected today with the "spirit of Porto Alegre." The World Social Forum, which originated in Porto Alegre, Brazil, represents a space of dialogue and interaction among peoples who believe that *another world is possible*. Our conference at Berkeley aimed to explore the extent to which *another United States is also possible*. In this book, which collects representative papers presented in the conference, we develop a transracial and transethnic dialogue about the decolonization of the U.S. empire in the twenty-first century. Scholars of different races, ethnicities, and fields of expertise reflect on the impending challenge to Latin@s and other minorities and racialized subjects in the United States: in the face of the crisis of world-capitalism, the crisis of U.S. authority in the world, and the increasing cultural and political changes that are expected as a consequence of the growth of the Latin@ population in the United States, how should we think about decolonization today?

The essays in this anthology aim to leave abstract universalisms and problematic versions of identity politics behind. The question of which alternative forms of knowledge, existing cultural/spiritual movements, and political projects can provide gateways for new forms of thinking beyond Eurocentrism and fundamentalism or beyond colonialism and nationalism is at the center of the political agenda today. Which decolonial ethical imperatives and utopian imaginaries are we going to build in order to confront the challenges of the post–Cold War, postsocialist and postnational liberation movements in the twenty-first century should be the main topic of discussion among people concerned for a future world beyond Eurocentered modernity, global coloniality and capitalism. Which alternative cosmologies and spiritualities can begin contributing to the building of what Enrique Dussel calls an ethics of liberation beyond Eurocentrism and white supremacy is a central part of the debate today. We need to imagine alternative decolonial worlds that might contribute to the future bifurcation of the present system toward a new decolonial egalitarian historical system beyond exploitation and domination. The Dusselian concept of "transmodernity" as opposed to the Eurocentered singular modernity and postmodernity is crucial to establishing decolonial transmodern dialogues among different ethico-epistemic traditions that provide alternative worlds to the imperial/global designs of the present "European/Euro-American modern/colonial capitalist/patriarchal world-system." The same can be said of decolonial proposals of women of color, who have insisted since the 1970s and 1980s that decolonization is an integral process that includes the reformation of subjectivity and "des-generación" (We owe the term to our colleague Laura Pérez). We would like to propose transmodernity as a simultaneous process of decolonization and des-generación that seeks to foster new, better, and alternative knowledges and ways of being human. We will be happy if this book contributes to such a task.

References

Ali, Tariq. 2002. *The Clash of Fundamentalisms: Crusades, Jihads and Modernity.* London: Verso.

Anzaldúa, Gloria. 1987. *Borderlands/La Frontera: The New Mestiza.* San Francisco: Spinsters/Aunt Lute.

———. 2000. *Interviews/Entrevistas.* A. L. Keating, ed. New York and London: Routledge.

Anzaldúa, Gloria, and Analouise Keating, eds. 2002. *This Bridge We Call Home: Radical Visions for Transformation.* New York: Routledge.

Balibar, Etienne. 1991. "Is There a Neo-Racism?" In Etienne Balibar and Immanuel Wallerstein, eds. *Race, Nation, Class: Ambiguous Identities.* London: Verso.

Basch, Linda, Nina Glick Schiller, and Cristina Szanton-Blanc. 1993. *Nations Unbound: Transnational Projects, Postcolonial Predicaments and Deterritorialized Nation-States.* Amsterdam: Gordon and Breach Publishers.

Christian, Barbara. 1985. *Black Feminist Criticism: Perspectives on Black Women Writers,* Athene series. New York: Pergamon Press.

Davis, Angela Y. 1998. "From the Prison of Slavery to the Slavery of Prison: Frederick Douglass and the Convict Lease System." In *The Angela Y. Davis Reader,* edited by J. James. Malden, Mass.: Blackwell.

Dussel, Enrique. 2002. *Hacia una filosofía política crítica.* Bilbao, España: Editorial Desclé de Brouwer.

Essed, Philomena. 1996. *Diversity: Gender, Color and Culture.* Amherst: University of Massachusetts Press.

Fanon, Frantz. 1988. *Toward the African Revolution: Political Essays.* Translated by H. Chevalier. New York: Grove Press.

Gilroy, Paul. 1993. *Small Acts.* London: Serpent's Tail.

Glazer, Nathan, and Daniel P. Moynihan. 1963. *Beyond the Melting Pot: The Negroes, Puerto Ricans, Jews, Italians, and Irish of New York City.* Cambridge, Mass.: MIT Press.

Grosfoguel, Ramón. 2002. "Colonialidad global y terrorismo anti-terrorista." *Nueva Sociedad* 177 (Enero–Febrero): 132–137.

———. 2003. *Colonial Subjects: Puerto Ricans in a Global Perspective.* Berkeley: University of California Press.

———. 2004. "The Implications of Subaltern Epistemologies for Global Capitalism: Transmodernity, Border Thinking and Global Coloniality." In *Critical Globalization Studies,* edited by William I. Robinson and Paul Applebaum. London: Routledge.

———. 2005. "Subaltern Epistemologies, Decolonial Imaginaries and the Redefinition of Global Capitalism." *Review,* vol. 29 (forthcoming).

Grosfoguel, Ramón, Nelson Maldonado-Torres, and José Davíd Saldívar. 2005. "Introduction." *Coloniality, Transmodernity, and Border Thinking.* Durham, N.C.: Duke University Press.

Habermas, Jürgen. 1987. *The Philosophical Discourse of Modernity: Twelve Lectures.* Translated by F. Lawrence. Cambridge, Mass.: MIT.

———. 1997. Modernity: An Unfinished Project. In *Habermas and the Unfinished Project of Modernity,* edited by M. P. d'Entrèves and S. Benhabib. Cambridge, Mass.: MIT Press.

Haney-López, Ian. 2003. *Racism on Trial: The Chicano Fight for Justice.* Cambridge, Mass.: Belknap Press of Harvard University Press.

Huntington, Samuel P. 1996. *The Clash of Civilizations and the Remaking of World Order.* New York: Touchstone.

——. 2004a. "The Hispanic Challenge." *Foreign Policy* (March–April).

——. 2004b. *Who Are We?: The Challenges to America's National Identity.* New York: Simon and Schuster.

Kaplan, Caren, Norma Alarcón, and Minoo Moallem. 1999. *Between Woman and Nation: Nationalisms, Transnational Feminisms, and the State.* Durham, N.C.: Duke University Press.

Lorde, Audre. 1984. *Sister Outsider: Essays and Speeches.* Trumansburg, N.Y.: Crossing Press.

Lowe, Lisa. 2001. "Epistemological Shifts: National Ontology and the New Asian Immigrant." In *Orientations: Mapping Studies in the Asian Diaspora,* edited by K. Chuh and K. Shimakawa. Durham, N.C.: Duke University Press.

Maldonado-Torres, Nelson. 2003. "Race, Religion, and Empire: Women of Color and the Decolonization of Spirituality." Distinguished Lecture Series. Department of Ethnic Studies. University of California, Berkeley. February 25, 2003.

——. 2004. "The Topology of Being and the Geopolitics of Knowledge: Modernity, Empire, Coloniality." *City* 8 (1):29–56.

——. 2005. "Decolonization and the New Identitarian Logics after September 11: Eurocentrism and Americanism against the New Barbarian Threats." *Radical Philosophy Review* (Fall).

——. Forthcoming. *Against War: Views from the Underside of Modernity.* Durham, N.C.: Duke University Press.

Mauer, Marc, and Tracy Huling. 1995. *Young Black Americans and the Criminal Justice System: Five Years Later.* Washington, D.C.: The Sentencing Project.

Mignolo, Walter. 1995. *The Darker Side of the Renaissance: Literacy, Territoriality and Colonization.* Ann Arbor: University of Michigan Press.

——. 2000. *Local Histories/Global Designs: Essays on the Coloniality of Power, Subaltern Knowledges and Border Thinking.* Princeton, N.J.: Princeton University Press.

Moraga, Cheríe, and Gloria Anzaldúa, eds. 1983. *This Bridge Called My Back: Writings by Radical Women of Color.* 2nd ed. New York: Kitchen Table: Women of Color Press.

Portes, Alejandro. 1996. "Transnational Communities: Their Emergence and Significance in the Contemporary World-System." In R. Korzeniewicz and W. C. Smith, eds., *Latin America in the World-Economy.* Westport, Conn.: Greenwood Press, pp. 151–168.

Quijano, Aníbal. 1993. "'Raza,' 'Etnia' y 'Nación' en Mariátegui: Cuestiones Abiertas." In Roland Forgues, ed., *José Carlos Mariátgui y Europa: El Otro Aspecto del Descubrimiento.* Lima, Perú: Empresa Editora Amauta S.A., pp. 167–187.

——. 1998. "La colonialidad del poder y la experiencia cultural latinoamericana." In Roberto Briceño-León and Heinz R. Sonntag, eds., *Pueblo, época y desarrollo: la sociología de América Latina.* Caracas: Nueva Sociedad, 139–155.

——. 2000. "Coloniality of Power, Ethnocentrism, and Latin America," *NEPANTLA* vol. 1, no. 3: 533–580.

Quijano, Aníbal, and Immanuel Wallerstein. 1992. "Americanity as a Concept, or the Americas in the Modern World-System. *International Journal of Social Sciences* 134: 583–591.

Said, Edward. 1979. *Orientalism*. New York: Vintage Books.

Saldívar, José David. 1991. *Dialectics of Our America*. Durham, N.C.: Duke University Press.

———. 1997. *Border Matters*. Berkeley: University of California Press.

Sandoval, Chela. 2000. *The Methodology of the Oppressed*. Minneapolis and London: University of Minnesota Press.

Wallerstein, Immanuel. 1974. *The Modern World-System*. New York: Academic Press.

———. 1979. *The Capitalist World-Economy*. Cambridge: Cambridge University Press and Editions de la Maison des Sciences de l'Homme.

———. 1984. *The Politics of the World-Economy*. Cambridge: Cambridge University Press and Editions de la Maison des Sciences de l'Homme.

———. 1991. *Unthinking Social Science*. London: Polity Press.

———. 1995. *After Liberalism*. New York: New Press.

———. 1996. "Neither Patriotism nor Cosmopolitanism." In Joshua Cohen ed., *For Love of Country: Debating the Limits of Patriotism*. Boston: Beacon Press.

———. 1998. *Utopistics: Or Historical Choices of the Twenty-First Century*. New York: New Press.

———. 2003. *The Decline of American Power*. New York: New Press.

Wynter, Sylvia. 2003. "Unsettling the Coloniality of Being/Power/Truth/Freedom: Towards the Human, after Man, Its Overrepresentation—An Argument." *New Centennial Review* 3, no. 3: 257–337.

PART II

Latin@s in World-Historical Perspective

1

Latin@s: What's in a Name?

Immanuel Wallerstein

"That which we call a rose, by any other name would smell as sweet," Shakespeare has famously told us. Is this true? And, if you change the name, is it still a rose? Or is the name an important part of the existential reality? Anyone who has followed ethnonational politics in the world-system cannot miss how often names change, how many quarrels take place about the change of names, and how many people refuse to accept name changes, persisting in the use of earlier terminology.

Are those in the United States who are to some degree related to those who were slaves to be called Colored people, Negroes, Afro-Americans, Blacks, or African Americans? May one of these people call himself or herself a Nigger? And should we capitalize these names or use lower case? Is the language spoken today by most people in Montenegro Serbo-Croat, Serbian, or Montenegrin? And on and on. You will notice immediately that these are not recondite scholarly debates but matters of passion and anger.

As we know, the term Latin@s is a relatively recent invention, especially with the @ sign. It is not an innocent choice. The @ sign is obviously the deference to the quite recent determination to develop and use nonsexist language. But whence Latin@s? It refers first of all to two different but related groups: those who come from and identify themselves with the countries of what is today called Latin America; and those within the United States who are descended from the first group. Or more or less, since no doubt there are a number of persons on the margin of both groups, about whom we could argue whether or not they should be included in the category, and such arguments have been rife.

Let us start with persons who come from the countries of Latin America. We immediately have a problem of which you are all aware. Which countries shall we include in Latin America? And what does Latin mean? It is usually said that this was an invention in 1865 of a French economist, Michel Chevalier, who was Minister of Finance in the government of Napoleon III. But Durán points out that it was already used in 1856 by two writers from Latin America: the Colombian José María Torres Caicedo and the Chilean Francisco Bilbao. Both were living then in Paris and, in Durán's view, were responding to an "impulse from the indigenist movement rooted in anti-Spanish sentiment" (1956, 61).

Chevalier obviously found this concept useful to his country. France was at that time occupying Mexico, and the concept "Latin" was intended to pull within a French sphere of influence all the countries in the Americas which shared the characteristics of a Romance language and were largely Catholic— that is, those countries that had been historically colonized by Spain, Portugal, and France. It was also intended to limit the political role of the United States in this region. For this reason and also because of its indigenist overtones, the term was resisted for a long time, both by scholars and officials in Spain and in the United States.[1]

The French were into using the term Latin a lot those days. In that very same year of 1865, the very same French minister persuaded Italy, Switzerland, and Belgium (but not Portugal) to enter an arrangement called the Latin Monetary Union, meant as a counterpart to and constraint on the role of the pound sterling in world monetary transactions. Greece joined in 1868 and Romania in 1889. Other countries were persuaded to mint their coins according to the union's standards. The list is motley, but politically understandable: Austria, Bulgaria, Venezuela, Serbia, Montenegro, San Marino, and the Papal State. The union disbanded in 1929. When, however, the Catholic Church consecrated the term Latin America in 1899, it restricted it to Spanish-speaking countries plus Brazil.

In the twentieth century, the term came into widespread and common political usage, albeit with varying definitions of the boundaries. Latin America was in competition with a number of possible alternative names. A quick survey of encyclopedias published in English, Spanish, Portuguese, French, Italian, and German shows no consensus whatsoever. Sometimes, one has to look under America, sometimes under "the Americas." English-language encyclopedias usually distinguish between North America and Latin America, Italian and German encyclopedias between Anglo America (or Anglosaxon America) and Latin America. But a Brazilian encyclopedia did not even have the term. It contained only North, Central, and South America. There is also Iberoamerica, Hispanic America, Lusoamerica, and of course the Western Hemisphere. As one can readily see, the terminology one prefers has implications both in the reading of history and in terms of contemporary politics.

The U.S. government has historically preferred that intergovernmental organizations be pan-American structures. Indeed, in 1945, Nelson Rockefeller, then U.S. assistant secretary of state for Latin America and a member of the U.S. delegation to the founding conference of the United Nations, was behind inserting a special clause in the UN Charter that legitimated the geopolitical role of regional organizations, thinking of the Pan-American Union about to transform itself into the Organization of American States (OAS).[2] When, however, several years later, the Mexican, Brazilian, and Argentine governments pressed the UN Economic and Social Council to create the Economic Commission for Latin America (ECLA), the United States fought the proposition, albeit unsuccessfully.[3] We know what an enormous intellectual and therefore geopolitical role ECLA was to play in subsequent decades, and one can well appreciate why the United States was unenthusiastic about the structure.

Later, however, when ECLA became tamer, it also changed its name to the Economic Commission for Latin America and the Caribbean. This reflected the ambiguous status of the various Caribbean countries—mostly English-speaking—in relation to the concept Latin America. And then there has always been the question of whether Haiti should be included in the term (because it is French-speaking) as well as Puerto Rico (because it is juridically part of the United States).

Still, despite nitpicking and blurred lines, most people in Latin American countries understand what it is to be a Latin@. It has clear political meaning. It symbolizes a certain militancy vis-à-vis the United States (and to a lesser extent today Western Europe). It is therefore a concept that has a left tonality. For this reason, some persons on the right in Latin America would prefer to think of themselves as Westerners, or Catholics, or even Europeans (in the sense of a putative pan-European identity). On the other hand, there have been some persons on the left, especially in those countries with a large population of *indios* who are uncomfortable with the concept, preferring a certain *indigenismo*.

The concept Latin@s in the context of Latin America is both militant outward (Latin@s as opposed to *Yanquis*) and unifying inward. We are all Latin@s together—Creole, ladino, indio; or *branco, pardo, negro*. It is doubtful that the concept Latin@s explains very much about, say, Guatemalan politics today.

When we come to the United States, the term has a different history. For one thing, it is much more recent. Fifty years ago, there were no Latin@s in the United States. Puerto Ricans and Mexicans were about the only categories in use. After Castro came to power and there began a migration of Cubans to the United States, there were also Cubans. In the 1960s, with the advent of the concept of affirmative action, the U.S. government created the official category of Hispanics, giving it a somewhat fluid definition: "all persons of Mexican, Puerto

Rican, Cuban, Central or South American, or other Spanish culture or origin, regardless of race."

Hispanics were one of four groups who were to benefit from affirmative action. De facto, one was a Hispanic if one had a traditionally Spanish surname. This led to two absurd consequences. In 1969, a certain Robert E. Lee went to a judge in Maryland and petitioned for a change of name from his English surname (and what a name in particular) to a Spanish surname. Once granted, he applied for advantages under the aegis of affirmative action. I am not sure how the government handled this request, which was probably difficult to reject legally. The other absurd consequence is that universities began to demonstrate that they had responded to demands of affirmative action because they had on their faculty middle-class white Argentinian refugees. Martha Giménez vigorously protested this clear evasion of the intent of affirmative action by her university in Colorado—to no avail, it should be noted.[4]

The 1960s were, however, a time of both militancy and demographic shifts. Young Mexican Americans renamed themselves Chicanos. There was beginning to be a serious Dominican migration to the United States, and later of course from many other Latin American countries. There were now second- and third-generation Puerto Rican migrants to the continental United States. The Puerto Ricans were no longer located just in the Northeast and the Mexican Americans no longer just in the Southwest. Both geographically and politically, there arose a demand for a unifying construct of these persons. This gave rise to the use of the concept, Latin@s.

This also gave rise to a debate as to whether Hispanics or Latin@s was the more useful concept. The debate was both academic and political. In academia, there was an illustrative argument among epidemiologists. In 1980, David E. Hayes-Bautista wrote an editorial for the *American Journal of Public Health* (1980) arguing that epidemiological studies that lumped together all Hispanics were deceptive because they failed to distinguish between the *Raza* of Indian origin and European Spaniards, and thereby removed the crucial variable of racial oppression.

In 1987, Hayes-Bautista and Jorge Chapa (1987) pursued the matter in the same journal in a more detailed way. In this article, however, it was no longer *Raza* and *indios* that were to be used to define Latin@s but persons "originating in a Latin American country" (p. 61), a category that, they argued, derived from the Monroe Doctrine of 1823. They said that the term Hispanics included Spanish, Portuguese, Cape Verdeans, and Filipinos, all of whom they wished to exclude, and did not include the English-speaking groups in Latin America, whom they wished to include. They insisted that Latin American was a geographical concept, not one based on ethnicity, language, or race.

In response, Fernando M. Treviño (1987) said he preferred the first article, based on *Raza* and *indios,* to the one based on the Monroe Doctrine. He pointed out that eliminating Filipinos was eliminating a group that was also "discriminated against" (p. 50). He concluded however, quite strangely, that Hispanics was a better term, even though he claimed he had no objection himself to being called a Latino. And the editor of the journal, Alfred Yankauer, neither a Latino nor a Hispanic, chimed in (1987), saying that, while he himself preferred Latino, he could obtain no consensus on this question among the editorial board.

Martha Giménez responded (1989) to this debate among the epidemiologists by questioning the utility of *any* standardized terminology. She said that the label Hispanic "abolished, for all practical purposes, the qualitative historical differences between the experiences and life chances of U.S. minority groups of Mexican or Puerto Rican origin, and those of Latin American and Spanish peoples." But then Giménez gave short shrift to Latin@s as well. Giménez pointed out that all these categories represented the "internationalization of minorities," and, as a result, "the devaluation and the denial of the unique historical experiences, struggles, culture, and identity of U.S. racial and ethnic minorities who are reduced to an abstract statistical category capable of indefinite expansion through legal and illegal immigration" (1988, 44). She asserted that these categories were what Marx had called an "imaginary concrete," and said they were "an empiricist grasp of a complex set of world-scale processes and relationships" (1988, 53).

The politics of this are quite clear, both within academia and within the larger U.S. political world. Latin@s are an identity group demanding rights they are denied and opportunities they do not have. Hispanics are the object of solicitation by the Republican Party. Centrist Democrats are not sure what this group is to be called. Anti-Castro Cubans certainly do not consider themselves Latin@s and probably hardly ever call themselves Hispanics. Haitians are not usually called Latin@s. And the few Brazilians that have migrated to the United States may not be either. As for those who have come from Spain, one group that purports to speak for them, the Spanish American Heritage Association, declared in 1980: "A Hispanic person is a Caucasian of Spanish ancestry. The Mexican Americans and Puerto Ricans are not Caucasians of Spanish ancestry, and therefore not Hispanics" (cited by Hayes-Bautista and Chapa 1987, 64).

University politics seem to have followed the larger political developments. There were never, to my knowledge, Hispanic programs, other than Spanish-language and literature departments. But in the 1970s, many Chicano and Puerto Rican studies programs were created. Later, most of them renamed themselves Latin@ studies programs, or something similar. One could show the same historical development for the concept Asian, which today, within the United States, embraces Japanese, Koreans, Chinese, Filipinos, Indians, and Bangladeshi, as well no doubt as many others. There is also the category Asian Pacific, which adds in the Guamanians and many other islanders. Individual Filipinos could, I guess, decide whether they preferred to be categorized as Latin@ or Asian Pacific in identity.

So, what's in a name? Obviously, quite a lot. Names define the boundaries of identity. Names define claimed historical legacies. Names define opposites or opponents. Names define what one is not. If one is a Latin@, one is not a Hispanic, or at least that is true for most people. And names of course symbolize alliances. Names are assertions of permanence, or at least of long-lasting structural situations and qualities. But in fact names, seen through a long-distance telescope, are very transitory, even transient. Names do not last too long, on the whole. But while they last, names are incredibly binding and bounding. They are in some ways akin to quick-dry putty. Coming at the right moment, they instantly affirm existential reality, and then last as long as they last—until I guess the putty dries out; that is to say, until the utility of the name exhausts itself.

Seen in the prism of April 2004, how important and effective is this name, Latin@? In the Western Hemisphere, Latin@ identity is at the heart of a crucial geopolitical battle. Faced with the rapid emergence of a triadic geoeconomic struggle between the United States, Western Europe, and East Asia, the United States is very anxious to enlarge and secure privileged access to markets and investment in the Western Hemisphere. The construction of the Free Trade Area of the Americas (FTAA) is no doubt the linchpin of this aspiration, and the North American Free Trade Agreement (NAFTA) was the first major step in arriving at this goal. In the United States, both Democratic and Republican politicians support this objective for the most part, and there has been only marginal difference here between the politics of the Clinton and the Bush administrations.

For a while, it seemed as if FTAA was virtually unstoppable. NAFTA had been adopted, a free trade agreement between Chile and the United States was signed, and others were being negotiated. Then suddenly FTAA got into trouble. Many things happened. Bush's Iraq adventures consumed U.S. governmental attention and gave space in Latin America for alternative views. The worldwide movement against neoliberalism showed its teeth first at Chiapas, then at Seattle in 1999, and subsequently morphed into the World Social Forum, commonly referred to as Porto Alegre. Lula and the PT won the elections in Brazil. The politics of the Lula government may have disappointed many on the left in terms of its position on the external debt and on internal land reform. But in terms of general foreign policy, Brazil has become a systematic organizer, first of all of resistance to the one-sided neoliberal objectives of the United States and Western Europe within the World Trade Organization (WTO), and secondly, and not least, to the FTAA, or at least to an FTAA on U.S. terms. By organizing the G21, Brazil brought about the failure of the Cancún meeting of the WTO in September 2003. And by promoting a potential merger of Mercosur and the Andean Community, Brazil brought to a stalemate the November 2003 meeting of the FTAA in Miami, which had been intended to further its construction.

What we are seeing here is a geopolitical assertion of "Latin America" in the world-system. It involves pulling away from Western Hemisphere structures and moving toward Latin American structures, ones that are also allied with what we used to call Third World structures. The game is scarcely over, and there is certainly no guarantee how it will come out. But Latin@ identity, that is Latin American identity, is at the center of the effort.

If we turn to the United States, again seen in the prism of April 2004, we read regularly in the newspapers that the largest growing electoral group in California, and indeed all over the country, is Latin@s. Well, actually, the newspapers seldom call them Latin@s. They are usually called Hispanics. Republicans are said to believe that, only if they can increase their now relatively low share of the Hispanic vote, can they reelect George W. Bush. And Democrats are working hard to consolidate their existing larger share of this group's votes, and expand it, first of all by more voter registration, and secondly perhaps by appealing to those younger Cubans who have been previously voting Republican but who now want a more flexible U.S. policy toward Cuba.

The question is, where is all this heading? In the case of Latin America, will Latin American identity be subordinate to a larger Third World identity (by whatever name that comes to be called)? Or will it be attracted by a link to "Latin" Europe, which after all is a connection that has many roots among Latin Americans—Catholicism for some conservatives; France as the locus of the Enlightenment for many left-of-center intellectuals; family links to Spain, Portugal, Italy, and even Germany for all sorts of people? And what is the content of *Latinidad* for a peasant militant in the Movimento sem Terra (MST) in Brazil, or for a Zapatista in Chiapas? Does the base militant even know the term? This is very far from being clear, as we look ahead into the next two decades.

A similar type of uncertainty surrounds the use of Latin@ within the United States. It is clear that there are many commonalities about the problems that Blacks and Latin@s face today. But it is also clear that there is a latent rivalry (well, not so latent), as each group pursues its own attempt to obtain rights it has been long denied. The future of a rainbow coalition (including of course also Asian Americans and Native Americans, and perhaps also Arab Americans) is as important and as tenuous as the future of common ties among Third World countries. Republican strategy is to hive off the upwardly mobile within these groups and particularly among the Hispanic/Latin@s. It has not been totally without success.

These are the games we play with names. But underneath these games lie the continuing polarizations within the capitalist world-economy, and the continuing different (even opposite) visions about the future, both of the capitalist world-economy as a system and, given its structural crisis, about the system that will replace it. And here we come to the final question. The deepest political struggle in the world-system today is that between what I call the spirit of Davos and the spirit of Porto Alegre. They represent two different visions and two different sets of objectives. But neither is as clearly defined about its middle-range objectives as it claims to be or even as it believes it is.

In this worldwide political struggle, the concept Latin@s can push us all, and particularly those who are encompassed within the concept, in two different, even opposite, directions. On the one hand, it can be a legitimate demand by oppressed groups, using a name that is ultimately founded on concrete local political realities. Latin@s can therefore move forward with others in a family of oppressed groups, and their movements, to find common ground and some kind of unity in objectives and action with other groups founded on other concrete local political realities. This is obviously the hope of those who participate in the World Social Forum with its base concept of the "open forum."

But of course it is equally possible—as we know from looking at comparable groups in the historical past and indeed in the historical present—that it can be the base of turning inward, of creating a fortress that protects the group more or less, and puts it in critical conflict with other similar groups. One should not underestimate the pressures that exist and will come to exist to move in this direction.

So, Latin@s as a concept and a discussion about "Latin@s in the world-system" is a double-edged sword that has to be handled carefully, intelligently, and with a sense of how much is at stake.

Notes

1. The first journal to be devoted to Latin American affairs in the United States was founded in 1918, and entitled the *Hispanic American Historical Review.*

2. At its founding in 1948, the OAS had 21 members, the 18 Spanish-speaking republics, Haiti, Brazil, and the United States. Today it has 35 members, the entire list of independent states in the Western Hemisphere. Essentially the OAS has added Canada and the English-speaking Caribbean states, plus Suriname, diluting its Hispanic character.

3. See Furtado (1985) for a detailed account of the contentious politics of creating ECLA by a leading figure in ECLA.

4. See Giménez 1988. In another article, Giménez recounts the "travesty of the concept" of affirmative action with this anecdote: "An interesting example of the effects of including well-educated South American professionals in the 'Hispanic minority group' is the recent award of a minority fellowship, by Boulder's local newspaper, to a high school senior 'minority' student, the talented and multilingual (speaking English, Spanish, French, and German) Argentine-born son of two Argentine university professors" (1989, 567n).

References

Corsanego, E. Durán (1999). "Latinoamérica o Hispanoamérica?" *Razón española,* No. 96, julio, 59–74.

Furtado, Celso (1985). *A fantasia organizada,* São Paulo: Paz e Terra.

Giménez, Martha E. (1988). "Minorities and the World-System," in Joan Smith et al., eds., *Racism, Sexism, and the World-System,* Studies in the Political Economy of the World-System, 11. Westport, CT: Greenwood Press, 39–56.

——. (1989). "Latino/'Hispanic': Who Needs a Name? A Case against a Standardized Terminology," *International Journal of Health Services,* XIX, 3, 557–571.

Hayes-Bautista, David E. (1980). "Identifying 'Hispanic' Populations: The Influence of Research Methodology on Public Policy," *American Journal of Public Health,* LXX, 1, April, 353–356.

Hayes-Bautista, David E., and Jorge Chapa (1987). "Latino Terminology: Conceptual Bases for Standard Terminology," *American Journal of Public Health,* LXVII, 1, Jan., 61–68.

Treviño, Fernando M. (1987). "Standardized Populations for Hispanic Populations," *American Journal of Public Health,* LXXVII, 1, Jan., 69–72.

Yankauer, Alfred (1987). "Hispanic/Latino—What's in a Name?" *American Journal of Public Health,* LXVII, 1, Jan., 15–17.

2

"Ser Hispano"

Un Mundo en el "Border" de Muchos Mundos

Enrique Dussel

No se trata de proponer una utópica "raza cósmica" como la que nos propone Vasconcelos, ni la "hibridez" de García Canclini, ni una historia interpretada literariamente como la de Octavio Paz en *Laberintos de la soledad,* sino más bien un ir descubriendo al *hispano* como "localizado" creativamente *entre* (el "in-between" de Homi Bhabha[1]) muchos mundos que van constituyendo, en el "border" intercultural[2], una identidad histórica, no sustancialista ni esencialista, sino dialécticamente creadora de sus propios componentes en el proceso mismo de la historia en continua integración de nuevos desafíos. Pero dicha experiencia histórica es al mismo tiempo normativa: debe ser descubierta y afirmada en su dignidad, mucho más cuando el estado actual de la comunidad *hispana* parte de una negativa autoevaluación de su propia existencia. La complejidad cultural del "ser-*hispano*" debe ser vivida desde una subjetividad, desde su intersubjetividad activa y creadora, que acepta los retos y los integra, y no los vive como simple dispersión o desgarramiento.

La estrategia de mi exposición en esta contribución, presentada de viva voz en el seminario de Pittsburgh, se sitúa en un horizonte pedagógico, comprometido, que intenta ser comprensible para un *hispano* no-universitario ni académico; para un *hispano* de la base social, a los que he expuesto este tema muchas veces, desde California a Caroliná del Norte en Duke, de Nueva York

41

a Chicago, y en tantas otras ciudades norteamericanas. Cuando el *hispano* descubre su compleja historia constitutiva reacciona al final de la exposición con un cierto enojo: "-¿Por qué no nos han mostrado esto nunca, por qué nos han ocultado nuestra historia en las instituciones educativas o de otro tipo norteamericanas?" A cuya protesta he respondido, aproximadamente: "-Difícilmente en alguna escuela primaria, high school, universidad, grupo sindical o religioso se mostrará al *hispano* esta existencia[3] tan rica, antigua y con tantas potenciales en la actualidad. El *anglo* protege celosamente su alegada superioridad cultural, política, religiosa." Deseo entonces guardar en esta contribución escrita el tono coloquial, comprensible al sentido común medio de los *hispanos* en Estados Unidos. Se trata como de un esquema para un curso, un seminario, una conferencia ante *hispanos* interesados en tomar conciencia crítica de su propia existencia.

El *hispano*[4], como todo ser humano[5], vive (existe) inevitablemente en un "mundo". Su "ser-en-el-mundo"[6] tiene por "mundo" uno que ha subsumido "muchos" mundos, cuyas historias no son cronológicamente simultáneas, sino que se han ido dando con diferentes ritmos, en diversos lugares, desarrollando distintos contenidos, cuyo horizonte denominamos el "ser-en-el-mundo-*hispano*", como facticidad concreta, actual, compleja, y de allí su riqueza intercultural integrada en una identidad siempre en formación, intersticial, nacida en un "border land" con gamas tales que pasan de una tonalidad a otra de manera continua, sin perder el experimentarse dentro de la solidaridad *hispana*. El *hispano* puede ser un indígena guatemalteco en Chicago, un mestizo mexicano en San Diego, un criollo blanco uruguayo en Washington, un afro-caribeño puertorriqueño en New York o cubano en Miami, un mulato de Santo Domingo en Houston, y muchas cosas más. Muchos mundos en un mundo. Un mundo que es hoy en la sociedad hegemónica norteamericana despreciado, dominado, empobrecido, excluido (más allá del horizonte del mundo *anglo* aceptable, más allá de la "línea" de la ontología heideggeriana, en el "border" donde comienza el no-ser, la nada de sentido de la alteridad levinasiana). Son los últimos de la escala social, cultural y epidemiológica (por ejemplo, los que tienen mayor porcentaje de Sida). El "mundo *hispano*" es como un fantasma, un espectro que ronda en la "exterioridad", pero que recientemente va mostrándose con nuevos rostros reconocibles, adquiriendo nuevos derechos gracias a su lucha por el reconocimiento de una existencia distinta, la que, pienso, podría servirle el tipo de narrativa que expondré, a fin de elaborar un mapa básico del tiempo histórico y de la territorialización de "su-mundo". Es un esquema que los maestros, líderes, militantes de las comunidades podrían usar para autoafirmar la dignidad menospreciada frecuentemente. Intenta ser una narrativa ético-pedagógica. No se propone denigrar al *anglo,* simplemente intentará dialécticamente afirmar, mostrar los valores del *hispano.* Puede que aparezca como apologética, y no está del todo mal ser apologista de los despreciados, ilegales, desconocidos, marginales.

Cada uno de los cinco "mundos" que sugiero los imagino como círculos, que coincide con los otros en torno al *hispano,* el que, por otra parte, guarda

una cierta exterioridad en referencia al mundo hegemónico. Todo *hispano* vive
dichos mundos en mayor o menor medida.

Valga para iniciar contar una anécdota, experiencia que viví hace años.
En la Universidad de Notre Dame, al llenar mi formulario de profesor, debía
responder una pregunta sobre mi "ethnicity"—que desconcertó por racista,
como es evidente-. Decía en primer lugar: "¿Es Ud. blanco (no hispano)?".
Después preguntaba: "¿Es Ud. afro-americano (no hispano)?", y así
sucesivamente "nativo (no hispano), y al final: "¿Es Ud. hispano?" Pregunté a
la secretaria: "¿Qué le parece que soy yo?". Al escuchar mi "acento" inglés me
preguntó: "¿Viene Ud. de México? Ponga *hispano*"[7]. Quedé entonces clasificado
"al final" (abajo) de las posibles "ethnicities". Esta anécdota creo que permite la
presente reflexión histórico-cultural.

1. El "mundo primero"[8]: Por parte de "madre"— el oriente extremo del Extremo Oriente

Cuando en Los Ángeles o San José uno encuentra a un mexicano, aunque
advierte rápidamente que se trata por ejemplo de un zapoteco de Oaxaca, que
habla su lengua amerindia y que quizá en poco tiempo llegue a expresarse mejor
en inglés que en castellano, descubre un hispano que, sin embargo, se diferencia
notablemente de muchos otros que también se identifican con esta comunidad
cultural, histórica y política.

En efecto, el hispano tiene siempre una cierta referencia originaria,
constitutiva con las culturas amerindias. Para el que pertenece por raza, lengua,
cultura, religión, historia a una comunidad indígena esta pertenencia es mucho
más experimentada. De todas maneras los *hispanos* reaccionan espontáneamente
ante un indígena procedente de América Latina como ante un miembro de su
propia comunidad. Puede observarse esto en el arte mural que llena numerosas
paredes (arte tan azteca y tan mexicano, que se inspira en los Rivera, Orozco u
O'Gorman de inicios del siglo XX) de los barrios *hispanos* de las ciudades
norteamericanas. El indígena aparece frecuentemente como un momento
simbólico en esas representaciones históricas. No es un despreciado "nativo",
sino que es el fundamento sobre el que se edifica una identidad histórica. Como
si quisieran expresar en sus obras los artistas populares: "¡Nosotros hemos estado
aquí *desde siempre*! ¡Venimos de Aztlán!". Este componente referencial es esencial.
El *hispano* dice relación a América como "su" continente (geográfico y cultural)
ancestral, originario, por "Malinche" (sea indígena o mestizo) su "madre", que
se enlaza con la "terra mater" (la "Pacha Mama" de los Andes o la "Cuatlicue"
del valle de México, la "tonanzintla": nuestra madrecita). Esa tierra es América
y fue originariamente *hispana,* por parte de madre. No fue la tierra "vacía" de John
Locke o Walt Whitman, sino que estaba "llena" de significado histórico-cultural.
El indígena es el que merece como nadie el nombre de "americano" (*American*).

Hemos expuesto en otras obras el movimiento en el espacio de nuestros pueblos originarios[9]. La humanidad efectuó un largo proceso civilizatorio en el continente afro-asiático (desde las culturas neolíticas en la actual Turquía, con ciudades desde el VII milenio a.C, y en la Mesopotamia, pasando por Egipto en el IV milenio, y apareciendo en las civilizaciones de la India o la China). Fue el "largo caminar" hacia el Oriente—del Occidente hacia el Oriente, contra la opinión eurocéntrica hegeliana-. Es en ese movimiento que deseamos insertar el origen de la historia cultural de los *hispanos,* ya que tienen por "madre" a la indígena, y nacieron en el "oriente extremo del Extremo Oriente" (este último occidental para América, más allá del Océano Pacífico, referencia central a las civilizaciones polinésicas a las que tanto deben las culturas amerindias), en el continente asiático, desde el cual, hace decenas de miles de años, a pie por Behring, siguiendo siempre hacia el este, se fueron introduciendo en América del norte (por Alaska) y llegaron veinte mil años después al sur (a Tierra del Fuego), por las más diversas y sucesivas rutas migratorias. En sus rostros está presente el Asia, el Asia oriental, el Pacífico occidental. Tenemos hoy seguridad que todas estas culturas fueron asiáticas, que pasaron por Mongolia, Siberia, las costas y las islas del Pacífico occidental, huyendo hacia el norte y expulsadas por pueblos más bravíos. Los esquimales fueron los últimos en llegar y quedaron todavía en Siberia y Canadá, quizá expulsados por pueblos turcos. La semejanza raciales, hasta faciales, de nuestros indígenas con los habitantes de Mongolia, Indonesia, Filipinas, Polinesia, Micronesia, son por demás conocidos.

Lo importante para una reconstrucción de la "conciencia crítico-histórica" de los *hispanos,* es que sitúen a sus ancestros originarios, no como venidos desde un "no-lugar", como caídos del cielo y estando aquí en América, en las playas de algunas islas caribeñas como "esperando" la llegada del "descubridor" Cristóbal Colón, que los investirá de un "lugar" en la historia. Ellos fueron los primeros habitantes de América, habiendo creado grandes civilizaciones urbanas (semejantes a las egipcias, mesopotámicas, del valle del Indo o del río Amarillo, y siguiendo cronológicamente su camino hacia el este), que ya habían "descubierto" todo el continente cuando se produjo la "invasión" europea en el 1492[10], viniendo desde el Asia materna.

El hispano debe experimentar existencialmente (subjetiva e intersubjetivamente) el hecho de haber estado en el continente americano, en sus valles, ríos, montañas, selvas . . . desde la comprensión de una historia de la humanidad razonable, de milenaria antigüedad, desde "antes" de todas las "invasiones" posteriores. Su "madre" (y su "padre" si es indígena *hispano*) dio nombre a todos los "espacios" y vivió la tierra, el sol, las nubes, los pájaros, los animales . . . desde sus mitos, desde antiguo, desde las "raíces". Deben poder saborear la dignidad de ser "los primeros", "los más antiguos" en referencia a todos los que vendrán "después". No para despreciarlos, ni para creerse superiores, pero sí para experimentar el don gratuito de haber sido los que recibieron a los que llegaron de otros "mundos", ofreciéndoles alimento (el "pavo" es un animal americano, amerindio) a los pobres

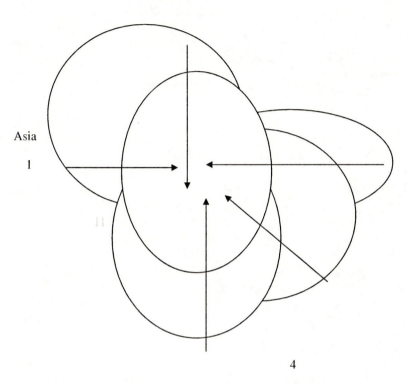

5 Estados Unidos

Asia

1

4

Africa

3 América Latina

Esquema 2-1. El *hispano*: un "mundo" como *border land entre* (in-between) muchos "mundos".

Aclaración del esquema 1. 1. Desde el oriente extremo del Extremo Oriente asiático. 2. Desde el occidente extremo del extremo Occidente europeo. 3. El extremo norte del Sur latinoamericano. 4. Desde el occidente del África. 5. El extremo sur del Norte anglosajón

que desembarcaban hambrientos (los que después celebrarán recordando la comida que les brindaron, pero olvidando el asesinato con el que pagaron a los que tan generosamente les dieron hospitalidad hasta con sus propios y escasos bienes, y en su propia tierra que les será expoliada).

Deben los hispanos conocer y apreciar del mundo amerindio no sólo la existencia de comunidades nómades (del norte en Estados Unidos o del sur del imperio inca), o de los plantadores de las praderas, del Caribe y del Amazonas, sino también a las imponentes culturas urbanas de la "América nuclear": a los mayas, a los aztecas, a los chibchas, a los incas . . . Civilizaciones de las que deben apreciar sus implantación en el espacio, sus hechos históricos, sus textos fundamentales, sus espléndidas estructuras culturales, políticas, religiosas, estéticas, comerciales, económicas, militares . . . Los *hispanos* deben estudiar esas culturas como un momento de la constitución de su propia identidad, que se va creando, modificando, creciendo en su paso por el espacio y el tiempo. En este caso la memoria es un momento fundamental de la creación de identidad solidaria.

2. El "Mundo segundo": Por parte de "padre"— el extremo occidente del Occidente extremo

Cuarenta siglos a.C., en el norte del Mar Negro, había pueblos que fundían el hierro, que domesticaban el caballo, y que sepultaban los cadáveres de los jinetes junto a sus caballos[11]. Era la cultura del "Kurgán" (al sur de Rusia). Siglos después podemos observar en bronce la estatua agresiva de un jinete con espada de hierro en su mano, es la figura de Francisco Pizarro en la plaza mayor de Lima. La cultura del caballo y el hierro había llegado a América. Es la historia de un pueblo que del este hacia el oeste llegó hasta nuestro continente.

España y Portugal eran el "finis terris" (el fin del mundo) de ese sistema antiguo, que comenzando por Japón o la China en el este, culminaba en el oeste con Europa. España, colonizada ya por fenicios en el segundo milenio a.C., provincia del imperio romano al final del primer milenio a.C. (cuya lengua indoeuropea, el "castellano" nacida en la Edad Media en la reconquista ante los musulmanes, es la que más semejanza guarda en el presente con el antiguo latín), albergará una Cristiandad en cuya plenitud (con Isidorio de Sevilla) será reemplazada por el Califato de Córdoba (otra gloria hispánica que ningún otro país europeo puede ostentar), centro cultural, filosófico (con Ibn-Rosh), teológico (con Maimónides), donde el Occidente obtuvo la traducción de las obras de los griegos al latín, a partir del árabe o del mismo griego, y que permitieron el clásico siglo XIII medieval de París. La nombrada "reconquista", comenzada en el 718 en una escaramuza guerrera que la tradición llama Covadonga, durará hasta enero de 1492, cuando los reyes de Castilla y Aragón ocupan Granada. La "reconquista" será continuada sin ninguna pausa como "conquista"de América.

Los países ibéricos inician así la "primera" Modernidad Temprana, ya que en el siglo XV será España, junto a Portugal que se le anticipa en la empresa por un siglos, la que producirá la apertura al Atlántico, constituyéndose en el "puente" entre el "Mundo antiguo" y la Modernidad (que España y Portugal originan, exactamente, con la "invasión" de las Indias occidentales, el Abbia Yala de los indios kunas del Panamá, llamada en honor al renacentista Americo Vespucci inadecuadamente "América").

Las culturas del extremo occidente (Europa) del continente afro-asiático, nunca fueron "centrales" con respecto a este gigantesco espacio civilizatorio. El territorio de conexión fue el imperio persa o el helenismo, el imperio bizantino o los sasánidas, región ocupada por último por el Califato de Bagdad ("centro" comercial del antiguo sistema desde el siglo VIII al XIII, los 500 años clásicos de la cultura islámica). Europa nunca fue hegemónica en este ámbito. Menos aún el norte de Europa sumida en la barbarie de los germanos hasta muy entrada la Edad Media. El polo fundamental de todo el inmenso continente, el de más peso poblacional, cultural, comercial, fue siempre la China y el Indostán, conectados al mundo bizantino por la civilización comercial musulmana (desde Filipinas hasta España, pasando por Malaka, el imperio mogol, los reinos del Medio Oriente, hasta el Egipto o Marruecos).

España y Portugal, por estar situadas entre el Mediterráneo y el Atlántico, reemplazaron la hegemonía de Génova o Venecia (ambas bizantinas) que habían conectado a Europa latino-germánica con el "sistema antiguo", porque habían logrado antes que ningún otro país del norte de Europa su unidad (Portugal ya en el siglo XIV, y España en el 1476 con la unidad de Castilla y Aragón). Contra lo que la historiografía posterior enseña, interpretación hegemonizada por el norte de Europa, España y Portugal fueron los países que inician la Modernidad, para las cuales el Renacimiento italiano fue sólo el despertar "Mediterráneo" por la caída de la Constantinopla griega. España y Portugal heredan el renacimiento, pero lo abren el ancho mundo del Atlántico (centro geopolítico de la Modernidad). Todavía bajo la hegemonía comercial de China y del Indostán, y contra un mundo musulmán-otomano que conectaba esas potencias con Europa, Portugal descubre el Atlántico sur-oriental con la Escuela náutica de Enrique el Navegante, que abre a Europa al "Mar de los Árabes" (el Océano Indico). España hace lo propio con el Atlántico tropical, gracias al genovés Cristóbal Colón, conectando al Caribe con Europa.

El choque cultural de lo más oriental de Oriente (Amerindia) con lo más occidental de Occidente (los países ibéricos) es el enfrentamiento inter-cultural más formidable de toda la historia mundial. La tierra había sido completamente ocupada y la humanidad se unía en un abrazo (mortal para los amerindios). Ese choque, y no "Encuentro de dos culturas" (eufemismo eurocéntrico), es justamente la entrelace de Malinche y Cortés, "dos mundos" de los muchos mundos que constituyen "el" mundo hispano. Abrazo incomprensible y sin embargo histórico, y asumido, y hecho carne desde hace 500 años. Abrazo cultural que el *hispano* lleva en su cultura, en su sangre, en su historia, y del cual el *anglo* nada puede comprender, ni experimentar, ni admirar. El *hispano* tiene una impresionante complejidad histórica americana. Tiene por "padre" un europeo latino, de comportamientos propios de la finura islámica (de la refinada Córdoba, Sevilla, Granada), tan lejana de la barbarie medieval europea.

La presencia española en América desde 1492 y de Portugal en Brasil desde 1500, anticipa por un siglo la invasión holandesa e inglesa a las costas norte del continente. Es el comienzo de la primera Modernidad Temprana, el despliegue originario del "Sistema-mundo" del que nos habla acertadamente I. Wallerstein[12]. América Latina (Amerindia + Países ibéricos) es moderna desde su origen. Sufre la Modernidad que siempre se inicia con la violencia de las armas (en América Latina, el África y el Asia), cuyo primer signo es la "conquista", que se inicia en el Caribe en 1492 y llega hasta el río Maule en Chile, aproximadamente en 1540. Cincuenta años en los que se ocupa la "América nuclear", que contiene la mayoría de la población del continente.

El hispano, sea mestizo o criollo, por parte de "padre" (el machista Cortés que domina a la delicada Malinche, princesa indígena, en la interpretación correcta de Octavio Paz en *El laberinto de la soledad*), que le permite remitirse a las culturas amerindias por su "madre", se refiere a una parte de sí mismo cuando piensa en la Europa moderna.

De todas maneras, el hispano se identifica con el español no en el sentido despectivo de los latinoamericanos (los "realistas", los "gachupines"). Pienso que geopolíticamente el *hispano* tiene interés en recordar a los *anglos* que son descendientes (y por lo tanto *hispanos*) de aquella España que hizo temblar a Inglaterra con "La Invencible" al final del siglo XVI. Carl Schmitt, cuando quiere dar un ejemplo de lo que significa "enemigo", cita un texto de Cromwell sobre los españoles[13]. España (no tanto Portugal que en muchos casos fue aliada posterior de Inglaterra contra España) desde antes del imperio romano, por estar situada en el Mediterráneo (y no ya como la Inglaterra en la Europa atlántica del Mar del Norte, germánica, medieval, nunca en contacto con las grandes culturas fenicias, egipcias, griegas y muy tardíamente parte periférica del imperio romano), fue para los anglosajones uno de sus oponentes históricos, en especial en el siglo XVI, debido a la hegemonía hispánica en Europa. La confrontación hispano-anglosajona tenía muchos siglos. El *hispano* entonces, por parte de "padre", despierta en el *anglo* muchos "malos recuerdos" (Shakespeare sabe que el "Manco de Lepanto"[14] inició la literatura moderna), al que no puede considerar simplemente un pueblo inferior, sino, por el contrario, un pueblo más antiguo, más numeroso, más desarrollado (todo esto, evidentemente, hasta comienzo del siglo XVII, cuando comienza la decadencia hispánica y el crecimiento de Inglaterra).

De nueva cuenta el *hispano* debería tomar conciencia que su lengua, su cultura, su tono religioso barroco, tiene un componente europeo que no puede negar, y que debería integrar a su pasado amerindio para constituir su inimitable personalidad histórica. Este "otro" *mundo* que vive como propio el *hispano,* y que se conjuga de manera creativa, viene a enriquecer al "primero".

3. El "mundo tercero": Como un/a "hermano/a" de descendencia "mestiza"— el extremo norte del Sur

El mestizo, el "pocho" en Los Ángeles del que nos habla Octavio Paz, es una mezcla racial y cultural tan antigua como la Modernidad. Ninguna otra raza o cultura le puede arrebatar esa dignidad, y ese estigma. Martín Cortés, el hijo de Malinche y del capitán español, morirá olvidado por una causa ajena como militar en España. Destino de un mestizo, símbolo del olvido de su origen y del sentido de su existencia.

El *hispano* es una síntesis (mundo tercero), un/a hermano/a de los latinoamericanos (el/la que llegaron al "Norte"), descendencia del mundo primero (Malinche) y del segundo (Cortés), o un criollo (un blanco nacido en América, y por lo tanto americano). Es uno de aquellos jóvenes criollos que, habiendo desde niños remado con piraguas por los inmensos e infinitos ríos del Paraguay guaraní, comiendo, durmiendo, vistiéndose como los indígenas, pudieron fundar las Reducciones jesuíticas[15], respetando las costumbres de los amerindios, sin propiedad privada, hablando sus lenguas, y viviendo los usos lugareños como propios. Los "españoles" que venían de Europa, no podían ya comprender el espíritu de estos latinoamericanos nacidos en tierras de este continente. Los *hispanos* son, por todo ello, "americanos" más antiguos que los que vendrán después, por parte de madre y como nacidos en estas tierras, por ser, como mestizos o criollos, habitantes de este continente desde finales del siglo XV. Los otros grupos que llegarán posteriormente a Nueva Inglaterra, no sólo los africanos, sino también los europeos de regiones no anglosajonas[16], tendrán plena conciencia de haber sido acogidos en tierra extraña y ya colonizada. Los *hispanos,* en cambio, tienen plena conciencia de que estas tierras americanas fueron por ellos habitadas "antes" que ningún otro grupo, incluyendo a los *anglos.* Y que fueron despojados de esas tierras, siendo declaradas "tierras vacías", y por ello excluidos, como los cananeos fueron excluidos de sus propias tierras cuando Josué ocupó Jericó, viniendo del desierto y habiendo sido esclavo en Egipto.

La historia de la vertiente latinoamericana del hispano se desarrolla como historia colonial del Caribe colombino hacia la "Tierra Firme", de Panamá a Venezuela, y hacia Florida. De allí va hacia el sur por Nueva Granada y por el Pacífico de Ecuador al Perú, a Chile, unificándose en el Plata con la corriente colonizadora del Atlántico sur-occidental de Asunción y Buenos Aires. Con Huancavélica y el Potosí la plata (descubierta en 1546 en el monte nombrado) inunda España, Holanda, Europa, y por las estepas y los navíos portugueses se acumula al final en la China (alcanzada igualmente desde Acapulco hacia Manila). Hacia el norte, el mundo colonial latinoamericano se expande en Centroamérica, en el México continental azteca, el ámbito yucateco-guatemalteco maya. Por último la corriente conquistadora va hacia el norte, hacia las minas de Durango, Saltillo, hacia California y la Pomería.

En 1620[17] toda la organización política latinoamericana había concluido, con sus virreynatos, sus audiencias, sus capitanías generales, cabildos, etc. La organización eclesiástica con más de treinta y cinco diócesis (fundándose en ese año en el norte la diócesis de Durango y en el sur la de Buenos Aires) había queda concluida prácticamente hasta finales del siglo XVIII. La civilización latinoamericana colonial estructura grandes universidades del rango de

Salamanca (en 1553)[18], decena de colegios universitarios, seminarios teológicos. La "ciudad letrada" crece barroca en el siglo XVII, y después ilustrada en el siglo XVIII.

Cuando en 1610, procedentes del Sur, llegando así al extremo norte de México, el extremo norte de América Latina, se fundaba la ciudad mexicana de Santa Fe en "Nuevo México" (así como México era la "Nueva España"), contemplamos en el actual territorio ocupado por Estados Unidos, su extremo sur, la región norte del mundo latinoamericano; mundo ya antiguo de más de un siglo, con todas sus bibliotecas (como la Palafoxiana de Puebla), imprentas, catedrales artísticamente imponentes, grandes palacios urbanos en las ciudades, espléndidos puertos amurallados (como los de la Habana, San Juan de Ulúa, Cartagena de Indias), caminos, acueductos, haciendas, ingenios . . . Todas estas instituciones son "anteriores" al origen del mundo anglosajón en el continente americano con la llegada de los Pilgrims. Las Reducciones jesuíticas de California y Misiones franciscanas en Texas, por ejemplo, nos hablan de la presencia de los hispanos en el extremo norte de una Latinoamérica que, desde la Patagonia, venía expandiéndose más allá del río Bravo.

El hispano es entonces un latinoamericano, un "latino", que como la cabeza del iceberg se apoya sobre una inmensa masa cultural, que yace oculta bajo las aguas, en la sombra de una historia, una población de más de cuatrocientos millones de ciudadanos, que como los Visigodos comenzaban a cruzar el Danubio rumbo al imperio romano bizantino (también allá eran "mojados" que iban hacia el sur, aquí hacia el norte).

De nuevo, estos latinoamericanos norteños, tienen conciencia de haber estado en estas tierras desde "antes" de la ocupación del desierto, antes de que se cruzaran los Apalaches, se extendieran por el río Misisipi y se alcanzaran Texas o California. Los hispanos/as son los/as hermanos/as latino-americanos/as del norte. Una nación latinoamericana a ser considerada como tal.

4. El "mundo cuarto": El afro-caribeño, un hispano más

Los *hispanos* contienen además en su "mundo" otro mundo de extrema vitalidad y muy antiguo también. Se originó cuando en 1520 en Santo Domingo los conquistadores terminaron con la extracción del oro de los ríos, ultimando igualmente a los indígenas taínos, y comenzando así el ciclo del azúcar. Para ello se trajeron los primeros esclavos africanos, procedentes de España y después directamente del África occidental[19].

Nació así el "mundo" de los trasterrados afro-caribeños, que se extendió por todas las islas, e igualmente por la Costa Atlántica de Centroamérica, por el norte de Venezuela y Colombia, las costas del Pacífico hasta Guayaquil en Ecuador, y el Brasil portugués, donde el azúcar y otros productos tropicales se convirtió en la mercancía más preciada del mundo luso-brasileño.

El afro-latinoamericano creció creando cultura, religión, mito, ritmo, junto al trabajo despiadado que exigían sus inhumanos propietarios. Ellos sobrevivieron gracias a su música, su danza, sus espíritus (orishas), su fortaleza impresionante. Cuando en el 1898 Estados Unidos anexionó las tres islas, colonias españolas, de Filipinas, Cuba y Puerto Rico, llegó ya al comienzo del siglo XX una población afro-caribeña a New York, en primer lugar. Eran los puertorriqueños. Todos los *hispanos* adoptaron los ritmos de la cultura afro-caribeña como propia. Tanto los *hispanos* de preponderancia indígena, como la mestiza o criolla blanca aprendieron la cadencia armoniosa del tambor africano. Por ello tenía alguna razón aquellas preguntas racistas de la universidad norteamericana cuando me interrogaban: "-¿Es Ud. afro (no hispano)?", porque el afro-caribeño es *hispano* y *también* afro. Su *hispanidad* no niega ni confunde su *africanidad*. Es "otro" mundo (el cuarto), que compone la conciencia *hispana* en Estados Unidos. Son los latino-caribeños, afro-caribeños de Puerto Rico o Santo Domingo con su "salsa", los cubanos con sus cultos de santería, el vudú de los haitianos, el ritmo de tambor de Haití, la macumba y el candomblé brasileños. El *hispano* es también afro, con sus bellos ojos frecuentemente orientales (de su "madre") y sus labios sensuales del África, moviendo en la danza sus caderas como sólo puede hacerlo un "latino". Es la complejidad creada "entre" los borders de muchos mundos, "entre" los intersticios de muchas culturas.

5. El "mundo quinto": El extremo sur del Norte

Inglaterra, las Islas británicas, tienen otra historia que España y Portugal. La Antigüedad y la Edad Media europea los dividió. Los franciscanos fundan Oxford y Cambridge. La "voluntad" contingente de Duns Scoto y el empirismo de los Bacon nos habla de otra tradición cultural que la de los dominicos, más inclinados a la "inteligencia" continental de París o Salamanca. El catolicismo barroco poco tiene que ver con el anglicanismo, el presbiterianismo democrático, el puritanismo utópico. La monarquía absoluta hispánica, fortalecida por la plata americana, derrota a su burguesía naciente española en 1521 en Valladar. Además, al expulsar a los seiscientos mil judíos, que debieron ser la clase financiera interior al imperio, fueron reemplazados por extranjeros, la Génova mercantil renacentista. En cambio, la debilidad de la monarquía inglesa permite la primera revolución burguesa triunfante en el siglo XVII, siendo esa misma burguesía ahora la encargada de organizar parlamentariamente el Estado, apoyar el comercio y desplegar la estructura colonial del creciente imperio inglés (que desde el siglo XVII, reemplazará lentamente a las potencias ibéricas). El anglo proyecta hacia el pasado el esplendor creciente británico de los siglos XVII y XVIII, y oculta cuidadosamente en las sombras al siglo XVI. El *hispano* debe partir del siglo XVI para autointerpretarse positivamente y poder resistir la humillación y la dominación presente.

En América los primeros anglosajones habían sido por su parte anticipados por los holandeses, ya que la "Nueva Inglaterra" había sido antes "Nueva Holanda", y "Nueva York" se había denominado "Nueva Amsterdam". Así, las primitivas comunidades utópicas que tanto admiró Tocqueville, que huían de una Inglaterra bajo el modelo del Leviatán de Hobbes, el Estado absoluto, fueron ya moderna, en el espíritu de la "segunda" Modernidad Temprana (de Amsterdam, Londres o Edinburgh). En el siglo XVIII los norteamericanos asimilaron creativamente a la Ilustración y realizaron "su" Revolución Industrial, no para disminuir la proporción del salario en el valor del producto, sino para permitir a los pequeños propietarios libres mayor producción. Las colonias inglesas participaron así en el origen de la Modernidad Madura, capitalista, liberal, industrial, y por ello no tuvieron en el continente americano ninguna otra potencia industrial ni militar que pudiera ser un oponente a su nivel. Su expansión era cuestión de tiempo, y el tiempo estaba con los anglos.

Cuando las comunidades de las Trece colonias de la costa atlántica del nordeste, emancipadas del yugo inglés en 1776 fueron ocupando el territorio mexicano, hacia el occidente (el largo camino hacia el "far West", que comenzó por la Luisiana -también parte originaria de Nueva España-, siguió hacia el sur con Texas, y hacia el oeste por Arkansas, Nueva México y California), incorporarán no sólo territorios sino también población hispana, que viniendo desde "antes" quedaron atrapados "adentro" de un "nuevo mundo" por ellos desconocido que venía del nordeste: el de los Estados Unidos de Norte América. Esta "inclusión"— que será seguida por una lenta dispersión *hispana* del sur hacia el norte, durante un largo siglo-, tendrá toda la característica de una "expulsión" (como la del pueblo elegido bajo Josué, que derrotaba a los cananeos en Jericó, ahora con rostros de indios o mexicanos: *hispanos*)[20]; expulsión no de parte de europeos extranjeros, sino que ahora de los propios americanos del norte que se expandirán ocupando territorios y manejando las poblaciones que quedaron en el sur, los *hispanos.*

Las poblaciones incluidas permanecerán indefensas, sin protección alguna. Como en el caso de la figura protagónica del cura Martínez[21], formado en el seminario de Durango en México, párroco de Santa Fe en Nueva México, elegido diputado para representar a su provincia en la ciudad de México en varias oportunidades, después en la asamblea independiente de Nueva México como Estado autónomo, y, por último, representante de New Mexico en Washington. Como sacerdote católico mexicano, en rebelión contra el manejo de la Iglesia por parte de "extranjeros" (no *hispanos*) será excomulgado por el obispo Lamy de San Antonio, de nacionalidad francesa (que no comprendía a la comunidad *hispana,* que era la mayoría de la población católica), obispo nombrado por un Vaticano que confiaba más en el gobierno norteamericano que en el mexicano. Quedó así todo un pueblo "como ovejas sin pastor."

Durante un siglo, desde 1848 hasta el final de la segunda guerra mundial (1945), el pueblo hispano fue ignorado, oprimido, eliminado. Su lengua era proscrita. Por su participación como militares en esa guerra y en las posteriores, por el aumento de su población, por la presencia masiva portorriqueña en el Este, mexicana en el Suroeste, y por último cubana en Florida, la importancia política de la comunidad *hispana* no podía ya ser acallada. El movimiento social y artístico chicano, el sindicalismo como el de Cesar Chávez, la presencia de organizaciones como "Padres" y "Madres" de sacerdotes y religiosas en la Iglesia católica, al igual que el nombramiento de muchos obispos *hispanos,* la aparición de líderes políticos, empresariales, intelectuales y artistas, dio a la comunidad *hispana,* poco a poco, el rostro de la mayor minoría de Estados Unidos. Movilizaciones como las realizadas contra al decreto 187 en California mostró ya una comunidad inicialmente conciente de sus derechos.

El futuro no está de ninguna manera garantizado. Su cultura compleja, rica y "americana" necesita ser creativamente desarrollada. Su presencia política debe adquirir mayor autonomía, para no inscribirse en el carro del poder sin exigir condiciones para el desarrollo de la propia comunidad. De todas maneras su reciente "aparición" en la escena pública es un hecho, determinante en la elección de los gobernantes de Estados Unidos por su implantación muy fuerte en Florida, New York, Chicago, Texas y California. Es la oportunidad histórica de innovar en la educación de los miembros de la comunidad, y las presente líneas son como el esbozo de un curso, un seminario, un libro de historia cultural, un esquema para enseñar al hispano tomar conciencia de su historia milenaria, centenaria, propia.

Los *hispanos* necesitan de América Latina, porque ahí están las nutrientes "raíces" de su mundo, la reserva vital de millones de "hermanos/as" que presionan desde su pobreza, pero también desde su esperanza contagiosa.

América Latina necesita de los hispanos. No necesita de *hispanos* que al hacerse presente en el sur, por ejemplo como diplomáticos o en funciones de empresarios o militares, puedan hablar la lengua de la cultura latinoamericana, pero para imponer la Voluntad de Poder del imperio de turno. Necesitamos de ellos para hacer presente en el gran país del norte una cultura americana, la del sur, que pueda mostrar al ciudadano norteamericano otros horizontes continentales más solidarios, responsables de la pobreza de millones, y de poblaciones que no deben ser consideradas como mercancías, sino como existencias dignas de seres humanos que nos ha tocado habitar este continente americano, el del sur y el del norte. Necesitamos de ellos para aprender a cómo convivir con una cultura *anglosajona* diversa, hostil, agresiva, cuya racionalidad se funda casi exclusivamente en la competencia del *homo homini lupus.* Pero que tiene igualmente inmensas reservas críticas con las que debemos organizar un frente para salvar la vida de la humanidad hoy en riesgo de un inmenso suicidio colectivo.

Notas

1. Véase Location of culture, Routledge, London, 1994.
2. Pero el "border" no como una línea, sino como un territorio espeso en significado como el "entrecruce" de horizonte de Gadamer; un "espacio" más que un límite; un "espacio" entre muchos mundos, que la subjetividad (intersubjetiva) del actor, los vive simultáneamente, articulándolos,

siendo todos ellos "mi mundo", "nuestro mundo", en la solidaridad del "estar-en-casa" (*zu-Hause*) hegeliano, pero "exterior" al mundo hegemónico de los *anglos,* en la "alteridad" (levinasiana).

3. En este caso, en el título, y a lo largo de este "paper", la palabra "ex-sistencia" será técnica, tendrá un significado sartreano o heideggeriano ("ex-": el punto de origen; "-sistencia": la trascendencia o el "estar" arrojado en el "mundo".

4. Hace veinte años los "hispanos" eran los ciudadanos blancos de Nuevo México que no deseaban ser confundidos con los "chicanos". Después se los denominó "latinos", y creo que recientemente se va imponiendo lo de "hispano". Es igualmente un tema a ser pensado la oportunidad política que esta comunidad cultural y política tiene para aceptar consensualmente esa denominación.

5. Esa mera exsistencia la denomina Heidegger bajo el nombre de "Dasein". Véase Martín Heidegger, *Being and Time,* § 9ss; Harper and Row, New York, 1962, pp.67ss.

6. *Op.cit.,* § 12; pp.78ss: "Bein-in-the-World".

7. Yo era ciudadano argentino de cuarta generación latinoamericana, cuyo origen es en parte alemán y en parte italiano.

8. Escribo "World first" y no "First world" por razones obvias, para evitar una confusión geopolítica.

9. Dussel, *The Invention of the Americas,* Continuum, New York, 1965; y también en *Latinoamérica en la Historia Universal,* Universidad del Nordeste, Resistencia (Argent.), 1966 (incluido en un CD que puede pedirse a *<dussamb@servidor.unam.mx>*, y en *Ética de la Liberación,* Trotta, Madrid, 2000, pp.15–98.

10. Esa experiencia de "llegar" a Amerindia por el oeste, debe hacerse vivir a los *hispanos* como una experiencia ontológica de la primera importancia.

11. Estos jinetes llegaron de la China y la India (por Kabul), hasta los medos y persas, griegos y latinos. Fueron los primeros "cowboys", que después surcaron los desiertos árabes, llegaron como vaqueros musulmanes a Andalucía, de allí pasaron a México (hacia el sur del continente como "llaneros" en los Llanos colombianos, y como "gauchos" en las Pampas argentinas). Por último pasaron al norte de México, y llegaron entonces al sur de los Estados Unidos. Su historia es ya la historia del "padre" de los *hispanos.*

12. Véase *The Modern World-System,* Academic Press, New York, vol. 1–3, 1980–1989.

13. Escribe Cromwell el 17 de septiembre de 1656: "The first thing therefore [. . .] is that: [. . .] Being and Preservation [. . .] Why, truly, your great Enemy is the Spaniard. He is a natural enemy [. . .] by reason of that enmity that is in him against whatsoever is of God" (cita C.Schmitt, *Der Begriff des Politischen,* § 7; Dunker und Humblot, Berlin, 1996, p.67)

14. Y no está de más recordar que aquella batalla del 1571 en la que participó Miguel de Cervantes, en la que España vence a los otomanos, es igualmente el final de la importancia del Mediterráneo y el comienzo de la hegemonía ya sin interrupción del Atlántico, el gran cambio geopolítico de los últimos quinientos años, que inicia España.

15. Véase mi obra *A History of the Church in Latin America,* Eerdmans, Grand Rapids, 1981.

16. Es interesante recordar, una entre tantas historias, las comunidades españolas judías que huyeron hacia Portugal tras la injusta expulsión del 1492. De Portugal algunas, como la familia de Spinoza, partieron en el exilio hacia las Provincias Unidas de Holanda. De allí pasaron a las islas caribeñas colonias holandesas, como la de Curação. La comunidad errante judía pasó por último a Nueva Amsterdan en Nueva Holanda. Dicha comunidad permanecerá cuando pase a manos de Inglaterra y se transformará en la comunidad judía de New York, muy anterior a los *anglos.*

17. Paradójicamente este es el año en que recién llegan los Pilgrims en el norte.

18. En Harvard hay una placa frente a la estatua del fundador, donde consta: "Desde 1636, primera universidad de América". En Santo Domingo se fundó en 1536 el primer centro de estudios de filosofía y teología en América, por parte de los dominicos. En 1540 en Tiripetío, Michoacán, Alfonso de la Vera Cruz funda la primera facultad agustiniana. En el nombrado 1553 se fundan las universidades de Lima y México con iguales prerrogativas que Salamanca, Paris, Oxford o Cambridge, en filosofía, teología, derecho y medicina. Los *hispanos* puede arrogarse, por parte de sus "hermanos" latinoamericanos el haber iniciado la vida universitaria en el continente.

19. Véase Robin Blackburn, *The Making of New World Slavery,* Verso, London, 1999.

20. El pensador hispano de Texas, Virgilio Elizondo, muestra la transformación del discurso de liberación del Moisés saliendo de Egipto con los antiguos esclavos (las comunidades utópico-cristianas que abandonaban Inglaterra o Irlanda, y que de la pobreza y la persecución entraban a la "Tierra prometida", en nombre del "Dios de los esclavos"), en el discurso que en el momento de la ocupación de la tierra, en cambio, empuñaban con Josué para justificar la conquista de la "Tierra vacía", o que había que vaciar, en nombre del "Dios de los ejércitos". Ese discurso será el permanente en Estados Unidos desde la ocupación del "far West" hasta la lucha contra el terrorismo de George W.Bush en el presente, inspirado en el "Western Design" de Cromwell, en el "Manifest Destiny" y la Doctrina Monroe, hasta las narrativas del expansionismo fundamentalista cristiano norteamericano.

21. Véase la obra colectiva de CEHILA, que dirigimos hace años, *Fronteras,* MACC, San Antonio, 1979.

3

Huntington's Fears

"Latinidad" in the Horizon of the Modern/Colonial World

Walter D. Mignolo

Huntington's Maps of Fear

Latinidad has a long history before entering with force into the everyday life of the United States in the twentieth century, and disrupting the U.S. national imaginary in which the state and the nation are equated with Anglicidad. Huntington's national identity politics in his recent *Who Are We?*[1] complements his previous global one. While in *The Clash of Civilizations?*[2] Huntington drew the line between the West and the rest of the world to assert the identity of the West in the global distribution of civilization, in *Who Are We?* he placed the accent on the continental distribution of identities. Underneath Huntington's thesis and fears (or the exploitation of fear to defend a modern idea of Western civilization and of the nation-state) there is a loud rumor that comes from the historical foundation of the modern/colonial world. The repressed rumor in *The Clash of Civilizations* comes from the final victory of Christians over the Moors in 1492 and the triumph of the Church—and of Christian Latinidad.

Although the reformation and the counterreformation created a schism in the very center of the Church, Catholics and Protestants could not escape their common roots: the moment when, in the third century A.D., and under Constantine, the Roman Empire and Christianity came together in an alliance that established the brass tacks for the future of Western Christians and capitalist empires since the sixteenth century (e.g., Spain, England, and the United States) as well as the Eastern Christian Empire, Russia, in which Moscow was declared the "Third Rome" at the beginning of the sixteenth century. Eastern Christianity fell at the margins of Latin Christianity. Clearly enough, in the map that Huntington reproduced in the first and short version of his thesis[3] the dividing line was traced, without equivocation, from the western margins of Russia, through the western sector of Belarus, Ukraine, and Romania, to the southeast, separating Croatia from Bosnia and Serbia. The line that begins in the northeast frontier of Russia ends significantly in Montenegro, leaving Greece in no-one's land, since Greece remains as the historical foundation of Western civilization. If the line was not clear enough for the distracted reader, Huntington wrote at the top of the map, and to the left and right of the line: "Western Christianity circa 1500," and to the right: "Orthodox Christianity and Islam." Western Christians, circa 1500, are as I already suggested coterminus with Latinidad. From the mid-seventeenth century onward, and above all with the concentration of capital in Holland and England, a reconfiguration of imperial/colonial domination world order took place and power shifted toward Protestant Christians and Anglicidad.

While the article published in *Foreign Affairs* had as a title "The Clash of Civilizations?" with a question mark, the book's title was assertive: *The Clash of Civilizations and the Remaking of World Order*. And while the map just described illustrated the article, in the book version maps of the world in 1920, the 1960s, and post-1990 took the place of the dividing line "circa 1500." One can see now that the rumor of the disinherited that will become "The Hispanic Challenge,"[4] is already there, in the shade of the maps introduced at the beginning of the book: the Braceros Program started around 1920; "Hispanics" as the fifth leg of the ethnoracial pentagon[5] emerged in "the 1960s" when massive immigration from South America (and the Third World) into the United States began, causing the end of the Braceros Program. In the 1960s there also took place a massive immigration of Puerto Ricans when the United States made of Puerto Rico a "showcase of developing underdeveloped countries"[6] and the project needed to relocate thousands of Puerto Ricans in order to clean house when the investing visitors arrived. And finally "the post 1990" not only witnessed the end of the Soviet Union, but most definitively the increasing numbers of immigrants from South America and Central America, many of them running away from countries under dictatorial regimes (that started in Chile in 1973) in conjunction with the advance of neoliberalism in the South. Southern immigration was a consequence of political repression and growing economic marginalization parallel to the growing concentration of capital in the hands of Southern elites, both of which were direct consequences of U.S. imperial designs. That is to say, one of the consequences of military, political, and economic invasion of the South by the U.S. government and corporations, was what Huntington conceptualized as "the Hispanic Challenge." The "Hispanic Challenge," in other words, is a direct consequence of the "Anglo Violence."

2. The Way "We" Were

The coalition of Christianity with Anglicity had significant consequences (from the late seventeenth century onward) for the remaking of the world order, for the geopolitics of knowledge, and for the future destiny of Latinity, in Europe. First of all, while England was taking over the economic and political dimensions in the legacies of the Spanish Empire, Germany was taking the intellectual lead in reconceptualizing the world (e.g., Kant and Hegel geopolitical imaginaries) and France saw the opportunity to take the lead of the Latin world in the south of Europe. "Latinidad" began to be displaced from the center of Christianity and equated with Catholicism, while Protestantism was linked with the changes from mercantile capitalism (mainly controlled by Spanish and Portuguese imperialisms and grounded in silver and gold) to free-trade capitalism (mainly controlled by England and France and grounded in Caribbean plantations and African slave labor).

French intelligentsia, state officers, and the Church were in a privileged position to exploit and use "Latinidad." The very notion of "Latinidad" as a secular and imperial identity politics served France's imperial designs well. In the first place, the separation of Church and State put France in a leading position vis-à-vis the ascending and competing imperial powers, England and Germany mainly. Secondly, the secularization of "Latinidad" allowed the French state to put itself in a leading position vis-à-vis previous and weak imperial powers (Spain, Portugal, and Italy—strong in its intellectual role, though less of an imperial power). And third, when French state politics, supported by its intelligentsia, promoted "Latinidad" in the ex-Spanish colonies in South America that had recently gained independence, it was because of the imperial conflict caused by the expansion of the United States toward the South, after buying Louisiana from Napoleon (in the 1830s) and prevailing in the war against Mexico in 1848.

Thus, "Latinidad" served France to place itself in the new imperial world order, in Europe, and in the Americas. By the end of the nineteenth century, "Latinidad" became more and more accepted by the self-colonized Hispanic American Creoles—and "Latin" America as the name of a subcontinent became indistinguishable from the political project of the Creole elite (landowners and plantation managers in complicity with the State) in their efforts to build nation-states out of the Spanish and Portuguese colonial ruins without realizing the differences between the nation-states being consolidated in impe- rial countries (France, Germany, England) and would-be imperial countries with a clear vision of its future (United States), and the consolidation of "de- pendent" countries, like those of "Latin" America, living under the spell of their recent "independence." The independence of "Latin" American countries in the nineteenth century was a political mirage: France was leading the imagi- nary of "Latinidad"; England—which had, after 1776, lost its colonies in the United States and the economic control of several Caribbean Islands—redi- rected its colonial ambition toward Asia and Africa and controlled the markets in South America and the Caribbean; the United States, as I already men- tioned, moved the frontiers several miles toward the South and took away from Mexico a vast territory extending from today's Colorado to California; which has been a vast "Hispanic/Latin" territory since the beginning of the sixteenth century, when it was still occupied by indigenous people of the Americas for several thousands of years before the arrival of the Spaniards. "Latinos" in South America, that is, "Latin" Americans, were recolonized by emerging empires while believing in their independence. Since 1848, and above all since 1898, as the result and consequence of the Hispanic-American War (in which Cuba and Puerto Rico were sandwiched), "Latins" in America (that is, Creoles from European descent; and mestizos who only recognize the Spanish or Portuguese past of their double descent), inaugurated a new imperial category that will be reproduced in independent countries in Asia and Africa after WWII: "the ben- eficiary colonized (and numerically minority) elite." Members of this elite sel- dom leave the country, and if they or their children leave for a while to study in Europe or the United States, most likely they return. They do not have any- thing to gain from migrating to Europe and the United States because their milking cows are not in the United States. It is this very elite that contributed to generating more and more marginalized people in their respective countries; marginalization that became obvious, clear, and loud since the 1970s, when in the United States the civil society and the State began to notice that there are more immigrants coming from the South. Who were these new immigrants? Mostly Mestizos from lower classes, sons and daughters of the large European migrations from the second half of the nineteenth century on. Since the 1990s a small number of indigenous people from the Andes and Central America were identified in Los Angeles. But, as far as we know, people of African de- scent living in the Andes (Bolivia, Colombia, Ecuador, and Peru) and the Car- ibbean Islands, who speak Spanish and Portuguese, form a significant number of the so-called Hispanic Challenge.

But then, what is "Latin" among Afro-Hispanics who practice Santería or Candomble (instead of practicing Christianity) and of African—not Euro- pean—descent? And what is "Latin" among the millions of indigenous people who have preserved traces of Christian symbols and rituals without changing their basic religious beliefs? And what is "Latin" about people, though they speak Spanish, whose life and sensibility are crafted in Tojolabal, Aymara, Nahuatl, Quechua, Quichua, etc.? Not much, I believe, based on personal conversations with indigenous and Afro leaders of social movements. Thus, in South America, "Latinidad" has several simultaneous functions in the imaginary of the modern/colonial world and in the structure of imperial/colonial domination. On the one hand, it served the goals of the beneficiary elite in the restructuring of the modern/colonial world order after the U.S. and French Revolutions. The Creole elite linked with France, openly, and with England in under-the-carpet negotiations of free trade and declared itself, in general, against the U.S. expansion toward the South. France took advantage of this moment and its circumstances.

The beneficiary elite was of course divided, as part of it remained faithful to the Spanish language, ideas, and traditions. They followed the lead of European "conservatives" (such as Donoso Cortés, who in 1852 published a book outlining the three major ideological frames after the French Revolution): Christianity, liberalism, and socialism (in its Saint-Simonian version, above all, but also of the early Marx). Colombia was one of the stronger defenders and followers of Hispanic traditions, as was Puerto Rico. In the Southern Cone, where Spanish influence was not strongly felt, the majority lined up with French ideas and against Spanish traditions. By the end of the nineteenth century, however, a line of dissent sprouted from the ruling "Latin" elite. Although antecedents could be traced to the third quarter of the nineteenth century, the most remarkable was the Cuban Jose Martí. Caught in New York, during the preliminaries of the Hispanic American war, he felt and witnessed at its highest, Anglo white supremacy/racism against Latin and Catholic (and also mestizos) in the South, who began to lose their "Latin" American whiteness to gain the color of U.S. "Latinidad." In this regard, and without forgetting 1848, it was in 1898 that white supremacy discourse was consolidated in the United States and there are good reasons why it was so. The Mexico–U.S. war was a war between nations, while the 1898 war was between empires, one in decay and the other on the rise. Hispanics on both sides of the Atlantic lost their whiteness then, one guilty of mixing with the Moors, and the other of mixing with Indians and Blacks. Jose Martí was and continues to be a canonical figure of "Latin" American dissenters and the foundational figure of Cuban identity. For Cubans, Martí comes before Marx. Marx provided Cubans a tool for the analysis of the logic of capitalism and a socialist (modern and Euro-centered) rhetoric to fight against it. Martí provides Cubans with the arms and tools to fight the coloniality of being infringed upon them by Spanish colonialism first and by the United States after the 1898 Hispanic-American War.

The second pillar of dissenting figures is Peruvian José Carlos Mariátegui. There are some significant differences between him and Marti. When socialism entered "Latin" America at the end of the nineteenth century (with the

wave of European immigrants) Mariátegui became very well acquainted with
Marx and Marxism, while Martí was acting and thinking at the crossroad of a
liberal imperialism on the rise (the United States) and the legacies and emanci-
pating ideals of liberalism inherited from the French Revolution. However,
one could say that for Peruvians—and for different reasons—Mariátegui comes
first and Marx second. Marx provided the Peruvian critical left (leaving aside
the experience of Shining Path), with a tool for the analysis of the logic of
industrial capitalism and to imagine beyond that and with a socialist rhetoric
to combat the rhetoric of liberal imperial modernity. However, Mariátegui's
contribution comes not from applying Marx but from experiencing, sensing,
and observing the colonial history of "Latin" America and of Peru. The crux of
the matter here is the heavy legacy of Spanish Christian and Catholic colonialism, the deep-rooted, long-lasting, strong presence of indigenous history, language, knowledge, and ways of life and the first decades of the rise of U.S.
imperialism after their victory in the Hispanic-American War (Mariátegui's
most influential writings date from approximately 1920 to 1930).

Thus, the "Latino/a" in South America is mainly the history of the population from Spanish and Portuguese descent; Creoles and Mestizos who assumed
European frames of mind and modes of living, followed in the periphery, the three
major macronarratives of the Enlightenment, in the background of the colonial
period during the Renaissance (1500–1800). Creole and Mestizo men built the
nation-state and the economy, since the beginning of the nineteenth century
following, in the margins, the guidelines of Liberal political theory [7] and of
Conservatism (e.g., secular conservatism) as well as the prolongation and ad-
aptation of Catholicism to the secular changes.[8] Jose Martí battles all his life,
from the age of 15, against Spanish colonialism in Cuba. Mariátegui faced
both the legacies of Spanish colonialism engrained in the "republication" State,
in Peru and in Latin America, and confronted the growing presence of the United
States. Although Mariátegui most often referred to Hispano-America and Martí
to Nuestra America, the idea of "Latin" America was floating. But it was floating
not so much in the subjectivity of people who dwelled in the Spanish-speaking
world of the Americas, as it was in the imperial rhetoric of French imperialism
assumed by France's state men and the intelligentsia, as well by their followers in
the Spanish colonies or ex-colonies, for whom the transition from colonialism
meant detaching from Spanish and Portuguese rules and to embrace British free-
market economy and French post-Enlightenment thoughts. All that noise made
indigenous people, as well as those of African descent, more and more invisible
until the 1970s, a period in which Latino/as in the United States began to make
their presence felt. Today, the Creole, mestizo, and immigrant population in South
America and the Caribbean, who align themselves with the dissenting tradition
inaugurated by Jose Martí and José Carlos Mariátegui, already joined forces (or are
likely to) with the indigenous movements, the emerging Afro-Andean movement,
and with the long tradition of Afro-critical thoughts in the British and French
Caribbean. Similarly, the strong presence of intellectual and activist women

toward the end of the 70s and 80s, like Domitila Vargas de Chungara in Bolivia and Rigoberta Menchú in Guatemala, began to break up the "Latinidad" as the logo of the culture, history, subjectivity, and political goals of a subcontinent that was founded in and by the Spanish colonization of the indigenous population, and the massive slave trade carried out by the Spanish, Portuguese, French, and British.[9] The "Latin" mentality of the nation-builders, imitators of European ideas and soldiers of British imperialism, since the nineteenth century (and since the 60s soldiers of U.S. imperialism), contributed to burying the force of a history that Marti and Mariategui began to uncover; that Domitila Vargas and Rigoberta Menchú[10] put on the table from the perspective and experience of indigenous women; and that from C. R. L. James to Sylvia Winters in the British Caribbean; and from the Haitian Revolution to Aimé Cesairé and Frantz Fanon in the French Caribbean. There is a third line, the Latin American Marxist tradition, whose agents still have difficulty today in bridging a dialogue with indigenous and Afro-thoughts and activism (as demonstrated by the interventions of Carlos Regalado in the First Social Forum of the Americas, Quito, July 25–30, 2004) and with the variegated spectrum of indigenous and Afro-descendant women (as demonstrated by Liliana Hecker in her intervention in the same Social Forum, Quito, July 25–30, 2004).

Interestingly enough, it is the dissenting line of thoughts, engrained in the colonial history of modernity, and in the Americas (inaugurated by Marti and Mariategui, and continued by Cesaire, Fanon, Sylvia Winters, Domitila de Chungara)—and not in the dissenting line grounded on Marxist thoughts—that make possible the productive dialogue between these complex traditions "beyond Latinidad" in South America and the Caribbean, and "Latino/as" in the United States that inaugurated a dissenting path based on the history of the United States with Mexico, Puerto Rico, and Cuba.

From this short story one aspect shall be underlined. "Hispanics," as the official classification from the State administration has it, keeps the links with Europe, although, as I would venture to say, 98 percent of "Hispanics" are from Latin America. On the contrary, when "Latino/as" des-identified with Hispanics, and in 1848 (the displacement of the U.S. frontier to the South), 1898 (Spanish-American [that is, U.S.] War involving Puerto Rico and Cuba, and to a lesser extent the Dominican Republic), and 1959 (Cuban Revolution—with the added complicity of the case), the links with Europe were cut: Latino/as in the United States are from "Latin" American—and not European—descent. The Gordian knot has been cut and an additional "element" has been added to the "Hispanic Challenge" to Anglo identity in the United States.

3. Why Hispanics Are Not White?

For four years now, I have been teaching an undergraduate seminar titled "Why Hispanics Are Not White? Globalization and Latinidad." One of the goals of the seminar is to help students understand that, on the one hand, "Latinidad" in the United States is not a national but a global issue that has been configured by the racial matrix that structures the imaginary of the modern/colonial world. How does it work? As I mentioned before, in 1995, historian David Hollinger analyzed "postethnic America" and the formation of what he aptly called "the ethnoracial pentagon": Whites, Hispanics, Native Americans, African Americans, and Asian Americans.[11] By 2004 a new post-9/11 category emerged. This is not the place to go into detail, but at the same time it should be kept in mind that the ethnoracial pentagon changed by the emergence of a new social actor in the global and national distribution of racism. Suffice it to say, then, that the ethnoracial hexagon was already preannounced in 1995, the same year of Hollinger's book, by the dividing line in Huntington's (in)famous article in *Foreign Affairs*.

Where is the ethnoracial pentagon coming from? It is well known that the "Hispanic" category as the fifth ethnoracial leg was introduced during Richard Nixon's administration, when the immigration from the Third World significantly increased in the United States as a consequence of growing dictatorial regimes and the lowering of the poverty line in Latin America as it was increasing in Europe as a consequence of decolonization of Asia and Africa. The restriction of immigration from South America put an end also to the Braceros Program that started in the 1920s as a solution for labor supply during and immediately after WWI. The key and interesting point of the ethnoracial spectrum, once "Hispanics" category was introduced, was that Hispanics—on the one hand—were not considered Whites and—on the other—that Hispanics did not belong to the same "foundational" logic of the ethnoracial tetragon: Hispanics did not enter into the spectrum as a "colored race" (whites, blacks, brown or red [Native Americans], and yellow) but as a "darkening brown, religion and language"; that is, as Mestizos, Catholics, and the Spanish speaking. But let's go back in time and trace the history of the ethnoracial configuration, how it became the foundation of the modern/colonial world racial imaginary and how it was transformed to end up with Latino/as in the colonial horizon of modernity that Huntington perceives as the "Hispanic Challenge."

Between 1500 and 1850 there was no "Latin" America. The territory that was named Tawantinsuyu, Abya-Yala, Cemanahuac by the people who inhabited it was renamed by Spaniards as "Indias Occidentales." (According to current theories they came from all over the Pacific coast of what the Europeans, in their Christian cosmology, named Asia but which was not yet recognized as such by the people who were living in the European-invented Asia.) "Indias Orientales" was the name of the area in possession of the Spanish in the Philippines and Molucas. Interestingly enough, the "arrival" of the Spaniards and Portuguese to the coast of Asia, navigating through the Magellan Strait, covered up and silenced the history of the people who, thousands of years before, crossed the Pacific toward the East and populated what—at the moment the Spanish arrived—had its own name. The Spanish and Portuguese, and then the Dutch, French, and British, all contributed to populate Indias Occidentales and the Caribbean Islands with a massive population of African slaves.

Today it is accepted that the earth is divided into six continents, but there are two ways of cutting the pie. In one case, the Americas is one continent (thus, we have Africa, America, Antarctica, Asia, Australia, and Europe). On the other, Europe and Asia are combined (Africa, Antarctica, Australia, Eurasia, North America, and South America). And you too can probably come up with another possible division. It doesn't matter how you do the division; the real issue is that all forms of the division come from a single and basic root: the Christian continental Triad. To make a long story short, the Christian T/O map that Isidore of Seville (570–636) attached to his famous work *Etymologiae* (The Etymologies). In the Christian T/O maps of the Middle Ages, the earth was divided naturally into three parts and each of them was attributed to one of Noah's sons: Asia to Sem, Africa to Sham, and Europe to Japhet. Obviously, for the Chinese, Indians, Persians, for people in the Mughal and Ottoman Empires in the fifteenth century, etc., such a tripartite division of the earth was either unknown or taken as the Christian way to conceive the world. The reason that America became the fourth continent was simply because those who did not know about it and "discovered" it were Christians, and for them the globe was divided into three continents.

In the sixteenth century, America was "incorporated" into the Christian cosmography and the globe now contained four continents; the Christian triad was thus transformed into the Christian tetragon. Interestingly enough, Bartolomé de Las Casas included, at the end of his *Apologética Historia Sumaria* (c.1552), a classification of "four kinds of barbarians." Las Casas did not equate types of barbarians with particular continents, but it is interesting to notice the transformation of the triad into the tetragon in a classification of "barbarians" that was mainly motivated by the Christian encounters with people they did not know, and who were not contemplated in their cosmological schemes. However, who truly translated Las Casas's tetragon (whether intentionally or not) and corresponded races to particular continents, was Immanuel Kant. Kant reinterpreted Las Casas's tetragon and made it more or less coincide with continents and with the skin color of people inhabiting them. Thus, for Kant, yellow people were in Asia; Blacks in Africa; Red (referring to the Indigenous people) in America, and White people in Europe. Consequently, Europeans in America, as well as their descendants, were considered whites in Kant's scheme. His tetragon lasted until the Nixon Era when Hispanics transformed the tetragon into a pentagon. As we know, "Hispanic" classification, issued officially from the State, managed to create a new category of racialized people within the frame of the Kantian tetragon.

Not all people classified by the State as Hispanics were happy and thankful for such identification. For why is it the privilege of the State to decide who people are? Why did the State use "Hispanic" as the category for people who came mainly from Latin America and not from Spain? Reasons for such decisions are not always given. But one can guess, based on the history of South America and the Spanish-speaking Caribbean Islands: that either the classification was decided because the officers of the Nixon administration were thinking of Spanish as the official language of most of the countries in South America (although there are as many speakers of Portuguese in Brazil than of Spanish in the totality of Spanish-speaking countries, including the corresponding Caribbean Islands), or a des-identification with Latin America came from the Chicano movements and the emergence of political projects (ethnicity, gender, and sexuality) that, from the start, linked des-identification with liberation. And I say *liberation* here instead of *emancipation* for a very particular reason.

The reasons of the State were colonial reasons in identifying a vast and heterogeneous population in the United States, based on the assumption that all of them speak Spanish and, therefore, if one speaks Spanish as the first language then one must be Hispanic (in the same way that speakers of English are assumed to be Anglo—which is the identity politics outlined by Huntington). This is the same logic that the Spanish state applied when it decided that those who lived in the lands that the Spanish Crown and Church took by assault were "Indians." Instead, the reasons that underlined the des-identification with, and delinking from, the State category of "Hispanics" (and therefore, to be detached from the fifth leg of the ethnoracial pentagon), were for liberation and, consequently, for decolonization. "Liberation" and "decolonization" both carry a meaning that "emancipation" doesn't. "Emancipation" entered the vocabulary of secular Europe in the eighteenth century, and the abstract idea was, in Kantian terms (which he equated with Enlightenment itself), was "man's emergence from his self-imposed nonage." (Nonage is the inability to use one's own understanding without another's guidance.)

What Kant most certainly had in mind was the emancipation of a particular class, the European bourgeoisie, from the tutelage of the Church and of the Monarchy. But most likely he was also thinking about men and, deducing from his racial prejudgments,[12] white European men, particularly Germans, French, and British, who were for him at the center and the top of the species (see section four of his *Observations on the Beautiful and the Sublime*). But "emancipation" acquired a second meaning linked to the "civilizing mission" of the second wave of imperial expansion of England and France, after Napoleon. "Emancipation," linked to the "civilizing mission" had deadly consequences since the European man became the "giver" who, in his civilizing mission, was helping the "primitives" (the term was introduced by Joseph Francis Lafitau who died in 1740, just a few decades before the time when Kant was writing), to enlighten and emancipate. The "civilizing mission" was then taken around the world (and still continues) under the presupposition that the further away you get from the heart of Europe (which for Kant and then Hegel was Germany, England, and France—and in that order), the less people are "prepared" to reach the beautiful and the sublime and, concurrently, to reach the highs of "European" rationality. "Emancipation," at that point, slips into genocidal reason, as Enrique Dussel has convincingly argued.[13] The introduction of the concepts of "liberation and decolonization" came precisely from those "primitives" (mainly from the Haitian Revolution and the independence of African and Asian countries after WWII) and, although not using these words, from Martí and Mariátegui's project; and more recently, Indigenous social movements as well as Afro-Caribbean and Afro-Andean. Latinos/as since 1970 began their own projects of liberation and decolonization, thus joining, directly or indirectly, a global network of conceptual (and, therefore, social, political, economic) liberation and decolonization.[14] The main difference between emancipation on the one hand and liberation/decolonization on the other, is that emancipation is what the White Man "gives" while "liberation and decolonization" are what the racially, sexually, and economically des-enfranchised—or, better yet, the "damnés" of Fanon[15]—want and have the right "to take."

Thus seen, Latino/as in the United States (and in the colonial horizon of modernity) are not exactly the people labeled as "Hispanic" by the State. According to the U.S. Census Bureau there are around 40 million Hispanics, which is a number larger than the population of Colombia or Argentina (around 35 million in each country), and close to the combined population of Ecuador, Bolivia, and Chile. As is the case in all these countries, the Hispanic population is not homogeneous in social status, political convictions, sense of self, and community. Not everybody in Bolivia, let's say, supports the neoliberal state, the Indigenous movements, or Marxist syndicalism. However, out of the struggle of Indian people for liberation and decolonization (because the "generosity" of the State is still deep-rooted in the same logic of the "giver" that justified Christian salvation, liberal emancipation, neoliberal freedom and democracy, Marxist socialist revolution, and Islamic universalism), a series of projects for liberation and decolonization emerged while rooted in the history of racialization and domination of the Indigenous experience, which doesn't assume a one-to-one relation between projects of decolonization rooted in Indian history and experience and Indigenous population. Part of the Indigenous population has joined the project of the Church (in a variety of different missions); others joined Marxist movements; still others work in complicity with peripheral neoliberal states. The same can be said about Latino/as. Latino/as project of liberation and decolonization does not necessarily "represent" the 35 million "Hispanics" of the national census!!!! It could or could not. On the one hand, it is up to those who have been classified as Hispanics to join Latino/as project of decolonization as their des-identification and liberation. It is not the task necessarily of Latino/a leaders to preach the gospel as the Church, Marxists, liberals, and neoliberals did and still do. Conversely, Latino/as contribution to decolonization in the United States and in their connection with other similar social movements around the world (for which the World Social Forum and the Social Forum of the Americas are becoming a place to "connect"), are not restricted to Latino/as. Here there are two common assumptions that must be dispelled.

One is that if a social movement and decolonizing project emerges from the historical experience of a racialized group it shall—of necessity—be limited to that racial(ized) group. Latino/as or Indigenous political projects are led by Latino/as and Indigenous people, but *not restricted to those who consider themselves Indigenous or to Hispanics who see themselves as Latino/as.* I am sure that Huntington will be ready to embrace any non-Anglo volunteer who would like to join his identity-politic political project, in the same way that neoliberals will embrace anyone who is ready to accept their belief system as justification for action.

The second is that those who belong to a racialized group have no choice but to identify themselves with the political projects of such groups. Thus, if you are Anglo and White, you cannot join a Black, Indigenous or Latino/as project and have no choice but to remain within the identity politics defended by Huntington. Both assumptions imply the need to uncouple political projects (which are elected and selected by the individual) from the social group "arranged" by the state by way of its language of classification, which serves to "manage" the population both nationally and globally. Latino/as, in this respect, are no longer a problem "just" of the United States but they are increasingly becoming a global issue. In that respect, due attention shall be paid to the fact that in nine years, Huntington will have made a significant contribution to invent the Muslims as paramount "challenge" to the Western civilization and as he now is inventing the Latino/as as paramount "challenge" to the United States

4. Back to Huntington's Fears

There is indeed good reason to expel Huntington's fears, whether they are deeply felt or strategically located. The emergence and growing presence of all kinds of Latino/as political and ethical projects present as good a reason to understand Huntington's fears as they help explain and understand the anonymous population he labels "Hispanics." And the real "fear" that Huntington would like to instill (paralleling the hegemony of fear we are living in) is perhaps returning to him as a boomerang, along with the hegemonic system of belief that underlies the rhetoric of neoliberalism. For, what is at stake in Latino/as critical and political project is that *we* are moving away from the system of belief and the logic in which Huntington has cast both the "challenge" of civilization clashes (in the aftermath of the exhaustion of "civilizing mission" possibilities) and the "Hispanic challenge." We are *delinking*. And we are delinking, but not in the terms of Samir Amin who conceived the project several decades ago.[16] Amin's delinking was *no* more than a fracture; it was only a change of content but not an effort in building of an-other logic, which means telling of an altogether different story—an*other* story.[17] Amin remained within the modern paradigm of the European Enlightenment and failed to understand that Marxism allows for a dissenting position only within the same cosmology in which the dissent is thought out; but it cannot truly be a delinking.

There is no point in entering Huntington's system and disputing his assertions and forecasts on his terms. It is always possible to make small changes in that mode but it only serves to maintain the existing rules. Delinking means that there are other games in town to play and *we* are no longer without alternatives. We are no longer condemned to complaining while staying within the system, playing according to its set rules. The point now is that *other* games are starting to be played, *other* rules are being created and implemented. And that is more than a good reason for the fearsome State and "civil" society to take seriously the fears that Huntington has spelled out for *them*.

The recent events involving the denial of a U.S. visa to Tariq Ramadan is another case in point that contests, without entering the preset game, Huntington's propagation of fear. Ramadan is not an extremist engineer but a scholar who knows as well the Q'uran and Muslim thoughts, as he knows Western philosophy.[18] His weapon is knowledge and his strategy is to play a different game. He, in a parallel location to the Latino/as in the United States, is a Muslim scholar in the West who is contributing to build another logic beyond the cage in which neoliberalism and Islamic Fundamentalists (as well as Russians and Chechens) are trapped. Linking and connections between projects that attempt to delink from hegemonic logic is the way to the future.

We have to recognize "Huntington's Challenge" but *we* shall not play into his logic and only contest his content. *We* have to start (*we* are starting) from the fact that another world is possible and that *we, engaged in Latino/as ethical, political, and epistemic projects* (as well as constructive Islamic ones), have another soup to cook. To look at the future without fear and with courage, cutting the umbilical cord from all kinds of Huntington's on the right and the left who still play in the post-Renaissance imperial and Christian logic as well as in their new secular, post-Enlightenment versions, once again, on the left and the right. Latino/as ethical, political, and epistemic project is one among many, around the planet, working toward an-other world, an-other logic, an-other sensibility celebrating life and love instead of preannouncing and enacting hatred and death.

Notes

1. The basic thesis of my argument here has been already advanced in previous publications. See, mainly, Walter D. Mignolo, *Local Histories/Global Designs: Coloniality, Subaltern Knowledges, and Border Thinking.* Princeton, NJ: Princeton University Press, 2000; Walter D. Mignolo, "The Larger Picture: Hispanics/Latinos (and Latino Studies) in the Colonial Horizon

of Modernity," in Jorge J. E. Gracia and Pablo De Greiff, eds., *Hispanics/Latinos in the United States*. New York: Routledge, 2000, pp. 99–124; Walter D. Mignolo, "Coloniality at Large: The Western Hemisphere in the Colonial Horizon of Modernity," *The New Centennial Review*, 2001, 1:2, pp. 19–54.

Samuel Huntington, *Who Are We? The Challenges to America's National Identity*. New York: Simon and Schuster, 2004. Of particular interest are Part II, "American Identity" and chapters 7 and 9 of Part III. The first is "Challenges to American Identity" and the second, "Mexican Immigration and Hispanization." The latter was published as an advance of the book under the title of "The Hispanic Challenge" in *Foreign Policy*, March/April 2004, www.foreignpolicy.com/story/cms.php?story_id=2495.

2. Samuel P. Huntington, "The Clash of Civilizations?" *Foreign Affairs* (Summer 1993), vol. 72, no. 3. This article was later reproduced with several responses (edited by Huntington) and published as: *The Clash of Civilizations? The Debate*. New York: Foreign Affairs, 1996. The book published a couple of years after the article is: *The Clash of Civilizations and the Remaking of World Order*. New York: Simon and Schuster, 1996.

3. Huntington, *The Clash of Civilizations? The Debate*, 1996.

4. In the article published by Huntington in *Foreign Policy*, a month or so before the publication of *Who Are We?* following a strategy similar to the article and debate on *The Clash of Civilizations* advanced in *Foreign Affairs* in 1993, and the publication of the debate, by the same journal, in 1996.

5. David Hollinger, *Postethnic America: Beyond Multiculturalism*. New York: BasicBooks, 1995—a publication that appeared nearly simultaneously with Huntington's *Clash of Civilizations*.

6. Ramón Grosfoguel, *Colonial Subjects: Puerto Rico in a Global Perspective*. Berkeley: University of California Press, 2003.

7. Natalio Botana, *La Tradición Republicana: Alberdi, Sarmiento y las ideas políticas de su tiempo*. Buenos Aires: Sudamericana, 1984.

8. Jeffrey P. Johnson, ed., trans., *Selected Works of Juan Donoso Cortés*. Westport: Greenwood Press, 2000.

9. There is by now an extensive bibliography on South America from the perspective of women, Creoles, Mestizas, and a few immigrants based in different countries. Of all the work being done, the most interesting from my argument are the ones crossing gender and sexuality with racism. That is precisely where "Latinidad" as masculine and "white" category began to break apart. See for instance one of the most important collections of articles in this respect: Silvia Rivera Cusicanqui, ed., *Ser mujer indígena, chola o birlocha en la Bolivia postcolonial de los años 90*. La Paz: Ministerio de Desarrollo Humano, 1996.

10. For instance, Sonia Saldívar-Hull, *Feminism on the Border: Chicana Politics and Literature*. Berkeley: University of California Press, 2000, in which Saldívar-Hull establishes links with politics of women in Latin America.

11. David Hollinger, *Postethnic America: Beyond Multiculturalism*, 1995.

12. Emmanuel Chukwudi Eze, "Color of Reason," in *Post-Colonial African Philosophy: A Critical Reader*, ed. Emmanuel Chukwudi Eze, Malden, MA: Blackwell, 1997.

13. Enrique Dussel, *The Invention of the Americas: Eclipse of 'the Other' and the Myth of Modernity*, trans. Michael D. Barber. New York: Continuum, 1995.

14. Although not directly related to my argument here, the case of the ex-Soviet Union colonies shall be mentioned. The "socialist revolution" had the same logic as "bourgeois emancipation" although with different content. The socialist revolutionaries with good "conscience" carried their own civilizing mission: to civilize the colonies meant for them to "convert" (or impose) socialism, as much as the British civilizing mission attempted to "convert" (or impose) liberal ideas that were being thought out and implemented in Europe. For reasons that I cannot explain here, liberating and decolonizing projects are not yet visible in either the ex-colonies or the states that remained under the Kremlin administration. Chechnya in particular is a case that deserves much more than a footnote. For my purpose here it should be kept in mind that, beyond

the eighty years of secularism under Soviet rule, Chechens are Muslims in their majority in a state in which Orthodox Christianity has a long history of complicity with imperialism, as long as Catholicism and Protestantism have in the West.

15. Nelson Maldonado-Torres, "Topology of Being and the Geopolitics of Knowledge: Modernity, Empire, Coloniality," *City: Analysis of Urban Trends, Culture, Theory, Policy, Action* (April 2004), vol. 8, no. 1., pp. 29–56.

16. Samir Amin, *Delinking: Towards a Polycentric World.* London: Zed Books, 1990.

17. There are many instances already around the world in which what I am saying can be substantiated, although this is not the place to expand on it. See Walter D. Mignolo, "The Geopolitics of Knowledge and the Colonial Difference," *SAQ* (Winter 2002), vol. 101, no.1, pp. 56–96; Catherine Walsh, "Interculturality and Coloniality of Power: An Other Thinking and Positioning from the Colonial Difference," in *Coloniality of Power, Transmodernity and Border Thinking,* ed. Ramon Grosfoguel, Nelson Maldonado-Torres, and Jose Saldívar. Durham, N.C.: Duke University Press, forthcoming; Maldonado-Torres, "The Topology of Being and the Geopolitics of Knowledge," in *City*; and, of course, pioneering works such as those by Frantz Fanon, Abdelkhebir Khatibi, Sayyid Qutb, Gloria Anzaldúa, etc.

18. See, for instance, his *Western Muslims and the Future of Islam.* London: Oxford University Press, 2004; and "Globalization: Muslim Resistances," Union Europea: Editions Tawhid, 2003.

PART III

Decolonization, Afro-Latin@s, and the African Diaspora

4

Afro-Latin@ Difference and the Politics of Decolonization

Agustín Lao-Montes

There finally seems to be a tendency in U.S. current scholarship and public culture to recognize the specificity of Afro-Latin@ difference.[1] A current wave of courses and publications on Afro-Hispanics and Afro-Latin@s is accompanied by public discussion on the relationships between Blacks and Latin@s as shown in such diverse publications as the *New York Times* and NAACP's *The Crisis*. Ironically, the new scholarly focus on Afro-Latin@s is matched with media highlights of Latin@s having more numbers than Blacks as part of a public discourse that pits one essentialized group against the other. These categorical representations that compare and confront "Blacks" to "Latin@s" tend to erase Afro-Latin@s from such simple equations of identity, culture, and politics. Against the grain of these terms of discourse, this article will explore some theoretical and political stakes involved in positing a particular thread of identification (and therefore of history and politics) that I will denominate Afro-Latin@ and/or Afro-Hispanic. Given our inquiry about Latin@s in the world-system in this volume, the focus of this paper will be on the specific locations of Afro-Latin@s within the world-historical pattern of the coloniality of power, and in the implications of their histories for the theory and politics of decolonization. The analysis will mostly draw from three historically rich and theoretically suggestive examples; namely Afro-Cuban politics and cultural movements since the nineteenth-century anticolonial war, the multiple meanings and locations of Afro-Puerto Rican Arturo Schomburg, and the critical values and limits of the trope of Caliban. But before examining such examples, it is imperative to interrogate the very notions of Afro-Latin@ and Afro-Hispanic, while drawing the analytical implications of doing so.

Afro-Latinidad: What's in a Name?

The hyphenated phrase Afro-Latin@ simultaneously signifies two complex and contested fields of identification; Africanity (or African-ness) and Latinidad. It is beyond the scope of this paper to develop a genealogy of these two identitarian discourses and their entangledness. Nonetheless, we should raise some key questions in order to specify our analysis and establish the argument. For instance, what are the spatiotemporal parameters and categorical character of Latinidad? Is Latinidad a transhistorical global civilizational attribute that defines a Latin civilization opposed to Anglo-Saxons as in nineteenth-century French imperial ideology? Is it primarily a hemispheric linguistic/cultural postimperial common ground, based on ancestry, which unifies the former subjects of the Spanish empire in the Americas? Or, is it more specifically, a U.S. territorially based, relatively recent panethnic designation for people of Latin American descent who reside in the United States?

Each of these possible interpretations of the time-space of Latinidad can also serve as premises to construct different analyses of its categorical status in relation to distinct discourses of race, ethnicity, nationhood, culture, and civilization. For example, in what we can call the Hispanic world (e.g., Spain, Hispanic America, U.S. Latino cities), people still celebrate Columbus Day as "El Dia de la Raza" (literally "The Day of the Race"). Can we situate this signification of Latinidad as "la raza" in the same semantic field with the 1960s Chicano slogan "Que Viva la Raza," and the 1970s salsa music/dance claim of unity of Latin@s as "la raza Latina"? Arguably, here "la raza," the same signifier, signifies three different ethnoracial discourses of Latinidad. In the first, the label la raza denotes a common Spanish heritage that connotes a Eurocentric genealogy that tends to marginalize "other" histories and sources of the Latin@ American self (e.g., African, Asian, Amerindian). Indeed, ideologies of Latinidad based on occidentalist discourses that ascribe primacy and superiority to White European history, culture, and identity are still hegemonic in Latin American countries as well as in U.S. Latino communities.

In contrast, the Chicano notion of "la raza" was conceived within a universe of discourse produced by a social movement seeking to challenge Eurocentric interpretations of history and culture, while opposing white racism in the United States, and affirming a Chicano memory and identity as conquered people of color (or internal colonies). For the most part, Chicano discourse imagined (and imaged) the nonwhiteness of la raza through a mestizo logic in which Chicanidad was conceived as a brown/bronze ethnorace (or nation), affirming itself against White supremacy, while entering in alliances with other negatively racialized ethnonational groupings (other Latin@s such as Puerto Ricans, and ethnoracial groups like Blacks and Asians). In this vein, most male Chicano discourses tended (and still do) to highlight the Amerindian element in order to trace a non-European/nonwhite ancestry, while also tending to marginalize the African elements in Mexican history and culture, as well as the significance of Afro-Latinidades.

Finally, statements such as "la salsa representando la raza latina" (salsa representing the Latin@ race), are enunciated from within a cultural imaginary in which Africa is often claimed as the root of the rhythm and the music. In the same song, called "La Raza Latina," the lyrics articulate an Afro-diasporic multicentered translocal/global geography of Latinidad: "Representando a las Antillas, a Puerto Rico, Cuba, Aruba, y Santo Domingo. Representando a las Americas, a Venezuela, Colombia, y Panama. Representando al Africa, con sus tambores viva la conga, viva el timbal. Representando la raza Latina, en todas las esquinas…"[2] Interestingly, this vernacular cosmopolitan discourse of the salsa of the 1970s is one of the few cultural settings in which Africanity came to be represented as one of the principal markers of Latinidad. In short, when speaking of Latinidad and its relations with Africanity, we should be very attentive as to how particular discourses of Latinidad entail specific significations of its civilizational, cultural, and ethnoracial content as a world-historical category and consequently as the way that it articulates with the prefix "afro" with its precise meaning of Africanity.

Africa, the African diaspora, and the prefix Afro, are also polyvalent words that signify highly contested and complex world-historical categories. Can we talk about Africa, in rigor as a relatively unified geohistorical continent, before the advent of modernity? Or alternatively, is what Mudimbe calls the "invention of Africa"[3] need to be conceptualized as part and parcel of the modern/colonial configuration of the hegemonic categories of time, space, language, and self that began to articulate a world-system in the long sixteenth century under the dominance of European empires? If Africa as a geohistorical/geocultural entity and category (as an epistemic and ontological reality) is an offspring of transmodernity, how should we conceptualize the relationship between the African continent and people of African descent throughout the world? Should we see Africa as an immutable mother and hence as the ultimate origin and source of unity and identity of all peoples of African descent in the world? Or alternatively, should we develop a more historicized concept of Africanity to account for continuities and discontinuities within continental Africa, as well as between the African continent and among people of African descent in different parts of the world? In the same register arises the question of how to theorize diaspora in the relationship to Africanity. Is the African diaspora composed by Africans outside of the continent, or is diaspora a condition that constitute Africanity itself in the context of violence, uprootedness, destabilization, and dispersal that came along with the institution of chattel slavery, the emergence of Africanist discourses of dark continent and of Negrophobia, but also with the rise of black social movements, publics, and cultural practices as "countercultures of modernity." To compare and contrast theories of the African diaspora is beyond the scope of this monograph.[4] The language of African diaspora is relatively recent, but black cosmopolitanisms have a long history ranging from early twentieth-century pan-African projects of return to origins and redemption of the homeland, to recent postcolonial and poststructuralist notions that understand African-ness as, either a transnational historical formation loosely linked by racism and racial politics, or as an imagined world that is strategically constructed out of disparate units and a play of differences. How are we to link Latinidad and Africanity in this highly contested and loaded domain of discourse?

I would argue that Latinidad and Africanity are modern/colonial categories of classification and identification that as such are mediated by (while they are constitutive of) world-historical processes of exploitation and domination, as well as by particular trajectories of political agency and genres of cultural expression. Hence, we would pursue a dialectic (and analectic) genealogic method according to which we should investigate the historical trajectories of discursive categories in relation to their power effects (within the local, national, and global patterns of the coloniality of power), and how they express and inform the constitution of forms of agency and subjection. Thus, Latinidad and Africanity are to be contextually defined, their analytical and political value being contingent to how they establish fields of identification in relation to particular configurations of geography, lineages of memory, and ethicopolitical projects, as we shall see. Paradoxically, modern/colonial categories of identity are relatively indeterminate, at the same time that they aim to be categorical, and therefore tend to be mutually exclusive. In this register, an important characteristic of any definition of Afro-Latin@ as a category is that it tends to remain outside of, or marginalized from, hegemonic narratives of both Africanity and Latinidad.

Latin@/Americanist hegemonic discourses of geography, culture, and identity, tend to be founded on a Eurocentric civilizational/racial logic within which Afro-Latin@ histories and cultures are either marginalized or entirely erased. The foundational ideologies of Latin@/American identity were premised on the same occidentalist discourses in which blackness was located at the bottom of the so-called great chain of being and Africa imagined as a dark continent situated at the margins of history and outside of civilization. These ideologies of identification correspond to ethnoracial hierarchies (economic, political, cultural) created in a colonial context, wherein Afro-Americans and

Amerindians and their cultures and knowledges, are subalternized and subordinated to Euro-American power. These are the world-regional, national, and local configurations of the global pattern that we call the coloniality of power. Arguably, Afro-Latin@s (or Blacks) are situated either at the bottom (as in the folklorized representation of the Puerto Rican Culture Institute of the African as the "third root"), or altogether outside of Latin@/Americanist world-regional and nationalist discourses. This clearly corresponds to the subaltern location of many Latin American peoples of African descent, not only because of racial hierarchies and racist cultures, but also within racialized regimes of labor exploitation and political disenfranchisement.

On the other hand, from the standpoint of Africanity, people of African descent placed in Iberoamerica tend to be left out of, or remain marginal within, most mappings of the Black Atlantic. This is partly because of a hegemonic Anglo-American outlook that even dominates definitions of the African diaspora, as well as the geographic contours of postcolonial studies and subalternism. Arguably, this excess of focus on the British Empire and on U.S. racial politics that is hegemonic in Black Studies, postcolonial critique, and subaltern studies tends to replicate imperial hierarchies of knowledge/power, within which Western European languages are dominant, and wherein Anglo-American hegemonies (Pax Brittanica and Pax Americana) are taken for granted as the main geopolitical frameworks for theory and politics. Furthermore, there is a tendency in both scholarship and activism, especially in the United States but also in Britain and the West Indies, to buy into the hegemonic ideology according to which "race relations" in Latin America have been characterized by mestizaje and racial democracy. Following these kinds of logics, Afro-Latin@s histories, cultures, and politics are barely registered in the emerging body of literature on the African diaspora in the Americas.

Given these theoretical and political tensions, a critical analysis of Afro-Latin@ as a category could potentially unpack and unleash contradictions in discourses of both Africanity and Latinidad. Such sort of critique could be crucial for problematizing and deconstructing key modern/colonial ideologies of identification enunciated by signifiers like blackness, Hispanidad, Afro-Caribbean, Afro-diasporic, African American, and Latin@ itself. To interpret how all of these signifiers of memory, identity, and culture intersect and are reciprocally embedded, I propose a cross-fertilization of the Chicana concept of borderland with the notion of African American as a set of overlapping diasporas.[5] Here diaspora is neither an essentialized cultural community spreading from a primordial homeland, nor a pastiche of entirely disparate locations, but a constellation of political movements, intellectual networks, and cultural genres, that are articulated by shared histories of racial capitalism and colonial subordination, and by political and aesthetic projects of self-affirmation and liberation. This world-historical postcolonial perspective can help us to reconceptualize the Black Atlantic and African American as a set of entangled diasporas wherein Afro-Latin@s had historically played important roles, while rethinking Latinidad as a global and hemispheric translocal category that should be defined and challenged by both the presence and marginalization of Afro-diasporic subjects within and beyond its borders. A fruitful angle for critique could be the ever-changing and contested politics of naming, as in who is included and excluded from the designation African American that replaced "Negro" and "Black" as the politically preferred self-designations for U.S. peoples of African descent. Is confining African American to the north a way of promoting the imperial reduction of America to the United States? It is playing in the liberal game of hyphenated ethnicization? Should we instead redefine the expression as Africans in the Americas? On the other hand, should we choose between Afro-Latin@ and Afro-Hispanic or do they reveal distinct dynamics and particular genealogies? Can the distinct yet intertwined categories of Afro-Hispanic and Afro-Latin@ suggest more fluid and complex understandings of both Latinidad and Hispanidad? A curiously revealing example is the sixteenth-century Black Latin grammarian and functionary of the Hapsburg Empire Juan Latino who, as put by Jose Piedra, acquired literary whiteness by mastering Castillian and marrying into a noble family, but who in his poetry also identified subtlety with the Black subaltern. Juan Latino, who can effectively be identified as Afro-Hispanic, was an important inspiration to Afro-diasporic intellectual Arturo Schomburg in the early twentieth century.

Arturo Alfonso Schomburg: Afro-Boricua Cosmopolitan

The life and legacy of Arturo Schomburg, a Puerto Rican–born mulatto who founded what still is the most important world archive of Black history, was a pillar of the Harlem Renaissance, and became president of the American Negro Academy, is a pregnant source for this discussion. The differential construction of Schomburg's biography by Puerto Rican, Black American, and Afro-Caribbean intellectuals is revealing of how distinct diaspora discourses define their subject and its space.

In Puerto Rico Schomburg is barely known, while in U.S. Puerto Rican memory he is top on the official list of great Boricuas, at the same time that U.S. Black historians remember him as Black archivist Arthur Schomburg. Jamaican historian Winston James[6] argues that Schomburg abandoned his Hispanic Caribbean militancy after 1898 and eventually let go of his Puerto Rican identity in favor of an Afro-diasporic one. But if we analyze Schomburg's work and his intellectual and political project, we should get a more complex view of his multiple locations and loyalties.

His long-lasting commitment to what we now call Afro-Latinidades[7] can be clearly seen in his struggle for inclusion of Afro-Cubans and Puerto Ricans in organizations like the Negro Society for Historical Research and of Afro-Hispanic writers in anthologies of Black literature. His research on Africans in early modern Spain pioneered the current revision of European history as multiracial since its very inception. His advocacy for translation of Afro-Latin@ writers like Nicolas Guillen revealed an effort to articulate an African diaspora as an explicit strategic project. Schomburg's leadership in the Prince Hall Mason Lodge was, as demonstrated by Jossiana Arroyo, another clear expression of his complex Afro-diasporic subjectivity, and particularly of his enduring connection to Afro-Latinidad. Indeed, Schomburg could not give up his Afro-Latin@ identity because his blackness was always contested in the United States, given not only his Puerto Rican origin but also because of his mixed ancestry and color (i.e., his ascribed mulatto self).

It was perhaps partly because of his border subjectivity that Schomburg was the one Black figure in the United States at the early twentieth century who kept good relations with often opposing characters like DuBois, Garvey, McKay, and Locke. But my main point is that his project of Black cosmopolitanism, standing from a recognition of diversity and complexity in the racial regimes and cultural practices in different African diaspora spaces, challenged narrow nationalist notions of both Africanity and Latinidad. He was in Lisa Sanchez's words a "transamerican intellectual"[8] who promoted a worldly diasporic project in which identity and community were conceived through and across difference. Schomburg's liminal location at various crossroads of Africanity and Latinidad made him a quintessential diasporic intellectual whose subject positioning and hence his epistemic outlook and political project was articulated from a standpoint of colonial difference (as in Walter Mignolo).[9] Schomburg's specific articulation of his colonial difference was Afro-diasporic and within this general terrain he always identified the particularity of Afro-Latin@ difference.

Schomburg's special interest in Juan Latino, and generally in Blacks in early modern Spain (in other words, Afro-Latin@s), reveal an interest in tracing a genealogy to Afro-Latinidades while registering their presence since the rise of modernity. This within itself implies a different reading (through the lens of Afro-Hispanic difference) of European history and of the very meaning of Hispanidad. On the other hand, Schomburg's use of the Amerindian word *Guarionex*[10] as a pen name, expresses his identification with subaltern resistance against European rule, at the same time that it reveals a nonessentialist notion of Africanity. In short, Schomburg's project was not simply one of inclusion of Afro-Latin@s in mappings of modern history, and particularly in cartographies of the African diaspora, but furthermore to disrupt and complexify our analyses of history and diasporic identity in light of the specificity of Afro-Latino difference.[11]

Afro-Latinidades within and beyond Caliban's Reason

We can also think the question of Afro-Latinidades through the trope of Caliban. Clearly a word play with canibal and the Caribbean, Caliban the savage who masters the language of the colonizer the curse back to him in Shakespeare's

Tempest became a conceptual character in Caribbean critiques of imperial power. Since the 1960s Caliban had been a key concept/metaphor in Caribbean postcolonial theory adopted across divides by intellectuals such as George Lamming, Aime Cesaire, Roberto Fernandez Retamar, Sylvia Wynter, and Paget Henry. Here I will only highlight three elements in this stream that José Saldívar calls the School of Caliban. First is that in spite of a shared intent of performing a postcolonial critique of Western thought and imperial domination, the very definitions of the subaltern space of Caliban and its relevant oppositional actors are not quite the same. Invoking Marti, for Fernandez Retamar, Caliban is the symbol of "Our Mestizo America" which means more Latin America than the Caribbean, while for Henry *Caliban's Reason* signifies a philosophical project indigenous to the Afro-Caribbean. Fernandez Retamar's Caribbean only marginally includes West Indian critical intellectuals while Henry's Afro-Caribbean is largely oblivious to Afro-Latin@s. In fact, Fernandez Retamar also does not recognize the specificity of Afro-Cuban difference. I propose that his reading of Marti as an anticolonial postoccidentalist thinker should situate Marti's antiracist subalternist sensibility within a history of Afro-Cuban militancy for racial and social equality that made the Cuban revolutionary army the first multiracial military in the Americas and the Cuban independence war the only insurrection of its time with the potential of becoming a social revolution, in this sense following the steps of Haiti. This specifically Afro-Cuban domain of politics continued with the organization of the first Black political organization in the Americas, the Partido Independiente de Color in 1910 that was crushed by a state racist massacre in 1912.[12] Another important absence in Fernandez Retamar's Caliban is the registration of 200,000 members of Garvey's Universal Negro Improvement Association in Cuba. It will be epistemic violence to claim, as some historians do, that these members of the UNIA were all Jamaicans with no significance in Cuban culture and politics.

The second point is that if there is a valuable critical edge in the allegory of Caliban, it is also problematic insofar as it is a master's trope that implies a from of critique by using the language and name given by the colonizer. Arguably, such paradox calls for a move toward a "post-Caliban period [where] we should create a new language and political categories" as put by Anthony Bogues. My contention is that there is need of a double critique or border thinking in which we should combine *Caliban's Reason* with post-Caliban's subaltern knowledge.[13] But Henry's project of an Afro-Caribbean Creolized philosophy composed by historicism and poetics will gain by integrating Afro-Cuban thinkers such as Juan Gualberto Gomez and Gustavo Urrutia, while Bogues' redefinition of Black radical political intellectual as prophetic should include Afro-Cuban spiritual traditions of healing and divination. This is not a mere call for inclusion but a quest for complexity in tracing the family resemblances[14] and linkages that define both the Caribbean and the Black Atlantic as geohistoric spaces in order to inform a coalitional politics of decolonization.

Finally, José Saldívar's Caliban names a Latin@ critical theory that redraws the borders of Our America across North-South divides for "a comparative cultural analysis of Latin American, Afro-American, African American, and Chicano/a writers." Saldívar's trans-American postcolonial perspective articulates a hemispheric field of cultural production and anti-imperial politics that moves from Marti to Anzaldúa. Caliban is gendered through the feminist gaze of Cherry Moraga where imperial power is seen through its patriarchal and heterosexist expressions. Moraga's identification with Sycorax, Caliban's mother, parallels Sylvia Wynter's claiming of Prospero's daughter Miranda for Caribbean feminism. As a border theorist Saldívar facilitates a critical space for multiple engagements, a diaspora space wherein Ntozake Shange can say "I write in English, French, and Spanish…cuz my consciousness mingle all New World African experiences." Zange, who was also considered a Nuyorican poet, represents a link between Chicanos and Puerto Ricans. Arguably, U.S. Latinidad as a grassroots signifier of negatively racialized peoples was primarily the product of the Chicano and Nuyorical movements of the 1960s. For the Young Lords, a Puerto Rican organization of the period, Latinidad was a project of decolonization that implied recasting an Afro-Indian heritage against the Eurocentric and Hispanophile dominant culture. This placing of the African together with the Indian is still an unlikely scenario in Latin America where indigenismo even in its radical manifestations tends to enhance the marginalization of Afro-Latin@s.

Afro-Latinidades and the Politics of Decolonization

To conclude I will briefly formulate five arguments on how Afro-Latinidad relates to the question of decolonization.

One, I propose that we conceptualize decolonization as a secular tendency of the modern/colonial capitalist world-system. Decolonization is the combined effect of everyday resistances, multiple struggles, and antisystemic movements. Because of the centrality of racial regimes in the matrix of the coloniality of power and given the enduring location of African and Afro-diasporic subjects at the very bottom of racial hierarchy, Black struggles and racial politics are crucial in the longue duree of world decolonization as exemplified by the Haitian revolution, the U.S. Black Freedom movement of the 1960s, and the anti-apartheid movement. In this sense, decolonization is a key concept for developing a subalternist perspective within world-system analysis.

Two, the multiple axes of the coloniality of power (labor exploitation, ethnoracial/ethnonational, cultural, and patriarchal domination) that correspond to the entangled logics of the system (politicoeconomic, geopolitical, geocultural) imply multiple and often uneven processes of decolonization. Given this, I contend that a theory and politics of decolonization/democratization should frame what Laclau calls the chain of equivalences among different movements in relation to the chains of coloniality. Hence the decolonization of mind, body, spirit, memory, identity, economy, and polity that we have been advocating in this conference should be at the heart of a formulation of a new analytics of the political and a new politics of liberation.

Three, if we frame U.S. Latino politics in terms of this ethicopolitical project of decolonization, Latinidad appears as a contingent and necessarily ambiguous political identity. I had argued that we need to distinguish ideologies of U.S. Latin@ power and that for Latinidad to be a useful standpoint for a transformative politics it needs to formulate its project and practice not simply in terms of ethnoracial empowerment, but in relation to global struggles against capitalist exploitation, imperial power, and patriarchal domination.

Four, regarding Afro-Latin@s (north and south), their multiple marginalizations (from Latin American polities, from narratives of U.S. Latinidad, and from many mappings of the Black Atlantic), lends their complex subalternity the possibility for challenging narrow nationalist and essentialist cartographies and ideologies of identity. Thus, Afro-Latin@s are engaged in a plurality of trenches from urban movements for racial justice in New York to political ecological movements claiming communal land and cultural rights in Colombia. The attempt to articulate an Afro-Andean discourse is redrawing the region and transcending Mariategui's project of an indoamerican socialism. Afro-Latinidad is also becoming a political signifier to build organization of people of African descent across the Americas. In these trans-American efforts diaspora could be shaped as a project of decolonization.

Fifth, to take Grant Farred's call to vernacularize Black intellectuals, we should vernacularize critical theory itself and vernacularize politics. This move implies what Mignolo calls a process of double translation to establish a dialogue based on reciprocity between the subaltern knowledges (let's say of the African diaspora in the Americas) and the cultures of scholarship and activism. An important example is the collaboration of vernacular intellectuals, scholars, and artists in hip-hop culture.[15]

To close, in the domain of critical political theory and transformative politics, I will like to suggest a counterpoint between Quijano's conceptualization of the global dominant as an imperial bloc[16] and Partha Chaterjee's recent move of developing postcolonial political categories grounded on the actual conditions and ongoing struggles of the global subaltern.

Notes

1. A shorter version of this paper was presented at the *Latinos on the World-System Conference* at the University of California at Berkeley, April 21–23, 2004.
2. "Representing the Antilles, Puerto Rico, Cuba, Aruba, and Santo Domingo. Representing the Americas, Venezuela Colombia, and Panama. Representing Africa, with its drums, long live the conga, long live the timbal. Representing the Latino race, in all the corners…"

3. Clearly, the epistemic invention of Africa as a continent corresponds to the birth of a global space in the long sixteenth century with the so-called discovery of the Americas, the early organization of the capitalist world-economy centered in the Atlantic, and the rise of European empires as transoceanic powers that corresponded to the organization of Spain as the first absolutist state in Europe. These world-historical developments, which mark the profound revolution that we call the advent of modernity, also entailed the emergence of modern/colonial discourses of the subject (and forms of subjection) and categories of the self such as "race" (and later ethnicity), as well as a new form of organization of state sovereignty and political community that eventually were articulated in notions of nationhood and nationality. As part of the geographic and historical knowledge produced within this overall process, the world was divided into continents, civilizations, and races in ways that were (and are) fairly continuous. Hence, the invention of Africa came along with the invention of Europe and the Americas, as well as with the emergence of racial discourses about blackness, whiteness, and native and mestizo Americans conceived both as racial and civilizational groups.

4. For two particularly suggestive analyses see Patterson and Kelley (2000), and Edwards (2001).

5. I can't develop this argument in this short monograph. We can see some first steps toward the same project in Clifford (1994). For the concept of "overlapping diaspora" see Lewis (1995).

6. See James (1998).

7. I use the expression Afro-Latinidades in order to define Afro-Latin@s as a domain of difference wherein there is a large variety in terms of expressive cultures, political projects, historical trajectories, and modes of identification.

8. See Sanchez-Gonzalez (2001).

9. For Mignolo, colonial difference is a general category that encompasses all forms of subjection of those subjects located outside of Europe (ot "the West") within the pattern of the coloniality of power. See Mignolo (2000).

10. Guarionex was the name of a Taino (Caribbean Antillean indigenous) chief who fought fiercely against the Spanish conquest.

11. In this segment I am highlighting how Schomburg's discourse and project express the specificity of Afro-Latin@ difference and the epistemic openings offered by its liminality. I do not engage in a critique of his work and politics, given that this is beyond the scope of this article. However, I want to clarify that in regard to Schomburg I use the expression Afro-Latino (and not Afro-Latina/o) given the masculinist character of his discourse (see Arroyo 2005).

12. For the Partido Independiente de Color see Helg (1995).

13. For a more detailed discussion of such questions see Lao-Montes (2004).

14. For the concept of family resemblances see Wittgenstein (2001).

15. For an excellent analysis of the multiple contradictions of significations of Africanity and Latinidad in hip-hop culture see Rivera (2003).

16. I take this formulation from Quijano's keynote speech at the *Latinos in the World-System Conference* at the University of California at Berkeley, April 21–23, 2004.

References

Anzaldúa, Gloria (1987). *Borderlands/La Frontera: The New Mestiza*. San Francisco: Spinters/Aunt Lute.

Arroyo, Jossianna (2003). *Travestismos Culturales: Literatura y etnografía en Cuba y Brasil*. Pittsburg: Nuevo Siglo.

Arroyo, Jossianna (2005). "Technologies: Transculturations of Race, Gender, and Ethnicity in Arturo A. Schomburg's Masonic Writings." In Mirabal, Nancy, and Agustin Lao-Montes, ed., *Techno-Futuros: Critical Interventions in Latina/o Studies*. San Francisco: Rowman and Littlefield (forthcoming).

Bogues, Anthony (2003). *Black Heretics and Black Prophets: Radical Political Intellectuals*. New York: Routledge.

Cesaire, Aime (1972). *Discourse on Colonialism*. New York: Monthly Review Press.

Chatterjee, Partha (2003). *The Politics of the Governed*. New York: Columbia University Press.

Clifford, James (1994). "Diasporas." *Cultural Anthropology* Vol. 9, No. 3: 302–338.

Edwards, Brent Hayes (2001). "The Uses of Diaspora." *Social Text* 66, Spring: 45–73.

Farred, Grant (2003). *What's My name? Black Vernacular Intellectuals*. Minneapolis: University of Minnesotta Press.

Fernandez Retamar, Roberto (2003). *Todo Caliban*. San Juan, P.R. : Ediciones Callejon.

Helg, Aline (1995). Our Rightful Share. *The Afro-Cuban Struggle for Equality, 1886–1912*. Chapel Hill: University of North Carolina Press.

Henry, Paget (2000). *Caliban's Reason: Introducing Afro-Caribbean Philosophy*. New York: Routldege.

James, Winston (1998). *Holding Aloft the Banner of Ethiopia : Caribbean Radicalism in Early Twentieth Century America*. London: Verso.

Laclau, Ernesto, and Chantal Mouffe (1985). *Hegemony and Socialist Strategy: Towards a Radical Democratic Politics*. London: Verso.

Lamming, George (1960). *The Pleasures of Exile*. London: M. Joseph.

Lao-Montes, Agustin (2004). "De-Calibanizing Caribbean Rationalities." *C.L.R. James Journal* (special issue on Paget Henry's *Caliban's Reason*).

Lewis, Earl (1995). "To Turn As on a Pivot: Writing African Americans into History of Overlapping Diasporas." *American Historical Review* 100, 3: 765–787.

Marti, Jose (1975). *Obras Completas* (27 Vols.). Havana: Editorial de Ciencias Sociales.

Mignolo, Walter (2000) *Local Histories/Global Designs: Coloniality, Subaltern Knowledges, and Border Thinking*. Princeton: Princeton University Press.

Moraga, Cherie (1983). *Loving in the War Years: lo que nunca paso por sus labios*. Boston: South End Press.

Mudimbe, Valentin. 1988. *The Invention of Africa: Gnosis, Philosophy, and the Order of Knowledge*. Bloomington: Indiana University Press.

Patterson, Tiffany Ruby, and Robin D.G. Kelley (2000). "Unfinished Migrations: Reflections on the African Diaspora and the Making of the Modern World." *African Studies Review* Vol. 43, No. 1: 11–46.

Piedra, Jose (1991). "Literary Whiteness and the Afro-Hispanic Difference." In Dominick LaCapra, ed., *The Bounds of Race*. Ithaca: Cornell University Press: 311–143.

Quijano, Anibal (2000). "Coloniality of Power, Eurocentrism, and Latin America." *Nepantla*, 1,3: 139–155.

Rivera, Raquel Z. (2003). *New York Ricans from the Hip-Hop Zone*. New York: Palgrave-McMillan.

Saldívar, José David (1991). *The Dialectics of Our America*. Durham, N.C.: Duke University Press.

Sanchez-Gonzalez, Lisa (2001). "Boricua Modernism: Arturo Schomburg and William Carlos Williams." In Sanchez-Gonzalez, ed., *Boricua Literature. A Literary History of the Puerto Rican Diaspora*. New York: New York University Press: 42–70.

Schomburg, Arturo Alfonso (1999, original 1925). "The Negro Digs up His Past." In
    Alain Locke, ed., *The New Negro. Voices from the Harlem Renaissance* (into. Arnold
    Rampersad). New York: Touchstone.
Shange, Ntosake (1983). *A Daughter's Geography.* New York. St. Martin's Press.
Wittgenstein, Ludwig (2001). *Philosophical Investigations* (The german text, with a
    revised English translation). Oxford: Blackwell.
Wynter, Sylvia (1971). "History and the Novel: Plot and Plantation." *Savacou* 5.

5

Black Latin@s and Blacks in Latin America

Some Philosophical Considerations

Lewis R. Gordon

The study of black Latinos and Latinas relates to the study of blacks in Latin America in a way that exemplifies at least three orders of knowledge in the contemporary academy: African American studies, Latino/a studies, and Latin American studies. Correlated with each are double consciousness and anti-black racism in the case of the first, borderland theory and its motifs of mixture in the case of the second, and the formation of New World modernity in the case of the third. Yet, as Claudia Milian Arias has recently shown, the first two distinct themes require much misrepresentation to maintain themselves as seg-regated orders of knowledge. The reality of at least New World Black studies, most known today as African American studies, includes Creolization and bor-ders that are often elided by reductive representations of black America. And, in similar kind, the doubled and antiblack realities of the Latino and Latina world, often marked by reference to Latin America as a region of mixture, are often elided by limiting borderlands and mixedness as *the* only paradigms of Latino and Latina Studies.

Milian Arias's approach is based on a conception of human studies that is attuned to the complex challenges of studying human communities. The ascription of "black" to such communities offers additional considerations. The purpose of this chapter is to explore some of those challenges in the Latino and Latina Studies and the Latin American contexts. Since there is much emphasis on the foundational discourses of borderland theory and mixedness (*mestizaje*) with emphasis on indigenous peoples in Latino and Latina Studies, most of this discussion will bring to the fore the anxieties over blackness that often have, even in this more thoughtful context, the effect of epistemic closure.

Let us begin with the study of blacks in Latin America. Such study requires taking seriously at least three conditions of possibility: (1) the geohistoricopolitical, (2) the categorial, and (3) dynamics of phobogenic imposition. Given the technical character of these terms, some elaboration is in order.

By *geohistoricopolitical,* I mean the emergence of "America" and the identities that are its consequence. Prior to the unique geohistorical dynamics that emerged as a function of Columbus's landing in the Bahamas in 1492, there was no "America," nor "Americas," and there was no reason for the populations already living in the Caribbean, the two New World continents, and the stretch of land that links them to think of themselves in such terms. As Enrique Dussel has so persuasively argued, the convergence of the New World with Columbus's arrival entails "America" as a fundamentally modern creation. That such an occurrence is geographical (a new, mapped out "place"), historical (a moment of such magnitude that it is epochical), and political (a reorganization of power in the public domain) entails its characterization as geohistorical-political.

The *categorial* here signifies processes of categorization. Since we are talking about kinds of people, this term refers to the anthropological consequence of the geohistorical-political designations known as the New World and the Americas. Among the results are people designated "black" or *negro* and, geolinguistically, "Latin" or, in the United States, "Latino" and "Latina" or, not very long ago, "Hispanic."

The *dynamics of phobogenic imposition* are quite simply conquest, colonialism, and racism, and the forms of consciousness that are their consequence.

These conditions provide us with the subjects of our study—the convergence of blacks and Latin America into blacks in Latin America to black Latin Americans. But before going further, we must make a distinction between such blacks in the New World from Africans in the New World. Africans, too, as V.Y. Mudimbe has shown in *The Invention of Africa,* at least in their continental designation "African," are products of the modern world. Prior to modernity, there was no reason for so many people on the continent called Africa to have considered themselves in terms of nomenclature from Roman antiquity. To think about the people, especially those South of the Sahara, in precolonial terms paradoxically requires the modern language of race. For although they may not have thought of themselves in terms of their skin color as black peoples or negroid peoples, it is very doubtful that their varied appearance over at least 219.5 thousand years could have been mistaken for the peoples we today call whites and northeast Asians. Paleoanthropological research has shown that until about twenty thousand or so years ago, there were only what modernity calls black people around, and going back about thirty thousand or so years, the only other hominids were neanderthals (who, incidentally, were morphologically white). As it turns out, paleoanthropologists and archaeologists such as Walter Neves, Hector Pucciarelli, Joseph F. Powell, Erik G. Ozolins, André Prous, Rolando González-José, and Renato Kipnis have been uncovering much evidence that the South American continent was populated by people as early as 40,000 years ago. Since the only homo sapiens at that time were what we would today call blacks, these scientists were compelled to admit that such people, after journeying from Africa through either South Asia and Australia or by simply following the currents to South America directly from Southern Africa, were black people. The question of blacks in South America is, then, at least a 40,000-year-old one.

The story of those early groups of blacks in the New World is yet fully to be told. The evidence suggests that the subsequent lighter Asiatic groups that entered the North American continent twelve or fewer thousand years ago made their way south and eventually conquered the darker populations already living there. The earlier group had to mix in for their survival, and there are only faint genetic traces of them remaining in South American indigenous populations. Such a story suggests that the violence that accompanies the convergence of "black" and "New World" is, unfortunately, at least several thousand years old.

The story of Afro–Latin American reality is, however, one about blacks who came to the New World from the moment of Spanish and Portuguese conquest onward. Although not all such blacks were slaves (Pedro Alonso Nino, for example, was a navigator on Columbus's first voyage), the reality of slavery in the economies and political institutions that followed has been so pervasive that all New World blacks are yoked to it. Thus, much of the understanding of blacks in the Americas is the constant problem and is problematic of labor, dehumanization, and resistance to exploitation. These considerations have a profound impact on the study of such blacks.

The study of blacks challenges many assumptions that are a function of the anxieties wrought by the circumstances, the phobogenic impositions, of blacks emerging as blacks. These assumptions are familiar social fallacies. Let us consider five. The first is the presumption of *homogeneity.* That is where one presumes that there are no differences between black populations. Heterogeneity, an important development of human culture by virtue of human creativity and the lived reality of choices, is here overlooked for the sake of lawlike generalizations that collapse into presumptions of unanimism. From such a view, there is no difference between one black and another black. Such a view does not reflect, at least, the way black peoples actually live.

The second is the *presumption of involuntary migration.* Here, it is presumed that black people never travel voluntarily. It is a consequence of the failure to recognize that not all black people were and are slaves. It occludes, as well, looking at black precolonial migration, and it occludes the complex migration patterns of African and black Pacific diasporic communities.

Third is the *notion of quantitative minorities.* The error here is presuming that the absence of black power is a product of being numerically outnumbered by whites. That Central America, South America, and the Caribbean have the largest number of blacks in the New World, and that those blacks and their mixed offspring are the majority population or a sufficiently large population, challenges such a thesis of smallness of number as cause for political impotence.

Fourth, and related to the third, is the *notion of involuntary mixture, especially from nonblacks.* The presumptions here are that mixed offspring emerge from involuntary relationships between blacks and nonblacks. Mixed children of black mothers and, say, white fathers are presumed products of rape or political economic pressures that result in white male privilege of access to all women. Those whose fathers are black and mothers are white are presumed to be products of some ineluctable lust on the part of black men or fever on the part of their white mothers. In effect, an atmosphere of illegitimacy is presumed over the heads of mixed offspring. Yet, as in our observation of voluntary migration, the error here is to presume that no cases of genuine agency exist. It is also based on the presumption that no members of the dominant group could actually fall in love with a member of the subordinated group. The truth of the matter is that human beings have always crossed sexual borderlines for such a reason, otherwise such injunctions would not have been necessary. The complex array of discussions in the recently published *"Mixed Race" Studies: A Reader* attests to the fallacy here.

And fifth, there is the *fallacy of stratified experience.* One need simply look at how courses on blacks in most institutions of higher learning are described in their catalogs to see this point. They are usually described as looking at "the black experience" or so-and-so "and the African American experience." It has become almost difficult to avoid referring to blacks without adding the credo of experience. Experience in the academy is, however, often placed against thought. The latter is where reflection, truth, and interpretation occur; it is what sets the conditions for even experience to acquire meaning. In effect, then, there is a uniquely colonizing dimension of this use of experience. In effect, experience, at least in this reductive sense, locks in blacks into an insidious relativism. It becomes an indication of blacks' inability to transcend themselves into a public sphere of knowledge, which is never really private because it is in principle communicable. Since white designations lack the proviso of experience, the scope of white intellectual explorations would here be intrinsically broader than those of blacks, for whites would have experience *and* thought. In effect, chaining blacks to experience leads to the conclusion that blacks do not think. This, many of us already know, is a familiar story.

If we bear these five fallacies in mind, the inevitable discussion of blacks in Latin America under the rubric of *race* would go in some surprising directions.

Today, it is nearly impossible to speak of race in at least the North American academy without a near knee-jerk appeal to social constructivism. Such a concept is treated as the official word on race as we see, for instance, in the official statements on race issued by the American Anthropological Association (1997) and the American Association of Physical Anthropologists (1996). We see here dynamics of phobogenic imposition at work. The latter (1996) statement, for example, stresses that human populations have always interbred, which supposedly rules out racial difference. Yet the same document acknowledges genetic and morphological differences between groups of human populations. There is, in effect, a straw man fallacy at work here. "Race" is called upon to meet criteria of difference between *species* instead of *intra*species differentiation. On an everyday basis, human beings do, however, use racial difference all the time, and they do so with a general level of accuracy that makes it questionable to appeal to the fewer instances of error. For example, I have two neighbors from the Dominican Republic. Both look like mixed-race black people, but the kinds of blacks they resemble are those in Northeast Africa or the Middle East. I remarked that my neighbors looked very Semitic. As it turned out, they revealed in conversation that both of them have fathers who were Arab. Although "Arab" is not properly a racial designation, there is a range of recognition of the kinds of mixtures that dominate morphologically in Arab populations, even though their descendants may only be culturally Dominican or Puerto Rican or Ecuadorian, etc. A similar observation could be made for Caribbean offspring of Sephardic Jews or, for that matter, Northeast Asians. Noticing the lineage manifested in such individuals need not be a function of a racist attitude against them. It could simply be an acknowledgment of being able to identify the communities from which they have *biologically* descended.

A problem with social constructionist arguments is that they often construct a social world that could not possibly have living people in it. A peopled world has embodied creatures with sense perception and the means of making distinctions that are not entirely reducible to socially intervening forces. The social world, in other words, brings meaning and organization to sense perception, but it cannot on its own change sense perception. For example, switching the word "red" with the word "blue" will not make one *see* as blue what one used to call red.

A further complication is that most social constructionist arguments exemplify a rather skewed conception of biology. Human populations are talked about as though they do not generate offspring and are not born from previous generations. The social constructionist language suggests that there is a greater randomness in morphological similarity between parents and children than empirical reality attests. Try as we may, some traits could only emerge in one group by having children from a member of a group or an offspring from a group from whom that trait originated. The fear, however, is that the admission of any biological factor would open up the floodgates of biological reductionism.

Such an extreme in thought is, however, easily identified as characteristic of bad reasoning. Since every human being is also a composite of cells, most of which keeps reproducing as long as he or she is alive, the biological must be taken seriously as *a* component of what human beings are. But the *meaning* of that component and the ability to transcend it in the form of creating a social world through which more meaning is generated and communicated suggests a complex story that entails also the social as *a,* instead of *the,* component as well. Bearing this conclusion in mind, race has been studied in at least three attuned ways as follows.

There is the relational or semiotic view of racial analysis. Here racial meaning is not intrinsic but a function of a relation between one designation and another. Take, for instance, the terms "black" and "white." Both are dependent on each other in that black is simply a darker or darkest distance from white. But white makes no sense except in terms of its distance from black. Mixture works its way on relative scales from one to the other. But the relativism here means that even if the designated blacks were to disappear, the commitment to a matrix of black and white would generate a new set of blacks so long as there is a series of nonwhites from which such a designation could flow. The same applies to the elimination of the upper end. From this point of view, racism should not, then, be equated with, say, white supremacy. For there is consistency between being against white supremacy and being antiblack. If this is correct, antiblack racism could be maintained in the wake of the elimination of white supremacy.

The relational view hints at the *grammar* of racial reality. Even where a matrix of black and white exists requires the addition of contingent forces of their discursive legitimacy. Here, the genealogical approach is useful, for it looks at how racism plays a role in the constitution of race and vice versa as part of the economy of power relations. The role of institutional power in the constitution of social meaning and the construction of concepts is brought to the fore in genealogies of race. A problem with both the relational and genealogical view, however, is the absence, in a nutshell, of how real live people play a role in the constitution of racial reality. The existential phenomenological focus on the noetic features of lived reality raises the question of how race and racism are *lived.* Whatever we may say is the ontological status of race here steps aside to the question of race *as meant* by the mechanisms of meaning in a living human world of human beings.

The dynamics of race and racism outlined thus far will now enable us to discuss some of the anxiety often stimulated by bringing up *blacks* in Latin America. The late Cuban singer Celia de la Caridad Cruz Alfonso (Celia Cruz) is both known first as black and Latin American and then as black and Latin@ (after migrating to the United States), because many of us have seen what she looks like while we listen to her music. But the absence of blacks on Latin American and Latin@ television (at least those on cable and satellite in the

United States), and the near lily-white portrayal of the recent Latin invasion of North American popular music suggests that white normativity—or at least some form of light-skinned mixed-race normativity—dominates the consciousness of Latin Americans, Latinos, and Latinas as a condition of appearance.

At this point, I would like to offer some tropes from two thinkers who have been influential in the study of black folk—one, a black scholar from the United States and the other, a black revolutionary psychiatrist from the Latin Caribbean: W.E.B. Du Bois and Frantz Fanon.

The exploration of fallacies in the study of black folk is furthered by Du Bois's famous reflections on what it means to be a problem in "The Study of the Negro Problems" and the first chapter of *The Souls of Black Folk.* He observed there that such people are often studied as problems themselves instead of as people who face problems in the world. When the people are the problem, the aim, then, is either to fix them or, failing to do so, get rid of them. Either version entails an intrinsic notion of wrongness and failure in black populations.

The lived reality of being problem people is one of constant contradiction. For the underlying problematic of being such a people is the racist ascription of them not really being people at all. To live the contradiction is possible by virtue of really being human beings. The result is a schism, as Du Bois observed, of two worlds requiring constant negotiation: The world of color and the white world. The correlate of these worlds is *double consciousness.*

There are many formulations of double consciousness, but the three I will offer here are (1) national, (2) epistemological, and (3) phenomenological.

The national formulation emerges when we realize that, save in avowedly black countries such as Haiti or Jamaica, the normative identity of most New World societies is either white or the lightest examples of mixture. The invisibility of blacks at the level of consciousness of the national self creates a tension of the meaning of a black national identity. To be so seems, at the level of nationality, to belong to two nations—to be black *and* the national norm. The familiar story of black Latin Americans having to live more as black than Latino or Latina in North America is not limited to the United States. If it were so, such blacks should have had no awareness of being black when they were living in Latin America. But the realities of black life in Latin America are such that a continued reasonable response to those who claim such ignorance is the ascription of self-delusion. The image of "real" Dominicans, Puerto Ricans, El Salvadorans, Mexicans, Chileans, Argentinians, Colombians, Costa Ricans, and Brazilians often finds its limits in black bodies. Blacks in those regions, save perhaps Panama because of the large numbers of Jamaicans who migrated there during the building of the Canal, and in Cuba versus Cubans in Miami, constantly encounter their black identity as an impediment to full citizenship. An ironic feature of this denial is that their blackness is often posed against mixed communities and supposedly purely white ones as favorable for national identity. Yet, such conclusions do not reflect the demographics of black communities in the Americas. What many New World blacks know is that most black communities are mixed communities. The instances of black families with *no* mixtures in their family lines are few, far, and wide between. Black nationhood as "pure" is lived by blacks as a fiction.

The epistemological consequence of such a contradiction is a constant struggle with national narcissism—between how such societies see themselves and how they really are. The correlate of those two views is one of national assumptions and national reality. This formulation is epistemological because it is about what and how we come to know things in and about our society and ourselves. Take, for example, Black Studies. In almost every mainstream academic setting, Black Studies is treated as a heavy particularized area of research with a "narrow" focus on the study of black people, while the mainstream departments that organize knowledge, almost exclusively around European perspectives and European-centered events, are presumed "universal." Because of the normativity of European civilizations, much about the rest of the world is often ignored. Yet, because of a claim to universality, the presentation of knowledge in such instances is almost never placed in formulations that reflect their de facto particularity. They are advanced as *the* exemplars of the human condition. Blacks, in other words, must speak for themselves, while whites speak for humanity. Beyond the clearly colonial epistemic features of this thesis is the problem of truth. For when students take Black Studies courses, they usually discover that the subaltern position of such studies requires more inclusivity: In studying the black world, they learn more about the white one, as well as that there are not only worlds that are black and white. Similarly, they relearn their national history in terms of the features of it that were rendered invisible by white normativity. The same for their literary canon, their philosophical canon, and various other disciplines. It is no accident that Black Studies often stimulate indignation in students. Students reach out to teachers with an implicit ethical expectation of the truth as the instructor best knows it. But such an ethics requires the instructor to be committed to truth, which requires making an effort at learning the actual scope of reality. Artificially narrowing the world to a single group manifests commitment to a false reality and the maintenance of the students' ignorance. When one studies history, for instance, one wants to know what happened, not what a system of racial ideology would like us to believe. That, for instance, archaeological evidence is showing that a "Europe and Asia = Civilization" approach to history is false suggests that we face the possibility of revolutionizing our understanding of history. Yet, most of this development is being ignored in most history departments worldwide. Instead, the continued lie of a stupid, "undeveloped" black past persists, and with that, the continued assault on the humanity of black folks worldwide.

There is a phenomenological dimension of double consciousness by virtue of its being a kind of *consciousness*. Phenomenology advocates the intentional view of consciousness, that consciousness is always consciousness *of* something. Through a suspension of our ontological commitments, we are then able to examine the complexity of phenomena. The phenomenological aspect of double consciousness, then, explores the phenomena that constitute such doubling. But more, phenomenology offers an understanding of perspectivity. It brings with it a theory of the body as an unsurpassable dimension of the situation of each of us in the world.

Du Bois's reflections bring to the fore the lived reality of a problematic consciousness. Such a consciousness finds itself embroiled in a dialectic of constantly encountering an alien reflection of the self in the social world. Fanon, in *Black Skin, White Masks* (a text that, given the author's organizing colonial experiences in the Latin Caribbean—namely, Martinique—should also be read as a Francophone Latin American text), presents a powerful portrait of what it means to live ensnared by the search for the self in an antipathetic other's eyes; what could be called *the dialectics of recognition.* Fanon showed that colonialism created a form of phobogenic imposition that infected intersubjective relations. This infection, whose scope included even the methods of inquiry offered by colonial disciplinary practices, can be characterized as epistemological colonialism—colonization at the level of knowledge production.[1] The alien black self is one of the products of such colonial practice. Yet, knowledge of the constructed aspects of a self fails to transform that self where the standpoint of appearance is always a colonial one. In effect, the search for recognition, of being valued as a self, of appearing, suffers from a psychopathological factor: Modern colonialism leaves no room for a normal black body. The basis of so-called recognition is stratified abnormality. The black is either flawed by virtue of not being white or flawed by virtue of appearing "too white," which is abnormal for a black. Such a "Catch-22" leads to a further problem: Since the Self-Other dialectic constitutes ethical relationships premised upon a hidden equality (each self is another's Other and vice versa), and since antiblack racism depends on a fundamental inequality (a human-below-human relation from the standpoint of the white, a human-other-human relation from the standpoint of the black), a system of unilateral ethical relations result, wherein blacks experience ethical responsibility in relation to whites but whites do not exemplify such reciprocity. The consequence is that racism destroys the Self-Other dialectic and collapses into the doubled world identified by double consciousness: a self-other *and* nonself–non-other structure. It is, in other words, the denial of the humanity of the black as *another human being* before the white. In effect, then, the struggle against at least the antiblack racism manifested by modern colonialism entails an effort to change what Fanon calls the *sociogenic* consequences of that world, to transform the society into both formal and substantive instances of reciprocal Self-Other dialectics of ethical relations between whites and blacks. Fanon's later well-known call, that we should change our material conditions and our *concepts* to set afoot a humanity that manifests healthier social relations, is a consequence of this argument.

The relevance of Fanon's thought to the study of blacks in Latin America pertains both to the understanding of black identity and the internal dynamics of liberation in Latin America and the Caribbean. Let us, however, embellish Fanon's thought a bit through taking a moment to consider his discussion of Negritude. The term itself was coined by Martiniquan poet Aimé Césaire, Fanon's *lycée* teacher and future foe. Fanon saw an exemplification of black resistance in Negritude poetry, whose content extolled the virtues of the night against the blinding forces of the sun. Africa, and indeed the black self, were valorized by Negritude poets such as Césaire and Léopold Senghor, the future first president of independent Senegal. Although he was waken from his poetically induced dialectical slumber by Jean-Paul Sartre, who pointed out in his essay "Black Orpheus" that Negritude could at best be a negative moment in a revolutionary dialectic that called for a universal struggle, Fanon found solace in his later observation, in *A Dying Colonialism,* that it was *blacks* who created Negritude. What this means is that Negritude should not be entirely rejected as a potential revolutionary force because it brought to the fore a central theme in Fanon's fight against stratified abnormality—the importance of agency or, in his terms, becoming *actional.* The historic reality of blacks in Latin America is that Negritude offers a voice of protest from within modernity. Examples of the continued impact of that voice are the writings of the Brazilian Negritude writers Abdias do Nascimento and Elisa Larkin Nascimento. That said, there is, however, an aspect of Fanon's treatment of Negritude that is in need of an additional consideration to solidify his thought in the Caribbean and Latin American contexts, and that is his treatment of black music.

Fanon's thoughts on black music are not as enthusiastic as those on written poetry. Consider this passage from his 1956 essay "Racism and Culture," reprinted in *Toward the African Revolution*:

> Thus the blues—"the black slave lament"—was offered up for the admiration of the oppressors. This modicum of stylized oppression is the exploiter's and the racist's rightful due. Without oppression and without racism you have no blues. The end of racism would sound the knell of great Negro music . . .
>
> As the all-too-famous Toynbee might say, the blues are the slave's response to the challenge of oppression.
>
> Still today, for many men, even colored, Armstrong's music has a real meaning only in this perspective.
>
> Racism bloats and disfigures the face of the culture that practices it. Literature, the plastic arts, songs for shop girls, proverbs, habits, patterns, whether they set out to attack it or to vulgarize it, restore racism.

Fanon writes as though the blues were *entirely* a function of racism and colonialism. I have argued in my essay, "Must Revolutionaries Sing the Blues?:

Thinking through Fanon and the Leitmotif of the Black Arts Movement," that such a conclusion is based on a failure to see the broader context of the blues. If the meaning of the blues were solely the lamentations of colonialism, slavery, and racism, then a prevailing mystery would be its continued impact on the lives of people who are not the colonized, the enslaved, and the racially marked. The blues is able to speak to nearly everyone in the modern world, if the popularity of all the music, dance, and poetry exemplified by it is considered, because the blues is about the tragic adult sensibility of life. It is akin to Friedrich Nietzsche's claims about ancient Greek tragedies in *The Birth of Tragedy from the Spirit of Music.* Based on his theory of health, where he argues that it should not be interpreted as the absence of adversity but the ability to handle such travails, Nietzsche's position is that the ancient Greeks faced life's suffering through transforming it into art. This form of art is not, however, one of escape but one of direct confrontation with life's challenges. The blues is no different. In the blues, life's suffering is made ironic by the willingness to live on in the face of so much temptation toward nihilism. Although it appeals to all ages, blues performance always exemplifies an aged sensibility. It epitomizes maturity in the face of absurdity.

Blues consciousness is the quintessential leitmotif of modernity. It speaks to the alienation of institutions that, as Michel Foucault argued in *Discipline and Punish,* make the soul the prisoner of the body, make the social world, the framework of freedom, the cage of despair. Just as Fanon calls for us to become actional and transform our social world, the blues reminds us of the tragic reality of everyone of us being responsible for it and ourselves; in effect, for each other.

This sense of responsibility leads to imploding forces. A feature of black people that is unmistakable in the modern world is their association with violence and their inability to assimilate. The violence is a function of what it means to live in a limited social world. When the social world is limited, there is little one could do but rely on one's physical reach, which increases the possibility of the forms of body-to-body encounters indicative of violence. Both Du Bois and Fanon were acutely aware of this dimension of oppression: Oppression collapses the body into itself. Liberation requires an effective transformation of our social effectiveness, our social reach. The problem is that the modern world has set assimilation as a condition for such reach, but for blacks, that means a form of disappearance. Blacks, *as blacks,* have thus exemplified a major inconvenience in the modern world: They are indigestible. No matter what the social and political systems put them through, they still come out—as Fanon observed in *Black Skin, White Masks,* when he says "Wherever the Negro goes, he remains a Negro"—black.

The contemporary situation does not look very good for blacks in Latin America. They have many of the travails of blacks in North America, but they lack many of the conditions of appearance in spite of their numbers. It is not that there is no political and academic effort to transform their situation. It is that the geohistorical political reality of the Caribbean's and Latin America's subaltern locations in New World politics prevails. The imposition of Anglo-American whiteness colors Mediterranean whiteness, which at least dominates Latin America, into a Creolized reality that expands the range of racialized subjects. Transforming the lives of blacks in Latin America, then, holds within it the transformation of Latin America itself. In the case of the Caribbean, this change has been more successfully so in nations that chose to become *black* ones. In the case of Jamaica, for instance, the national identity has offered a conception of dread, as Paget Henry has argued in "Rastafarianism and the Reality of Dread," that addresses at least Fanon's demand of building new concepts. And what is Latin American music without the conga speaking to its soul?

These reflections lead us, now, back to the work of Milian Arias, who observed these limitations as exemplars of *border imposition* in the Latino and Latin@s and North American black contexts. Added to Du Bois and Fanon should be the importance of borders as the circumscription of social reality, as advanced by Gloria Anzaldúa. I have intentionally focused on the complexity of blackness in this chapter primarily because Anzaldúa's thought has been forwarded primarily in terms of a conception of Latino and Latina identity as a consequence of a Latin America that highlights mixtures of whites with indigenous American groups from a more Asiatic line. The blackness of Latin America, which stands as the largest black population in the New World, is heavily misrepresented in such instances, and as a consequence, so, too, is the blackness of the Latino and Latina populations of North America. Yet, this is a criticism of *implementation* of a correct insight. Blacks in Latin America and black Latinos and Latinas do face many borders, as the discussion up to this point attests. A positive consequence of studying these borders and their dynamics of geohistorical, categorial, and phobogenic imposition is the role it plays in the continued struggle to address the invisibility of such communities.

Conclusion

These remarks are mostly prolegomena. It has simply been my hope here to outline a set of concepts that I hope might be useful for the study of blacks in the Caribbean and Latin American and black Latino and Latina contexts. The path from conceptual outlines to race and then to the aesthetics of the leitmotif of modernity and borders is meant as a stimulant to new considerations on the problems faced by blacks in this trying world. They have offered much to the modern world's material infrastructure and cultural life; far more, as Anna Julia Cooper observed in "What Are We Worth?" than has been invested in them and their descendants. Yet, as the epistemological message of double consciousness suggests, even a repressed contradiction is all the more present by virtue of its absence exemplifying a limited point of view. The study of blacks in Latin

America and black Latinos and Latinas beckons us, in the spirit of Fanon's closing encomium of *Black Skin, White Masks,* to make of us those who truly question.

Note

1. The ideas that my colleagues Paget Henry, Nelson Maldonado-Torres, Claudia Milian Arias, Rowan Ricardo Phillips, Kenneth Knies, Jane Anna Gordon, and I have been working on over the past decade come out of Du Bois's and Fanon's insight on the colonization of knowledge and the need to construct new kinds of human study. See the references for some of the relevant work.

References

Anzaldúa, Gloria. 1981. "La Prieta." In *This Bridge Called My Back: Writings by Radical Women of Color,* edited by Cheríe Moraga and Gloria Anzaldúa; foreword by Toni Cade Bambara. Watertown, MA: Persephone Press.

———. 1999. *Borderlands/La Frontera: The New Mestiza,* 2nd ed. San Francisco: Aunt Lute.

Baraka, Amiri. 1963. *Blues People: Negro Music in White America.* New York: William & Morrow.

Césaire, Aimé. 2000/1972. *Discourse on Colonialism,* translated by Joan Pinkham. New York: Monthly Review Press.

Cooper, Anna Julia. 1988. *The Voice of Anna Julia Cooper, Including "A Voice From the South" and Other Important Essays, Papers and Letters,* edited by Charles Lemert and Esme Bhan. Lanham, MD: Rowman and Littlefield Publishers Inc.

Du Bois, W.E.B. 1903. *The Souls of Black Folk: Essays and Sketches.* Chicago: A.C. McClurg & Co.

———. March 2000a/1898. "The Study of the Negro Problems." *The Annals of the American Academy of Political and Social Science* 56: 13–27.

———. 2000b. "Sociology Hesitant." *Boundary 2* 27, no. 3 (Fall): 37–44.

———. 2000c/1897. "On the Conservation of the Races." In *The Idea of Race,* edited by Robert Bernasconi and Tommy Lott. Indianapolis: Hackett.

Dussel, Enrique. 1996. *The Underside of Modernity: Apel, Ricoeur, Rorty, Taylor, and the Philosophy of Liberation,* translated and edited by Eduardo Mendieta. Atlantic Highlands, NJ: Humanities Press.

Dzidzienyo, Anani, and Rhett Jones. 1977. "Africanity, Structural Isolation and Black Politics in the Americas." *Studia Africana,* no. 1 (Spring): 32–44.

Ellison, Ralph.1986. *Going to the Territory.* New York: Random House.

Fanon, Frantz.1967a/1959. *A Dying Colonialism,* translated by Haakon Chevalier with an introduction by Adolfo Gilly. New York: Grove Weidenfeld.

———. 1967b/1952. *Black Skin, White Masks,* translated by Charles Lamm Markman. New York: Grove Press.

———. 1967c. *Toward the African Revolution,* translated by Haakon Chevalier. New York: Grove Press.

Fernández-Armesto, Felipe. 1987. *Before Columbus: Exploration and Colonization from the Mediterranean to the Atlantic, 1229–1492.* Philadelphia: University of Pennsylvania Press.

Finch, Charles S. III., 1991. *Echoes of the Old Darkland: Themes from the African Eden.* Decatur, GA: Khenti, Inc.

Fischer, Sibylle. 2004. *Modernity Disavowed: Haiti and Cultures of Slavery in the Age of Revolution.* Durham, NC: Duke University Press.

Fontaine, Pierre-Michel, ed. 1985. *Race, Class and Power in Brazil.* Los Angeles: UCLA Center for Afro-American Studies.

Foucault, Michel. 1995. *Discipline and Punish: The Birth of the Prison,* 2nd ed., trans. Alan Sheridan. New York: Vintage Books.

Gordon, Jane Anna. Forthcoming, 2005. "Challenges Posed to Social-Scientific Method by the Study of Race." In *Not Only the Master's Tools,* edited by Lewis R. Gordon and Jane Anna Gordon. Boulder, CO: Paradigm Publishers.

Gordon, Lewis R., ed. 1997. *Existence in Black: An Anthology of Black Existential Philosophy.* New York: Routledge.

———. 2000. *Existentia Africana: Understanding Africana Existential Thought.* New York: Routledge.

Henry, Paget. 1985. *Peripheral Capitalism and Underdevelopment in Antigua.* New Brunswick, NJ: Transaction Books.

———. 1997a. "African and Afro-Caribbean Existential Philosophies." In *Existence in Black,* pp. 11–36 (see Gordon 1997).

———. 1997b. "Rastafarianism and the Reality of Dread." In *Existence in Black,* pp. 157–164 (see Gordon 1997).

———. 2000. *Caliban's Reason: Introducing Afro-Caribbean Philosophy.* New York: Routledge.

Hernández, Tanya Katerí. 2003. "'Too Black to Be Latino/a': Blackness and Blacks as Foreigners in Latino Studies." *Latino Studies* 1, no. 1 (March): 152–159.

Ifekwunigwe, Jayne O., ed. 2004. *"Mixed Race" Studies: A Reader.* London: Routledge.

Knies, Kenneth. Forthcoming, 2005. "Transcendental Phenomenology and the Idea of Post-European Science." In *Not Only the Master's Tools,* edited by Lewis R. Gordon and Jane Anna Gordon. Boulder, CO: Paradigm Publishers.

Maldonado-Torres, Nelson. 2001. "The Cry of the Self as a Call from the Other: The Paradoxical Loving Subjectivity of Frantz Fanon." *Listening: Journal of Religion and Culture* 36.1 (Winter): 46–60.

———. 2002. "Post-Imperial Reflections on Crisis, Knowledge, and Utopia: Transgresstopic Critical Hermeneutics and the 'Death of European Man.'" *Review: A Journal of the Fernand Braudel Center for the Study of Economies, Historical Systems, and Civilizations* 25, no. 3: 277–315.

———. Forthcoming, 2005. "Toward a Critique of Continental Reason: Africana Studies and the Decolonization of Imperial Cartographies in the Americas." In *Not Only the Master's Tools,* edited by Lewis R. Gordon and Jane Anna Gordon. Boulder, CO: Paradigm Publishers.

Mignolo, Walter. 2000. "The Larger Picture: Hispanics/Latinos (and Latino Studies) in the Colonial Horizon of Modernity." In *Hispanics/Latinos in the United States,* edited by Jorge J. E. Garcia and Pablo de Greiff. New York: Routledge, pp. 99–124.

Milian Arias, Claudia. 2001. "Breaking into the Borderlands: Double Consciousness, Latina and Latino Misplacements." Doctoral Dissertation. Providence: American Civilization, Brown University.

————. 2002. "New Languages, New Humanities: The 'Mixed Race' Narrative and the Borderlands." In *A Companion to Racial and Ethnic Studies,* edited by David Theo Goldberg and John Solomos. Malden, MA: Blackwell Publishers, pp. 355–364.

————. Forthcoming, 2005, "Differences Are Relational: Dialoguing with African American and Latino Studies." In *Not Only the Master's Tools,* edited by Lewis R. Gordon and Jane Anna Gordon. Boulder, CO: Paradigm Publishers.

Nascimento, Elisa Larkin. 1980. *Pan Africanism and South America: Emergence of a Black Rebellion.* Buffalo, NY: Afrodiaspora.

Neves, Walter A., and Hector Pucciarelli. 1998. "The Zhoukoudian Upper Cave Skull 101 as Seen from the Americas." *Journal of Human Evolution* 34, no. 2 (February): 219–222.

Neves, Walter A., Joseph F. Powell, and Erik G. Ozolins. 1999. "Modern Human Origins as Seen from the Peripheries." *Journal of Human Evolution* 37, no. 1 (July): 129–133.

Neves, Walter A., André Prous, Rolando González-José, Renato Kipnis, and Joseph Powell. 2003. "Early Holocene Human Skeletal Remains from Santana do Riacho, Brazil: Implications for the Settlement of the New World," *Journal of Human Evolution* 45, no. 1 (July): 759–782.

Nietzsche, Friedrich. 2000. *The Birth of Tragedy from the Spirit of Music,* translated and edited by Douglas Smith. Oxford: Oxford University Press.

PART IV

Indigenous People in the Americas

6

Indigenous Struggles over Autonomy, Land, and Community

Antiglobalization and Resistance in World-Systems Analysis

James V. Fenelon and Thomas D. Hall

They tore off our fruits, they broke off our branches, they burnt our trunks, but they could not kill our roots.—Popol Vuh[1]

Indigenous peoples are involved in struggles over local autonomy, land tenure, community relations, and socioeconomic "development" that are often seen as antiglobalization efforts when viewed through the lens of world-systems analysis. In many parts of the world, these struggles take on definitive forms of decolonization strategies, none more poignantly than Mexico and other Latin American countries. In this chapter, we consider the situations and perspectives of indigenous peoples in Mexico and America "Profunda" (first) and then make comparative analyses with other cases and struggles by Indigenous peoples in India, New Zealand, and the United States.

Mexico Profundo:

The recent history of Mexico, that of the last five hundred years, is the story of permanent confrontation between those attempting to direct the country toward the path of Western civilization and those, rooted in Mesoamerican ways of life, who resist. (Bonfil Batalla 1996, xv)

Following Bonfil, the struggles of indigenous peoples extend back through time and space, from before conquest and invasion, within the Americas for five centuries. Bonfil furthers states that it is only after European invasion and the installation of the colonial regime that the country becomes "unknown territory" whose contours and secrets need to be "discovered" (1996, 8–9). Thus essential features of indigeneity also become a partial foundation, however denied, for the nation-state and new cultural forms built over those who preceded it. Bonfil thus identifies this as "De-Indianization," a "historical process through which populations that originally possessed a particular and distinctive identity, based on their own culture, are forced to renounce that identity, with all the consequent changes in their social organization and culture" (1996, 17). We argue, however, that what Bonfil identified was a targeted cultural destruction of individual "Indian" or indigenous communities, nations,[2] cultures, and collectivities for the purposes of domination. These were then rebuilt on racialized concepts of "the Indian" that no longer has these diverse relationships, but only represents the primitive and undeveloped. Thus, stark contrasts on the nature of the land, autonomous sociopolitical relationships, and community as a collectivity, emerge in relationship to "modernity" and capitalist expansion over increasingly large territories. "The clear and undeniable evidence of our Indian ancestry is a mirror in which we do not wish to see our own reflection" (Bonfil Batalla 1996, 18).

The America Profunda meetings held in Mexico City, December 2003, illustrate these relationships that are central to indigenous life throughout the Americas:

All of the nation states of the American continent were defined, organized, and created by means of the extermination, denial and marginalizing of the peoples that existed in territories encompassed by their notion of national sovereignty... The resistance of the Indian peoples, first against the colonial powers and later against the nation states that took their place, was a continual source of tension and conflict... [not recognizing treaties]. [They] adopted a policy of incorporation into the nation state which denied the existence of the Indian peoples as peoples and their rights. (Esteva y Rengifo, *America Profunda* 2003, 7–8)

These meetings of scholars and indigenous leaders from throughout the Americas identified that "Government, based on its monopoly of violence...

was a hierarchical power structure…" We also found an indigenous homeo-morphic equivalent of (*autoridad*) in which "Communal authority is the whole community in its assembly" including the elders, and others who shared in decision making. "The central idea is to maintain harmony within the com-munity" (Governance panel, *America Profunda* 2003).

In respect to globalization, participants also found that "We are suffering the consequences of neoliberal politics." They observed that powers all over the world, "allied to the transnational corporations, apply the politics of the so-called Washington consensus, at an unsupportable human and environmental cost…" One main conclusion the group found was that there seemed to be in a "process of formation, at the grassroots, a *Consensus of the Peoples*" (*America Profunda* initial findings 2003).[3] Extending out from these observations, we can identify the conceptual foundations of indigeneity.

Indigeneity

The America Profunda group called American indigenous communities "*Pueblos Indios*" for convenience, as to identify important differences from other groups resisting cultural domination and potential erasure or assimilation. We refer to the United Nations definition for our usage:

> Indigenous communities, peoples and nations are those who have a con-tinuous historical connection with precolonial societies that preceded the invasion… that have the determination to preserve, develop and transmit to future generations their ancestral lands and their ethnic identity. . . . (Jose Martiniez Cobo 1987)

One of the basic relationships of indigenous peoples is having a relation-ship to the land (Bonfil 1996, 88). This relationship is often sacred, it rarely has direct economic value. Land is usually held collectively, rather than individu-ally. This orientation to the land is in direct opposition to how modern, capitalis-tic society approaches land, with direct economic values and individual title.

> The larger problem for the Indians was the struggle against breaking up the communal lands. The Liberals made private property sacred … the commu-nal ownership of land in Indian communities became an obstacle to be re-moved. (Bonfil 1996, 100)

Bonfil, as do a host of scholars working on indigenous peoples of the Americas, identifies other areas of social organization that differ markedly from dominant groups and mainstream "modern" society, including medicine (34) community service, *cargo* systems in Mexico that are "simultaneously civil, religious, and moral" (36). Thus we observe that it is the collective nature of indigenous life which appears to be at conflict with modern social systems, invading and incorporating the indigenous. This collectivity includes the land, distributive economics, shared decisionmaking, and the community. Invasive systems want to take over the land, stratify the economy to build a power elite, centralize political systems into hierarchies they control, and relate all social issues to ever-larger urban areas that dominate in all arenas the surrounding communities. Since indigenous peoples utilize alternative systems of social organization, and do not dissolve relationships, they are seen as obstacles, and if they resist, they are seen as "enemy."

In seeing the "Indian as Enemy" Bonfil observes:

> The radical denial of the imaginary Mexico... The struggle over land, involved one side, which wanted free trade and individual property, while the other side protested the land was communal and inalienable. (1996, 103–104)

With ensuing conflicts over resources, and increasingly played out over culture, indigenous peoples literally become the enemy, both of dominants and later civilization itself. Value systems, one placing private property and maximized economic profits as its mainstay, and the other with community relations, come into sharp conflict, with violence employed by the invasive systems, and often by the defending systems. To "civilize" is meant to pacify them, domesticate them, "end *their* violence" (Bonfil 1996, 105).

Western colonial powers and later the United States created a "minority" ethnic group—the "Indian"—while they tried to destroy the culture, history, and knowledge of individual Native nations or cultures. Even as this process occurred, place names and land-based knowledge systems evolved from the previous indigenous systems. In Mexico, we refer to the "Day of the Dead" posters and celebrations, which in Oaxaca represent "pre-Hispanic origin of the celebration of the dead."[4]

Layers of domination—500 years and more in Mexico—reveal Bonfil's Mexico Profundo, the indigenous "Indian" foundation even as oppression stratifies every aspect of life—cultural, political, economic, and social. Therefore the indigenous represents both the foundation of the society itself, and the "enemy" to be overtaken and destroyed. Once we dispel the notion of primitive people without historical memory, we need to address how indigenous peoples understand these histories, often denied and/or distorted by dominant historical perspectives. Murals painted over the walls in the barrio Santo Domingo (Mexico City), in their cultural center "La Escuelita" that is itself the site of considerable resistance, demonstrate the detailed knowledge and perspectives of these relationships, even among more "urbanized" peoples of indigenous background.[5]

Overview of the Analysis

We have identified four organizational principles or themes found in indigenous people's cases under review in this and in our previous studies (Hall and Fenelon 2004):

- Economic relationships that are redistributive, partially or wholly.
- Political relationships of "cultural sovereignty" and "community autonomy."
- Environmental relationships that are symbiotic, less destructive than capitalists.
- Community as inclusive relationships that tend toward common goals.

Globalization and Indigeneity: World-Systems Analysis

In earlier works we have made a set of points about world-systems analysis (Hall and Fenelon 2003, 2004). First, even the most localized forms of resistance cannot be understood without careful attention to larger system or global processes. Yet, conversely, world-system analysis cannot be used in a "one size fits all" mode. Rather, it is the complex interactions and conjunctures of specific cases that shape the processes of incorporation and resistance to incorporation (Carlson 2001). Further, we argue that too little attention has been paid to how events in peripheral areas have affected core areas. Thus, to understand these processes requires a multitiered analysis that attends to highly local conditions, regional conditions, national or state conditions, and global or world-system conditions, and their interactions.

In our attempts to search for regularities or patterns within these complexities, we attend to several levels of social change, often moving in opposite directions:

- there have been long-term, almost glacial, shifts in the realities and meanings of ethnicity, indigeneity, and nationality;
- that in the last century or so, all of these have become far more fluid;
- they are far more contested politically, socially, economically, and culturally;
- the velocity and patterns of social construction of indigenous identities (and other socially constructed identities) have shifted significantly.

Indigenous peoples are especially problematic and salient to our understanding of social processes in the world-system because:

- by their very continued existence they pose a major challenge to neoliberal capitalism on the ground, politically, and ideologically;
- they offer a variety of models of how societies or groups might participate in the world-system while remaining distinct within it;

- they may point to ways in which the current system might be transformed into something more humane (Hall and Fenelon 2003, 2004).

Within these broad outlines we note that the struggles of First Nations in the United States and Canada generally revolve around various forms of legal sovereignty based in treaty relationships, development of racialized "minority" groups, and historical changes. In the rest of the Americas and globally, indigenous peoples established unrecognized autonomous zones and communities in their various locales, usually at some expense. Key examples are Miskitos in Nicaragua, and Mayan-descent Zapatistas in Mexico. These indigenous peoples who are still considered or treated solely as "minority" groups within their nations are the most vulnerable, and often form resistance groups and/or rebellious movements, such as *Communidades Indigenas* in Oaxaca.[6]

The key issues here are: (1) Sovereignty is recognized in First Nations, though they are historically within genocidal states; (2) Minority or conflicted autonomy in Latin America, although historically *mestizo* states, confers neither sovereignty claims nor clear legal protections for its indigenous peoples; (3) We need to use comparative cases both within the Americas and more globally to understand these issues more fully. We pursue this with several cases.

The Maori peoples in New Zealand borrowed from the English pattern, leading to a central Waitangi Treaty of 1840, over which issues of sovereignty are fought. Thus, they are a particularly apt comparison for First Nations in Canada and the United States. The Warli and Gond "tribals" (*adevasi*), indigenous peoples in western and central India, existed over three thousand years, within classically Tributary systems of India followed by colonial imposition, so that these indigenous peoples appear closer to Latin America, although they are "scheduled tribes" (*adevasi* total make up some 9 percent of the population, close to 69 million people) in contemporary parlance (Bijoy 2001).

Based on initial observations, we identify at least four major points of convergence: (1) we observe a recognition of indigenous autonomous existence and routes they are taking toward social transformation; (2) we delineate how new states adopted policies of incorporation that denied the existence and rights of the indigenous peoples; (3) We note how indigenous peoples emphasize communal authority in all spheres of society; and (4) we observe processes of grassroots formations, such as the "Consensus of the Peoples" in *America Profunda*, and identify the continuance of indigenous struggles in urban environments and in removed and segregated locations:

> There was spatial segregation, which expressed the nature of the colonial order.... while the Indian barrios formed the periphery. Drastic regulations existed to assure the residential separation of colonizers and colonized (Bonfil 1996, 48).

This last point has particular salience with U.S. policies of Termination and Relocation, reservations and reserves in North America and New Zealand, increasing tendencies now in South America, and "copycat" policy formations with the Bedouin Arabs in Israel,[7] with all forms found with *adevasis* in India, especially urban relocation and reserves.

Additionally, we observe how modernity is reformulated, in traditional societies, and with social structural fusion of movement dynamics transcending individual peoples. For instance, the Zapatistas have significantly supported women's rights and movements, within their communities and externally, presenting themselves as working to benefit others, not themselves, evidenced in signs and murals at their headquarters at Oventik.[8]

Perhaps the most important aspect of indigenous struggles that links to world-systems analysis is the connectedness that many movement groups seek with other indigenous peoples. For Zapatistas this may mean making invitations referred to as international *Encuentros* and Intercontinentals, which is illustrated in the mural of four hands united from four directions on their headquarters building in Oventik, Chiapas.[9] The mural includes *Democracia* (democracy), *Libertad* (liberty), *Justicia* (social justice), and *Paz* (peace) over the hands in fists. The image is a medicine-wheel design with "*Unidad y Victoria*" over the circle. The colors are from Lakota traditions, which differ from those of Maya. Thus, two different indigenous traditions and social movements are connected in their vision and struggle. It is this set of relationships to which we now turn.

Comparative analysis:

We critique *America Profunda* from a number of perspectives. First, that the basis of indigenous resistance and consciousness is integral to Latin America. Second, we compare Zapotec resistance with the Maori in New Zealand, with the Gond and the Warli in India, with the Wampanoag in the United States; with the Zapatista movement, and with Lakota resistance. We then review overall indigeneity and its intersections with globalization.

1. Basis of indigenous resistance/consciousness integral to Latin America

Indigenous peoples represent significant percentages of the population of many Latin American countries, and in some cases, when grouped together, they constitute the majority. This is certainly the case in Bolivia, where the Indian Movement *Pachacuti* (led by Felipe Quispe Huanca, an *Aymara*), initiated protests in Bolivia that contributed to the downfall of the sitting president:

> "We believe in the reconstruction of the Kollasuyu, our own ancestral laws, our own philosophy... We have... our political heritage (that) can

be successful in removing and destroying neoliberalism, capitalism and imperialism.

It is community-based socialism… That is what the brothers of our communities hold as model… In the Aymara and Quechua areas, primarily in La Paz, we have been working since 1984 on fostering awareness of community-based ideologies. …" (*Washington Times*, March 3, 2004)

Felipe Quispes speaks of movements arising throughout "Indian" Latin America, shared struggles that are based on a diversity of indigenous peoples and nation-states. While each is reconstructing traditions unique to its own culture, and often relative to the specific lands they inhabit, they are also finding commonalities across many fronts, notably in opposition to cultural domination and capitalist expansion over their lands. Even as the essence of a community, economic cooperatives, shared decisionmaking, and land tenure relations vary, indigenous peoples rely on these foundations both to resist in their individual situations, and increasingly in global networks (Ramirez 2003).

Ecuador is an outstanding example, with recent protests and insurrection rising to levels of revolutionary activity, some of it in concert with mainstream military forces, leading to the Quito accords, and ultimately a broken alliance. Indigenous peoples are often in the middle of social unrest and rebellion, especially when there are high numbers and they are well organized. Unfortunately, all too often they are left out of resolutions and agreements arising out of these conflicts.

Mayan-descent peoples in Guatemala, in the states of Chiapas and Oaxaca, Mexico, are moving away from Liberation Theology to new indigenous "Liberation Philosophy," which is partly based on traditional understandings of culture, the land, and community. These are epistemological movements that reject not only the hierarchy of European social orders, but the very nature of their social organization (Maldonado 2002).

Nicaragua Miskito communities realized the "autonomous" zones of *Zelaya Norte,* first in armed conflict with the Sandinistas who were in low-intensity war with Contras funded by the United States (part of resistance to capitalist globalization as socialism, but more importantly as community responsibility and resisting privatization), and later with coalition governments. This has led to a series of legal challenges by Nicaraguan indigenous groups, all of which furthered the causes of resistance and revitalization.

Mapuche peoples in Chile have also organized their resistance along cultural lines, again relating their struggle to community and land. While many of these interethnic conflicts find flash points around some major economic activity, such as mining or land appropriation for large-scale agricultural development, their underlying issues remain focused on maintaining traditional lifestyles in order to retain community cohesion.

2. Examples of indigenous communities resisting domination[10]

Zapotec *Pueblos Indios,* mostly in the state of Oaxaca, Mexico, have used a variety of strategies or tactical approaches toward the incorporating process of the state and its economies, ranging from outright assimilation to relatively direct secessionist autonomy. *Yavesia,* a Zapotec community in the Sierra Juarez highlands, has formally organized their economy to resist the deforestation that nearby communities have experienced, developed a natural water bottling operation, and formalized women's cooperatives, maintain a fishery, and have computer programs including GIS mapping for their young students to learn about the land and history of their people. Additionally, they formally receive delegations from other indigenous communities throughout Mexico, and study like-minded social movements such as the Zapatistas for applications to their situation. All decisions are taken in community meetings that include everyone, and they employ *cargo* systems that can even demand people return from work in the United States.

Maori people in New Zealand have been battling colonialism and discrimination for some two hundred years now, maintaining their sense of community, as in their *marae,* their treaty relations as in the Waitangi Tribunal, an adapted communal decisionmaking, and quasimodern redistributive economics realized with a few *Iwi* or *Hapu* settlements, now in corporate form. Even so, Maori mostly exist in the lower-stratification levels with significant institutional inequalities in all sectors of the society. Discrimination levels have recently increased over such resource issues as the Foreshore and Seabed debates, wherein Maori have a constitutional right to control land collectively, although *Pakeha* (white) people and the government want to enforce private property and new legislation. Maori leaders and scholars now state "Maori have never said we owned the seabed" when debating the Foreshore legislation (Waitangi Tribunal 2003). For Maori, their relationship with the land was one of belonging to it, not one of "owning it." Further, they believe that "*Ranguini,* our sky father... and *Papatuanuku,* our earth mother..." make up *Aotearoa* over which they have a "role as *kaitiaki*" or guardians / stewards of the land[11] (Marsden 2003).

Gond peoples in central India, largest of the "scheduled tribes" first so identified by the British and later accepted by the Indian government, are in constant conflict with governmental and privatized corporate forces, over the land, their community leadership, medicinal plants, and forest rights. As with the Warli below, they are often labeled as "encroachers" upon their own traditional lands, since they do not have formal recognition of title or treaty right. In fact, this is an inherited condition from British colonialism:

The British in 1793 commenced the forced restructuring of the relationship of Adivasis to their territories as well as the power relationship between Adivasis and 'others' (Bijoy 2001).

These practices have continued, with a special focus on cultural destruction or erasure, leading to denial by the government of India at the United Nations that it even had so many indigenous peoples (the largest number in the world) and no legal standing for important social structures, such as the *Ghotul* with the Gond and land creation stories with the Warli literally calling their origin place "mother earth" (Prabhu 2004). Warli families maintain the practice of allowing animals in the house, not differentiating between humans and other life forms. Villages north of Dahanu experience near constant conflict with corrupt "foresters" selling rights to private companies, and with government law calling their villages "encroachment" on their traditional, now timbered forest lands. Movement organizations have arisen, for the most part nonviolent, who represent Warli and other indigenous peoples' rights to land and access to roads and schools, periodically having to fight off large squads of police and militia who want to remove them to cities. Even more interesting is that many of these communities, and the movement groups, have regenerated extremely large Teak forests, that they protect and now have limited government agreements on cutting rights. When these forests mature, activists expect another round of conflicts with private companies and government agents.

There remains an intersectional analysis of Marxist revolutionary praxis in India, in both the Gond and Warli situations, that should be discussed at this point. Marxist groups have enlisted indigenous support, sometimes whole villages, to causes that do not represent the qualities delineated above, ultimately leading to sharp conflicts with these groups as well. In many ways, as with the Miskito in Nicaragua, this shows that it is the qualities of being indigenous which underlies these struggles.

Wampanoag peoples in the United States represent our last comparative cases, having a struggle that is over 400 years of colonialism and repression, and with many of the recognition issues discussed above. The Mashpee Wampanoag, survivors of those who saved the Puritans first coming to what is now known as New England at Plymouth, maintain their traditions and history as an unrecognized people, even as the Aquinnah Wampanoag have won recognition legal battles with an official reservation land base. Aquinnah people are working from a "tribal council" that, like other peoples, will not give up any more land. They are replanting beach dunes to their original forms, have reestablished a shellfish operation using traditional methods, and are employing cooperative ventures, including joint-use agreements, across Martha's Vineyard island areas, notably their "sacred cliff" lands as a major tourist point. Revitalization in this situation includes their struggles for "tribal sovereignty" recognition, maintenance of what was oral tradition history, and economic development that does not run counter to their traditional values.

3. Resistance (Tzotzil, others) and the Zapatistas in Chiapas, Mexico

We must remember that in the original Zapatista declaration, a primary and critical target was NAFTA and incursion of global capital that worsened conditions in the region. One reason the Mexican military could not conduct an all-out assault against the Zapatista revolt was the possibility of other indigenous movements arising, especially in Oaxaca and Guerrero. Our first condition, the basis of indigenous resistance and consciousness being critical to Mexico and Latin America, was demonstrated in these set of conflicts. The next two years were full of movement activity and attempts at counterinsurgency. The San Andreas Accords appeared to settle some demands, but the government started supporting paramilitaries in the area, destabilizing the pacific communities and softening Zapatista support in some sectors. One well-known example of how violent these actions became is the massacre at Acteal, an unarmed Tzotzil highland village that followed their Christian or Catholic practices, but supported the idea of Zapatista developments.[12]

Zapatista communities began to organize in new ways that attempted to respect traditional culture, but sowed new patterns as well, including equality and involvement for women, direct challenges to local and state authorities, and community self-defense. Conflicts took various forms, forcing Zapatistas to struggle with the local paramilitaries, corrupt government officials, military forts built throughout the region, restive localities, peasant organizations, and a depressed economy. One of the last interactive responses established by the Zapatistas was to form and run offices of "Junta del Buen Gobierno" that heard local issues and resolved them for the betterment of harmonious relations within the community, similar to restorative justice systems of North American Indian Nations like the Lakota, who actually wrote them into their treaties in the nineteenth century.[13] These are near-perfect examples of mediating social structures that place community relations as the highest value, and that use personal property as a variable.

Community organizations in Los Altos and other contested regions where conflicts between Zapatista and government-supported forces were common, thus transformed basic sociopolitical relations so they were both modern and responsive to contemporary issues, and yet were traditional and sensitive to local indigenous concerns. The municipal sign at *San Pedro Polho* represents this well, by identifying itself as an autonomous rebel community that banned drugs, stolen property such as cars, and alcohol abuse as threats to local lifestyles, and more importantly has the phrase *"Aqui el pueblo manda y el gobierno obedece"* (here the people speak and the government obeys...).[14]

What we have observed in the Zapatista case, and will now identify with other indigenous peoples under discussion, is how new social forms arise out of high conflict situations between indigenous communities and movements and dominant nation-state governments and private corporate groups intent on wresting profits from their land and labor. These tend to respect the four categories previously identified as being generically important to indigenous peoples, and yet also interact with modernity and contemporary political realities. The Warli also developed such mechanisms, in response to internal colonialism established by the Indian government that clear-cut forests for private timber companies, legalized bond labor, and attempted land takings on a massive scale. These Warli and Gond resistance groups have regenerated Teak forests, rebuilt ancient cultural traditions that produced community cohesion, and produced socioeconomic activity that would be redistributed among all its members and could support legal challenges as well. Lakota resistance was also based on agreements after armed conflicts, as in the 1868 Fort Laramie Treaty, which noted the sanctity of the Black Hills, *ina maka* as a grandmother, and honored kinship relations and honorable defense of the people. As discussed earlier, Intercontinental *Encuentros* held by the Zapatistas with the Lakota and other indigenous peoples have also produced new social transformations and connections.

4. Overall "Indigeneity" in the face of globalization

There is great diversity of cultural practices and social formations of indigenous peoples that is further complicated by their individual geographic and political placement, even with the few cases we have presented here. However, we can identify certain aspects of Indigeneity that have been consistent across these cases, and hypothesize as to why these seem more powerful explanations for what is occurring on a global level.

These are the four major organizational social structures with indigenous peoples:

(1) Decisionmaking (political systems) that is consensus driven, often without any formal leader but rather a spokesperson who is controlled by a council of elders;

(2) Economy (redistributive on communal level) that shares with all its members and has focus on families and group property, valuing social prestige to honor and mark success;

(3) Land tenure (cultural/historical ties, group control) usually as a kind of a collectivity, often without private ownership, sometimes sacred, and rarely if ever sold to outsiders;

(4) Community cohesion (autonomous, self-determination) with a focus on harmonious relationships, often on kinship levels, with the greater group good as the primary value.

New forms of indigeneity are arising in various international contexts, albeit based on traditional concepts merging with modern social forms. A rising consciousness and connectedness of disparate groups in global struggles, intersecting with an immense presence of the Zapatista perspective on the Internet, has contributed to global forms of indigeneity. The Maori have been linking with American Indian organizations; Lakota and other U.S. Indian Nations have traveled to Miskito extensively with the Zapatistas and other resistance forces in Mexico. The *Adevasi* in India, while often more isolated, are increasingly connecting with international organizations.

Collaborations between Marxist resistance/revolutionary forces have increased, over the past two decades, but may well be in decline now, with the Zapatistas becoming more indigenous in their orientation. Miskito resistance to the Sandinista domination in Nicaragua was a classic case in the opposite direction. The Zapatistas representation are offset by nonviolent indigenous groups such as at Acteal, though they support the ideals. Strong Marxist groups in India better demonstrate these tensions, with the Warli people—more loosely with the Gond—actually coming into direct conflict over their ideological and movement orientations.

Indigenous groups have existed for thousands of years in cultural dominance systems, and maintained their identities and struggles, often resurfacing in later regimes. *Adevasi* in India definitively represent this, and to a lesser extent the resurgence of many indigenous peoples and their movements in Mexico illustrate this continuity.

All of these struggles look quite different from a "bottom-up" perspective rather than from a "top-down" approach. Fieldwork and significant experience on site and with indigenous peoples is the only way to get this perspective, since it resides in particular cultures, historical situations, and sociopolitical realities of the people themselves. However, we have identified four major categorical or conceptual areas of analysis, which appear to be consistent for most indigenous peoples, at least in terms of issues. So, we conclude by reconsidering these in world-systems analysis.

Conclusions

Questions remain on the meaning, experience, and praxis of indigeneity, which we can only elaborate on by continued ethnographic work, including indigenous perspectives, from the people themselves. While much of indigenous resistance is systemic in nature, it can utilize modern social configurations and technology, which is both additive and transformative of traditional forms of indigeneity.

Specificity on a comparability of indigeneity in Latin America, with First Nations, demonstrates not only a diversity of perspectives noted above, but close analysis of sociopolitical development in their respective nation-states and regional issues, inclusive of status of sovereignty claims and autonomous governance. These are markedly diverse across the western hemisphere, and appear especially contrastive between North America and Central and South, or Latin America (with Mexico). There is an interconnectedness between these movements, and peoples, that appears to be neoliberal in some guises, and is antiglobalization in others (Sklair 2002).

Alignments with Marxist revolutionary movements or ideologies of social change look to be instigated by expediency rather than coalitions. Indigenous peoples seem to be focused on revitalizing and rebuilding a sense of community and an orientation to land, instead of political reformulation. In many cases, apparently including the Zapatistas (now, anyway), there is no longer interest in changing nation-state politics, but a strong, overriding focus on establishing autonomy over local society and living relationships.

We need to analyze their specific situations in terms of models presented herein (local economy, community, decisionmaking, land tenure), attenuated with the complex relationships indigenous peoples have with nation-states and in any regional conflicts. Struggles spanning international politics, such as the Pashtun in Afghanistan/Pakistan, Kurds in Iraq/Turkey, Bedouin Arabs and Palestinians in the Middle East, or Quechuan peoples in the Andes, further complicate any understanding of ongoing dynamics.

New forms of social struggle and structure are arising on the ground as we speak, meaning that indigeneity, local autonomy, and indigenous communities will continue to change and interact in the modern world-systems in ways that may befuddle us at times, and just as often will enlighten us on the past, present, and future of our diverse world.

Notes

1. Quote from "America Profunda," composed of "more than 125 persons of 23 peoples, coming from 15 countries of three continents over several days in Mexico City, to reflect together about our realities and perspectives" (December 6–9, 2003). The preliminary draft documents, as the meetings and symposium itself, was run, organized, and facilitated by Gustavo Esteva (*Centro de Encuentros Y Dialogos Interculturales*, CEDI) and Grimado Rengifo (*Programa Andino de Tecnologias Campesinas*, PRATEC).

2. Described as "culturicide" by Fenelon, James V. 1998. *Culturicide, Resistance, and Survival of the Lakota ("Sioux Nation")*. New York: Garland.

3. This "Consensus of the Peoples" (America Profunda initial findings, 2003) include these elements: Radical Pluralism; Personal Dignity; Autonomy; New Political Regime; Subordination of the Economy; Radical Democracy; Conviviality; Communality; Creation of a New World; Autonomy in Exchange; Socialization; Service and Reciprocity (each defined and explicated in the initial findings document).

4. Plate 1: "Day of the Dead" poster (revealing Mexico Profundo), picture taken in Oaxaca, Mexico, November 2003. *http://fs6.depauw.edu:50080/~thall/hp1.htm* (first in a series of 5 plates found at this site, referenced in this paper, all photography by James V. Fenelon).

5. Plate 2: Mural of 500 Years of Indigenous Life, photograph taken at "La Escuelita" cultural center, barrio, Santo Domingo, Mexico City, Mexico, December, 2003, *http://fs6.depauw. edu:50080/~thall/hp1.htm.*

6. Plate 3: Indigenous Resistance and Rebellion (poster/banner), hung in central square of Oaxaca City, Oaxaca, Mexico, November 2003. *http://fs6.depauw.edu:50080/~thall/hp1.htm.*

7. Abu-Saad, Ismael, Harvey Lithwick, and Kathleen Abu-Saad. 2004. *Preliminary Evaluation of the Negev Bedouin Experience of Urbanization*. Beer Sheva, Israel: Negev Center for Regional Development.

8. Plate 4: Oventik, Zapatista headquarters, Signs and Buildings Oventik en Los Altos, Chiapas, Mexico, December 2003. *http://fs6.depauw.edu:50080/~thall/hp1.htm.*

9. See Plate 4, above, for a photograph taken of this mural painting at the Oventik headquarters hall.

10. This information was "collected" as quasiethnographic, on-site "fieldwork" by author Fenelon, during interactive visits arranged by the Indigenous Perspectives program (Boston University, IHP) in Fall 2003, with indigenous communities in Oaxaca and Chiapas, Mexico; in north and south Aotearoa, New Zealand; Dahanu and east-central Maharashtra, India; and coastal Massachusetts, United States of America. We find this work supplements, in key and critically necessary ways, scholarly analytical modes of inquiry.

11. "Mangapouri Stream Research and Restoration Project," lecture/presentation by Pataka Moore and Caleb Royal, at *Te-Wananga-o-Raukawa* (college) at Otaki, Aotearoa, New Zealand, October 2003.

12. Site visit at Acteal, Chiapas, in December 2003, and lectures by Raymundo B. Sanchez, San Cristobol. For discussion, see Ramirez (2003).

13. Plate 2, referenced above, refers to these "Junta del Buen Gobierno" offices at Oventik and Zapatista communities throughout the contested *Los Altos* region.

14. Plate 5: Zapatista Community Sign, San Pedro Polho Los Altos region, Chiapas, Mexico, December 2003. *http://fs6.depauw.edu:50080/~thall/hp1.htm.*

References

Bijoy, C.R. 2001. "The Adevasis of India—A History of Discrimination, Conflict and Resistance." *Indigenous Affairs, International Working Group for Indigenous Affairs (IWGIA)*, Copenhagen, Denmark, 1/01, March 2001, pgs. 54–61.

Bonfil Batalla, Guillermo. 1996. *Mexico Profundo—Reclaiming a Civilization* (translated by Phillip A. Dennis). Austin: University of Texas Press.

Carlson, Jon D. 2001. "Broadening and Deepening: Systemic Expansion, Incorporation and the Zone of Ignorance." *Journal of World-Systems Research* 7:2(Fall):225–263. E-Journal http://jwsr.ucr.edu/index.php.

Cobo, Jose R. Martinez. 1987. *Estudio del problema de la discriminacion contra las poblaciones indigenas* (vol. V, Conclusiones, propuestas y recomendaciones). Nueva York: Nationes Unidas.

Fenelon, James V. 1998. *Culturicide, Resistance, and Survival of the Lakota* (Sioux Nation). New York: Garland Publishing.

Hall, Thomas D., and James V. Fenelon. 2003. "Indigenous Resistance to Globalization: What Does the Future Hold?" Pp. 173–188 in *Emerging Issues in the 21st Century World-System: Vol. I: Crises and Resistance in the 21st World-System*, edited by Wilma A. Dunaway. Westport, CT: Praeger.

——. 2004. "The Futures of Indigenous Peoples: 9-11 and the Trajectory of Indigenous Survival and Resistance." *Journal of World-Systems Research*, 10:1(Winter):153–197.

Maldonado Alvarado, Benjamin. 2002. *Autonomia y Communalidad India, enfoques y propuestas desde Oaxaca.* INAH, Secretaria de Asuntos Indigenas, CEDI, Oaxaca, Mexico.

Marsden, Maori. 2003. *Woven Universe: Selected Writings of Rev. Maori Marsden.* Te Ahukaramu (ed.). Charles Royal, Estate of Rev. Marsden, Te Wananga-o-Raukawa, Otaki.

Prabhu, Pradip. 2004. "Nature, Culture and Diversity—The Indigenous Way of Life." in Smitu Kothari, Imtiaz, and Helmut Reifeld (eds.), *The Value of Nature—Ecological Politics in India.* New Delhi: Rainbow Publishers.

Ramirez, Gloria Munoz. 2003. *EZLN: 20 y 10, el fuego y la palabra.* Mexico: Revista Rebeldia.

Sklair, Leslie. 2002. *Globalization: Capitalism and Its Alternatives,* 3rd ed. Oxford: Oxford University Press.

Waitangi Tribunal. 2003. Te Manutukutuku, No. 59 (September). Wellington, NZ: Waitangi Tribunal (government publishing, http://www.waitangi-tribunal.govt.nz).

7

Running for Peace and Dignity

From Traditionally Radical Chicanos/as to Radically Traditional Xicanas/os

Roberto Hernández

The Twenty-Eighth Annual Political Economy of the World-System (PEWS) conference, thematically titled "Latin@s in the World-System," posed several questions, among which were: How to think about decolonization of the American Empire in the twenty-first century? Which traditions, imaginaries and identities will prevail within the Latin@ population? And how can Latin@s build a different relationship among themselves and with other groups...? My focus lies on three main themes: historical silences and distortions of the Chicano Movement, questions of spirituality and *indigenismo,* and lastly, a consideration of an ongoing spiritual run called the Peace and Dignity Journeys and the role Latinas/os, youth in particular, have been playing in it.The purpose of this essay is twofold. First, it is an attempt to delve into the complex role of indigenismo and indigenous spirituality amongst Chicanas/os specifically, and Latinas/os generally. While not much scholarly attention has been given to the matter, this piece is meant as a starting point that will hopefully lead to more questions, rather than an exhaustive effort. Secondly, and just as important, I situate my work within the framework of Chicana/o Studies, and in so doing, I aim to intervene critically in the sometimes dogmatic formulations of Chicano historiography and knowledge production generally. Historian Emma Pérez' analysis is thus useful, as she suggests four frames through which Chicano history has usually been articulated:

1. Ideological/Intellectual: "Chicanos are heroes/intellectuals."
2. Immigrant/Labor: "Chicanos/as are immigrant laborers" and/or "Chicanos/as are colonized workers."
3. Social History of the Other (as History of the Same): "Chicanos/as are also social beings, not just workers"; and
4. Gendered History: "Chicanos are also Chicanas."[1]

These frameworks, Pérez argues, limit the lens by which we view history, as well as its content. Taking heed from Pérez, my intervention for an indigenista perspective in Chicana/o Studies, which I hope will become evident in this essay, also draws from "dialogue about the nature and direction of Chicano social science research" reached at the first NCCSS meeting (then National Caucus of Chicano Social Science) in 1973. I point here to the first of five points of consensus:

> Social science research by Chicanos must be much more problem-oriented than traditional social science has been. Chicano research should aim to delineate the social problems of La Raza, [and I would add methodological, ontological and epistemological considerations] and actively propose solutions. Analysis should not be abstracted or disembodied from such pressing social concerns. Social science scholarship cannot be justified for its own sake: it must be committed scholarship that can contribute to *Chicano Liberation* (my emphasis).[2]

While the five points of consensus were meant to outline a vision of the nature and direction of Chicano social science research, such vision has yet to be realized and it is arguable whether it is followed today. Also arguable is what was and is meant by "Chicano Liberation" and the limits of social science research. Although the subject of much debate in the 1960s as it is today, it is in thinking through this debate that epistemic and ontological considerations become crucial, as does the breaking away from strict disciplinary boundaries that define our sense of knowledge and knowledge production.[3] Nonetheless, this paper is guided by a spirit of "committed scholarship" aiming to constructively and "actively propose solutions," in this case to political, ideological and TemporalSpatial questions of decolonization, spirituality and coloniality. By TemporalSpatial, I am referring to the five kinds of TimeSpace (episodic geopolitical, cyclico-ideological, structural, eternal, and transformational)

Immanuel Wallerstein depicts in his study of historical systems.[4] I also borrow from Walter Mignolo's assertion of the "epistemic potential" of Chicano and Latino Studies,[5] to argue that the vision of liberation and decolonization has accompanied such programs since their inception, but has not been fully realized, in part, due to a failure to recognize the extent, depth, and reach of the coloniality of power, as Anibal Quijano describes contemporary power relations.[6] In other words, I am here proposing that it is through knowledge production from an indigenous or indigenista perspective that we may further the process of decolonization from the structural TimeSpace of the capitalist world-economy, which has lasted over 500 years, built, in part, on the suppression of indigenous knowledge and spirituality. Such a perspective entails a necessary break from Cartesian and binary logics that inform Western rationality which would, in turn, lead to significantly different relations to questions of land, ownership, social relations, modes of production and value.[7]

Using the ongoing debates about identity politics and the political utility of nationalism as a departure point, this paper thus examines the history and historiography of the Chicano Movement. Contrary to most scholarly considerations of the period, which reduce it to a moment of nationalist fervor, I explore different tendencies that coexisted and continue today. I take the perspective and argue that heterogeneity has been a significant source of Chicano organizations' strengths, yet their inability to come to terms with such heterogeneity has also been at the root of their own limitations. In particular, I consider the origin of the Chicano Movement as a union of multiple organizations and struggles of similar, yet by no means identical, political persuasions, as the originating tension that has emerged time and time again as point of contestation, albeit in different manifestations. While I briefly consider the nationalist-internationalist debate that took center stage in the 1980s, my focus is the more recent engagements with decolonial *indigenismo* among Latinas/os, as informed since the 1960s.

Michel-Rolph Trouillot shows how history, its production and public memory reflect power relations since "Power is constitutive of the story . . . [it] does not enter the story... It precedes the narrative proper, contributes to its creation and to its interpretation..."[8] Therefore, he continues, if one is to uncover the hidden stories, an inevitable series of questions arise: why, how, and by whom have the stories been silenced? Or told? The answers lay in an interrogation of power in its many manifestations, in this case a consideration of representations of the Chicano Movement made by participants who entered academia, as informed by the ideological perspective that has maintained a hegemonic position, namely nationalism.

As Black youth were breaking with their reformist-minded predecessors of the Civil Rights Era, affirming *"Black Is Beautiful"* stances, young Mexicanas/os were abandoning the assimilationist and reformist organizations and mobilizing to the thunderous chants of *"Chicano Power!"* and *"¡Viva La Raza!"*[9] At the forefront of the shift to a nationalist and militant politics (among other ideological tendencies) were youth frustrated with the inaction to the brutal injustices their communities were facing; namely police brutality, inadequate housing, job/wage discrimination and poverty. A major signifier of such a shift toward self-determination was the process of self-naming. In the 1960s many young Mexicanas/os began calling themselves Chicanas and Chicanos. They also adopted the concept of "Aztlán" (a "mythical" place from which the Aztecs were said to have migrated south to Tenochitlán) in reference to the Southwest of the United States, a land that had previously been a part of Mexico. Aztlán, or the Southwest, therefore became a symbolic home to the Chicanas/os, many who romantically saw themselves as descendants of the Aztecs and hence fighting for their homeland.[10]

On the heels of the now-famous National Chicano Youth Liberation Conference in Denver, Colorado, in March of 1969, where El Plan Espiritual de Aztlán, the subject of much recent criticism from the conservative right, was drafted, a second unrelated conference was convened by members of Chicano Coordinating Committee on Higher Education (CCHE) and held a month later in Santa Barbara.[11] From this conference came plans on the part of the students present (over fifty student leaders who were selectively invited) to drop the names of their respective organizations and in exchange collectively take on the name of a new organization, Movimiento Estudiantil Chicano/a de Aztlán (M.E.Ch.A.). Many of the students present were concerned with finding a way of operationalizing El Plan de Aztlán, which among other points, called for "UNITY" as its first point of action—a concept that would prove to be extremely problematic.

While high school students in Los Angeles and elsewhere had already been walking out of schools in protest of a failing educational system, what was significant about this conference was the formalization of the initiative that students took. In other words, while the Santa Barbara conference undoubtedly marked the birth of M.E.Ch.A, the self-representation of the event, *which continues today*, also reveals the vanguardism that has come to characterize many Chicano organizations. It is here that I differ with Carlos Muñoz' argument in *Youth, Identity, and Power*, perhaps the most widely read volume on the Chicano Movement: "The adoption of the new name, and its acronym, M.E.Ch.A., signaled a new level of political consciousness among student activists. It was the final stage in the transformation of what had been loosely organized, local student groups into a single structured and unified student movement."[12] While adopting one name was a significant move, rather than accepting this romanticized view of events, I would argue the language of the Plan de Santa Barbara illuminated the fact that there was still a lack of unity on goals, principles and strategy. Instead, El Plan was very loosely and ambiguously written, as it spoke more to the multitude of varying perspectives present than to one single unified voice. While potentially positive if embraced for its heterogeneity, problems soon arose from the insistence on a cultural unity despite clearly varying views and class differences that existed. Although it did provide the necessary inspiration to further "movement" activities, different people, informed by distinct ideologies, took with them different readings of the Plan.

The loosely and ambiguously written Plan de Santa Barbara thus illustrated the initially generalist approach to a definition of Chicano Nationalism that was itself still emerging. While it was useful for creating a sense of social cohesion, its ambiguous nature remained and conflicts over ideology, among others, some new and some old, would arise. It was from these two initial conferences that the concepts of cultural nationalism, Aztlán, and Chicano/a were being solidified and thus became the hegemonic discourse of the Chicano Movement.

A significant part of the utopian-vision-in-progress was due to writings of a young poet, Alurista, whose poem "El Plan Espiritual de Aztlán" galvanized the moment; but from this poem, too, emerged different, diverging tendencies. Alurista has since gone down in history as a Chicano icon, despite his own later, *and lesser known,* rewriting of "El Plan Espiritual de Aztlán" in which he makes his own indigenous epistemological location more explicit. Few knew much about Alurista, at the time a student in San Diego; what mattered most was his poetry. A point that must be elucidated, however, is that Alurista, whose real name is Alberto Urista, was himself an immigrant from Mexico City who had come to the United States with a clearer understanding of Nahuatl language and cosmology than most urban Chicanas/os.[13] So while the terms Aztlán and Chicano were becoming popularized, appropriated and romanticized for the purpose of the political mobilizations of the Chicano Movement, underlying Alurista's poetry was nonetheless an entirely different cosmological understanding of one's relation with the land and of the term Chicano itself, which I argue posits the condition of possibility for a distinction between what I will propose as "cultural nationalists" and "indigenistas."

Black scholar activist, Robert Allen, in *Black Awakening in Capitalist America,* writes how in the 1960s several parties with diverging interests were using the concept of "Black Power" in dramatically different ways. Allen distinguishes between the cultural nationalists, revolutionary nationalists, and bourgeois nationalists. Of the three, for example, the latter's concept of Black Power was equated with Black Capitalism and shared the support of Richard Nixon.[14] It is here, I argue, a similar analysis of the Chicano Movement can be sustained, and thus shift in an attempt to elaborate it in regards to the Chicano/a experience of the 1960s.

In the July/August 2002 issue of *Monthly Review,* Jorge Mariscal and Betita Martinez, respectively, elucidate the internationalist tendencies of the Chicano Movement, rooted in 1900's labor struggles.[15] These coexisting tendencies came to a clash in the 1980s, embodied in the League of Revolutionary Struggle (LRS, known as Liga) and M.E.Ch.A. While accepted Chicano history and popular lore maintains Liga were "outside communist agitators" attempting to "infiltrate" a presumably unified (nationalist) movement, Mariscal and Martinez' historical contextualizations help demonstrate Liga members were part of already existing internationalist tendencies *within* the Chicano Movement. Contrary to prescriptions of the period as solely a nationalist movement, Mariscal and Martinez attempt to rescue a more sophisticated politic that existed. Mariscal elaborates the point in relation to Chicano Studies, which we still see reflected today in the numerous interest-based caucuses and ideological persuasions of the National Association of Chicana and Chicano Studies (NACCS). Mariscal states, "As Chicano Studies programs developed . . . during the early 1970s, ideological divisions would distinguish 'revolutionary,' 'nationalist,' and more traditional faculty and curricula."[16] The heterogeneity made itself evident once again in the recent (2004) creation of an Indigenous Caucus. Nonetheless, a nationalist imaginary, of one variation or another, has always dominated, among Chicana/o intellectual circles, albeit at odds with Chicana feminist, internationalist, poststructuralist and indigenous scholars since the inception of Chicano Studies.

Such divisions exist not only among faculty and curricula. They are also evident among students and activists in the community. However, rather than consider the ideological divisions as a sign of decline as it is usually portrayed and in which there exists the logic of a fading authentic moment, I believe it is more useful, and, in fact, historically accurate, to speak of such divisions as the anxiety and inability to come to terms with the wide range of perspectives that coexisted alongside an often monolithic Chicano cultural nationalism. It was such inability to grasp a sense of a heterogeneous community, which led two major organizations in the 1970s, the August 29 Movement (ATM) and Centro de Acción Social Autonomo (CASA) to rival, for example, not (only) over ideology, but over what was the correct form Chicano Liberation would take: an independent Chicano nation in the Southwest or a return of the Southwest to Mexico.[17] Both, however, had totalizing stances that included the outright erasure of the native populations in the Southwest. While some took to forms of nationalism that in effect erased the existence of native peoples such as the Chumash, Tohono O'odham, and Kummeyay of the Southwest, others took a different approach. It is to these few, but important, examples I will turn my attention.

As an initial attempt to delve into the complex role of *indigenismo* and indigenous spirituality amongst Chicanas/os specifically and Latinas/os generally, I interrogate two aspects of said concepts, which for explanatory purposes I propose as a distinction between symbolic and concrete engagements with indigenous cultures and teachings. By symbolic and concrete engagements and commitments, I mean to distinguish between what I earlier posed as "cultural nationalists," on the one hand—those who simply invoke pre-Colombian imagery and symbols for political purposes, yet may discount indigenous perspectives, lived experiences, struggles and living peoples themselves—and *"indigenistas,"* on the other—those who do actively engage and maintain spiritual and political commitments (this too is heterogeneous which I will touch on later) with the respective teachings of (their) traditional communities in a conscionable and respectful way. Another distinguishing characteristic of the latter group is their tendency to be more historically attuned and acknowledging of how different colonial histories and racialization processes have constructed present-day relations with other native peoples and one another in given spaces as negotiated by geopolitical borders. That is to say, I make a distinction between various reactionary political forms of cultural nationalisms and those who learn and make spiritual commitments to their own native teachings. As such, I focus on how some of the debates around *indigenismo* have thus manifested themselves in the context of discussions around the Chicano Movement and more recently, Latinas/os generally.

It is necessary, however, to acknowledge the numerous "indigenista" groups, many with their own distinct and often varying politics regarding *indigenismo* and spirituality. In this regard, it is difficult to speak of one monolithic form or manifestation of *indigenismo,* so I will limit myself to groups in California, Arizona and Colorado. I similarly will attempt to account for tendencies within the cultural nationalist organizations that are "officially" ambivalent and/or maintain often contradictory negotiations with indigeneity, M.E.Ch.A. in particular.

As Mariscal and Martinez remark about leftist tendencies, I contend that there have also always been, albeit limited in numbers, "indigenista" tendencies among the participants of the Chicano Movement. Perhaps most notably are the Arranda, Enrique and Sanchez families of San Diego and Arizona who have been involved with the Peace and Dignity Journeys, and Rocky Rodriguez and others in Colorado who were part of the Occupation at Wounded Knee in solidarity with the American Indian Movement. There were also several young Chicanas/os in the San Francisco/Oakland Bay Area who accompanied the group "Indians of All Tribes" in the November 1969 takeover of Alcatraz Island and others who joined Native students in creation of DQ University, a Native Chicano community college near Sacramento a few years later. There are also numerous groups of people who have been involved with Danza Azteca (Aztec dancing which is itself a form of prayer) and other forms of ceremonies. These examples point to a different understanding of, and relationship to, the term "Chicano/a" and, furthermore, the necessity to outline an *indigenista* conceptualization of the term Xicano/a.

Contrary to being the "derogatory term from the 1930s" as it is commonly described, the term Chicano is derived from the word *Mejicano* or Mexican, which is itself rooted in the word *Mexicano* (with the "x" being pronounced as "ch") within the Nahuatl language from which it stems. *Mexicano* was thus in reference to the *Mexica,* or Aztecs as later called by the Spanish colonists, and was derived from the union of four terms: *meztli* (moon), *xictli* (bellybutton), *cayotl* (offspring, child of), *noxt* (yes!). Although translations rarely do justice to actual meanings of words, it is from these root words that *mexica* translates roughly to "children from the bellybutton of the moon." Likewise, *xicano,* from its Nahuatl base can be taken to mean an affirmation "Yes! I am a child of the bellybutton/earth!" So while in the 1960s young Mexicanas/os took to the streets and proudly proclaimed themselves Chicanas/os, underlying this affirmation was a radically different cosmological understanding of one's relationship to self, the land, the earth and all living things, that Xicanas/os have now consciously embraced.

On the other hand, there are cultural nationalist groups who although identify with the cultural referents of what is perceived as an indigenous past, do not extend such significance to an indigenous living present. While cultural nationalist groups, whose public presence is most known, make use of pre-Colombian imagery and symbols, they by and large discount an "indigenista" perspective and fail to connect with those who have engaged in and with the respective teachings of traditional communities as well as ongoing struggles of living native peoples, north and south. Marginalized from the annals of Chicano Movement history have been the internationalist tendencies and, I would argue, also strands of indigenismo.

In a parallel observation, Maria Tere Ceseña's work on the role of *Danza Azteca* in Chicana/o communities, elucidates a similar point. She argues that through the presidency of Lazaro Cardenas, the years of consolidating the Mexican Revolution via Jose Vasconcelos' conceptualization of *La Raza Cosmica,* the State adhered to a "political rather than cultural [and much less 'biological'] affiliation" to "*lo indigena*" generally, and Cuauhtemoc specifically, erecting numerous statues in his honor, while denying the present-day indigenous reality of its own population. She interestingly notes that while revering this indigenous "past" in the process of modernizing Mexico through the narrative of Mestizaje, Emiliano Zapata, an indigenous hero of the Mexican Revolution, has never been "formally" revered by the state.[18] While the terms political, cultural and biological are, in fact, very loaded and at times cannot be extricated from one another in their functional roles, what Ceseña argues resonates with is my assertion that cultural nationalists generally have taken to a political—albeit often defined, imagined, and/or manifested as cultural—affiliation to an indigenous identity, while not always being in tune with ongoing struggles of indigenous peoples today, beyond that of symbolic solidarity, if at all.

Instead, despite real histories of infiltrations on the part of the FBI's Counter Intelligence Program (COINTELPRO), the obscure rendezvous with Liga in the 1980s led several nationalist organizations to institute rigid surveillance discourses, which has resulted in the blacklisting and ousting of those with internationalist and/or indigenista tendencies. Such organizations have adopted language warning against dual loyalties, ironically resembling the fundamentalist ranting of Samuel Huntington's warning of a Mexican "cultural threat" to the United States and President George W. Bush's paranoid assertions: "You are either with us or you are against us!"[19] Such similar proclamations by Chicano/a organizations are indicative of a presumed regime of truth, fearing the looming demise of a "pure" or authentic moment or form; a negation of a long history of heterogeneity and failure to come to grips with that history. So while Partha Chaterjee has described nationalisms as rational responses to colonialism,[20] they, along with fundamentalisms, are not precolonial or premodern. Instead, as Minoo Moallem describes, they are "a by-product of the process of modernization and in dialogue with modernity. [While], fundamentalism's impulse is to counter modernity, ... as a moment of modernity fundamentalism is discontinuous with related premodern discourses."[21] Moreover, fundamentalism opposes difference and claims cultural unity and homogeneity—a cultural unity and homogeneity that may have never existed—rather than accepting difference and working with similarly allied interests to achieve one's goals.

While there are now those that question what came out of the social upheavals of the 1960s—and, in fact, many of the legal/material benefits have begun to be eroded—I argue that what emerged may not yet be as visible or even tangible. By this I mean the experience of Chicanas/os making community with other Native peoples, north and south, and learning different native teachings; a situation that existed prior to the 1960s yet began occurring much more so as a result of the political agitations of the period. While at times it has been hard for some Chicanas/os and Latinas/os to trace their indigenous blood, others have had families, who whether openly or discreetly, kept family genealogies indicating their indigenous lines. Historically speaking, however, many Chicanas/os have not always known their own lineage and have had to search through family albums and converse with relatives not always willing to acknowledge their own Indian blood. Although during the 1960s, the tendency was to romantically identify with the "Aztec Warrior/Princess" iconography popular in Mexico, pushed in part by the state, many Chicanas/os have since come to a better understanding of the complexities of colonization in regards to the multiplicities of native ethnic communities and cultural identity, searching further into their own family histories and learning their respective languages and teachings.

Examples such as those aforementioned, who have since continued to build and influence the building of more community circles,[22] set the stage for ongoing conversations between what is often called the North and South. Although some modernist historians have confused this issue of spatial manifestation and place the distinction of North and South at the U.S.–Mexico border, which presupposes the eternal existence of the geopolitical divide and modern nation-state while not acknowledging the border divides native communities themselves,[23] by North and South I am referring here to the continents. It is from these conversations that have been occurring with more frequency and intensity in the last four decades, across the North and South that, when an elder in the North had a vision of an Eagle and Condor with their necks intertwined, an image long known in the South, the spirit of the Peace and Dignity Journeys was set in motion.

The image of the Eagle and Condor is an image illustrative of the Prophecy of the Confederation of the Eagle and Condor nations—the Eagle representing the north, the Condor representing the south. The intertwined necks thus signify a "reunification" of native nations across the continent. With the proposed celebrations of 500 years of the Columbus voyage nearing, "In 1990 over 200 representatives of native nations from throughout Turtle Island (South, Central and North America) met in Quito, Ecuador to discuss, strategize, and take action on issues affecting Indigenous People."[24] Once there, Elders from across the continent discussed the prophecy and the coming together of indigenous nations after centuries of colonization. "Inspired by this prophecy, elders proposed Peace and Dignity Journeys as a way to realize this unification. Through spiritual running and networking, indigenous peoples as a united force, from all over Turtle Island [would] reclaim peace and dignity by honoring indigenous values, ways of life, and current struggles of resistance to modern colonization."[25] A commitment was made that every four years runners would gather at the northern and southern tips of the continent, Chickaloon Nation, Alaska and Tierra del Fuego, Argentina, and run south and north, respectively, until meeting near the center of the continent. The first three runs, in 1992, 1996, and 2000, met in Teotihuacan, site of Mexica pyramids (and a new Wal-Mart) near Mexico City. The fourth run, underway at the time of this writing, will meet in Kuna Nation, Panama, in late 2004. As the anticipation of the Quincentennial celebrations/protests of Columbus' "discovery" of the New World began mounting and the indigenous summit in Quito, Peru, came and went, a new generation of young Chicanas/os who had begun referring to themselves as Xicana/o, had also been developing an *indigenista* perspective, looking beyond the limits and silences of an Aztlán-based cultural nationalism, embracing instead a hemispheric-wide mode of indigenous solidarity, cognizant of the 500 years of global capitalism that informs this historical system.

In an insightful essay entitled "Bucking the System: The TimeSpace of Antisystemic Movements," Richard Lee distinguishes between resistance in the short term and in the longue duree. Speaking of the capitalist world-economy or modern world-system as its own historical system with an internal logic, with which social actors must grapple to affect long-term social change, Lee suggests that since the nineteenth century, "To be antisystemic increasingly meant resisting the exclusions of liberal universalism"[26]; short-term and short-sighted movements. Lee however points to "new" movements engaged in a "retargeting of action away from the nation-state" such as those founded on ecological/environmental, racial and gendered concerns, as long-term resistance movements.[27] He argues these examples work through a TimeSpace of transformation of global capitalism and, furthermore, as "challenges to the premises of inequality associated with the structures of knowledge that began to emerge in the 1950s and 1960s" and continue to inform this historical system.[28] It is thus that I suggest indigenismo exists and makes its presence alongside the Peace and Dignity Journeys in the context of transformational TimeSpace—resistance and social change in the longue duree aiming to change the structures of knowledge that dictate how we think of ourselves in relation to the land, property, value, and each other.

As these younger *indigenistas* began organizing within M.E.Ch.A.s since the early 1990s, two trends emerged. On the one hand, there are those who have taken a cultural nationalist view of *lo indigena,* and on the other, there are those who have had a much more considerate and respectful view of, and relationship with, indigeneity across the Americas. I thus argue that in contrast to the cultural nationalists, there is a strong movement of youth in particular who have been increasingly brought up exposed early on to indigenous teachings, which they have, in turn, taken on as the guiding framework upon which to focus their energies, politics and lives.

While some critics have argued that these developments are New Age or appropriation of presumed "authentic" Northern teachings and past, the young Chicanas/os respond by invoking memory and a history of colonization that has resulted in generations of mestizaje. Others argue indigenismo is nostalgia for the past. Mike Davis, in a recent talk on the rise of Pentecostalism and other popular religious movements among the urban slums, demonstrated a typical Marxist approach to religion and spirituality, one of inexplicability to "new" questions being posed to Marxism and the Left generally.[29] However, what we find is not "new" turns toward the religious or spiritual, but rather a continuation of reliance, perseverance and resistance based on spirituality occurring in a context the Left has also failed to come to grips with. This is not "new," but a significant shift in paradigm from modernist notions of nationalism forcing one to ask: What is the intersection of spirituality and politics? What are the politics behind spiritual resistance? Or is it spirituality guiding politics? Can the two even be separated from one another? These questions are not meant to follow in the romanticizing footsteps of some cultural nationalists, but rather to provoke more questions to build on a topic long ignored.

So, while Josefina Saldaña-Portillo, in an essay "Who's the Indian in Aztlán," unjustly compares the mestizaje of Chicanas/os with the one invoked by the corporatist Mexican State in the 1930s, she also makes a generalized remark about M.E.Ch.A. not supporting the Zapatistas by their failure to include them in one of their four points of action the 1999 national conference.[30] Saldaña-Portillo's generalization, however, speaks more to her not being in tune to the changing internal dynamics of M.E.Ch.A., which includes factions of cultural nationalists and indigenistas. She fails to realize the existence of an internal shift to an orthodox reading of the group's founding documents on the part of the cultural nationalist leadership at the time, which suggested M.E.Ch.A. could only support specifically "student-oriented" causes. Saldaña-Portillo also bases her own characterization on an idealized notion of the Zapatistas as the "authentic Indians" while obfuscating a history of colonization that resulted in the mestizaje, deterritorialization and detribalization of many, including those who call themselves Xicana/o.

The 1999 M.E.Ch.A. decision, in fact, came again on the heels of a split within the organization at the University of California, Berkeley, in November 1998, which has come to be emblematic of the larger debate I have here tried to shed some light on.[31] Such knowledge would, in contrast, clarify that several chapters and individuals do openly support the Zapatistas, among other native struggles, and in fact have themselves a different understanding of mestizaje and *indigenismo* than the corporatist approach to mestizaje of the Cardenas presidency and Mexican State, to which Saldaña-Portillo compares M.E.Ch.A., Chicanas/os generally and the work of *indigenista* Gloria Anzaldúa, *Border-lands/La Frontera: The New Mestiza* specifically.

Ironically, a much-anticipated recent book by Ernesto Chavez, *¡Mi Raza Primero!: Nationalism, Identity, and Insurgency in the Chicano Movement in Los Angeles, 1966–1978*, reinscribes the nationalist historiography and truncates any sense of continuity to the Chicano/a Movement by placing its time frame as 1966–1978. It thus adds to the tendency to dismiss the 1960s as "a thing of the past" with no lasting consequences. Instead, as we look toward the future of Chicana/o and Latina/o Studies and questions of decolonization of the capitalist world-system, what would help would be an acknowledgement on the part of movement scholars and participants alike to recognize and accept its heterogeneity, drop orthodox readings of "founding documents" and open up to communication and dialogue with all Latinas/os, including those that work from what I have tried to shed light on as an *indigenista* perspective. Similarly, any approach to a question of decolonization must necessarily work from spirit keeping in mind both as a short-term, as well as a *longue duree* approach, such as those that the networks created by the Peace and Dignity Journeys have been working to create, strengthen, and solidify since the early 1990s. In conclusion, Roland Wright in *Stolen Continents: The New World Through Indian Eyes Since 1492,* draws from native conceptualizations of TimeSpace and time immemorial to suggest that as a matter of example, if we take the time native peoples of this land have survived and lived here prior to 1492 to signify a month, then Columbus arrived on these shores only yesterday. In other words, the structural TimeSpace of colonization and global capitalism is a relatively recent phenomenon and as historical systems they are not eternal. On the other hand, the eternal TimeSpace of the indigenous stories and knowledge and the related transformational TimeSpace of the Peace and Dignity Journeys are by their nature "antisystemic movements" rather than the "mysticism" and "romanticized mythology" they are often accused of being.

Notes

I write this piece upon my homecoming to Huichol land in Jalisco. I begin this way in the spirit of the Peace and Dignity Journeys and reunification of north and south. The title has thus emerged from conversations with numerous elders, friends and colleagues. What I will share herein I write with permission of my elders, the Peace and Dignity Medicine Staffs and their caretakers. *Noxtin nomecayotzin...*

1. Emma Pérez, *The Decolonial Imaginary: Writing Chicanas into History* (1999), pp. 8, 13–23.

2. "National Caucus of Chicano Social Science Newsletter," vol. 1 no. 1 (Summer 1973), n.p. Reprinted as Appendix II, in Reynaldo F. Macias, ed., *Perspectivas in Chicano Studies* (1977), pp. 214–220.

3. For more on the complicity of social sciences with colonialism and the need for undoing disciplinary divisions of knowledge, see Immanuel Wallerstein, *Unthinking the Social Sciences* (1995).

4. Immanuel Wallerstein, "The Inventions of TimeSpace Realities: Towards an Understanding of our Historical Systems," *Geography*, LXXIII, 4, October 1988, reprinted in *Unthinking Social Science*, pp. 135–148.

5. Remarks from seminar on *Liberation Theology and Coloniality*, University of California, Berkeley, April 21, 2004.

6. Quijano describes "coloniality of power" on three levels (nation-state, global and imaginary), which mutually reinforce one another. My focus herein is on the third: "thinking" and epistemology. For more on "coloniality of power" see Anibal Quijano, "Colonialidad del poder, cultura y conocimiento en América Latina."

7. Few published works have begun to outline such a perspective. For more see Roberto Rodriguez, *The 'X' in La Raza* (1997); *Codex Tamuanchan: On Becoming Human* (1998); and Patrisia Gonzalez, *The Mud People* (2003).

8. Michel-Rolph Trouillot, *Silencing the Past: Power and the Production of History* (1995), pp. 28–29.

9. See Muñoz, *Youth, Identity, and Power: The Chicano Movement* (1989), especially chapters 1 and 2.

10. For more on Aztlán, see Rudolfo Anaya, ed., *Aztlán: Essays on the Chicano Homeland* (1989).

11. Muñoz (1989), p. 79.

12. Ibid.

13. Personal conversations with Alurista, San Diego, 1996.

14. Robert Allen, *Black Awakening in Capitalist America: An Analytic History* (1969).

15. Jorge Mariscal, "Left Turns in the Chicano Movement, 1965–1975," and Elizabeth "Betita" Martinez, "A View from New Mexico: Recollections of the Movimiento Left."

16. Mariscal (2002), pp. 62.

17. Ernesto Chávez *¡Mi Raza Primero!: Nationalism, Identity, and Insurgency in the Chicano Movement in Los Angeles, 1966–1978* (2002), pp. 109–110.

18. Maria Tere Ceseña, "Mexicanidad North of the Border." Paper Presented at the *Crossing Borders Conference*, held at the University of California, San Diego, March 5, 2004.

19. Doug Thompson, "Bushes Erratic Behavior Worries White House Aides," *Capitol Hill Blue* (June 4, 2004).

20. Partha Chaterjee, *Nationalist Thought and the Colonial World: A Derivative Discourse* (1986).

21. Minoo Moallem, "Transnationalism, Feminism, and Fundamentalism," in *Between Woman and Nation: Nationalisms, Transnational Feminisms, and the State*, ed. Caren Kaplan, Norma Alarcon and Minoo Moallem (1999), p. 323.

22. For more on recent Chicana/o indigenous identity formations see Patrisia Gonzales and Roberto Rodríguez, "Column of the Americas," distributed by Universal Press Syndicate and a compilation of their earlier columns, *Gonzales/Rodríguez: Uncut and Uncensored*, published by Ethnic Studies Publication Unit at UC Berkeley in 1997.

23. For such consideration of North-South relations see Patricia Penn Hilden, "How the Border Lies: Some Historical Reflections," in *Decolonial Voices*, ed. Arturo J. Aldama and Naomi H. Quiñonez (Bloomington: Indiana University Press, 2002), pp. 152–176.

24. *Peace and Dignity Journeys 2004*, Foldout brochure (San Francisco, California, 2004), p. 2.

25. Ibid.

26. Lee (2002), p. 30.

27. Ibid.

28. Ibid.

29. Mike Davis, "Spectres of Superurbanization: Marx and the Holy Ghost." This talk was part of *The City: An Interdisciplinary Lecture Series*, held at the University of California, Berkeley, February 5, 2004.

30. Saldaña-Portillo, Josefina, "Who's the Indian in Aztlán?: Re-Writing Mestizaje, Indianism, and Chicanismo from the Lacandón," in *The Latin American Subaltern Studies Reader,* ed. Ileana Rodríguez (2001), pp. 402–423.

31. Daniel Hernandez, "Differences Cause Split in MEChA" *The Daily Californian* (November 30, 1998), p.1.

References

Allen, Robert. 1969. *Black Awakening in Capitalist America: An Analytic History.* Garden City, NY: Doubleday.

Anaya, Rudolfo, and Francisco Lomeli, eds. 1989. *Aztlán: Essays on the Chicano Homeland.* Alberquerque: University of New Mexico Press.

Ceseña, Maria Tere. n.d. "Mexicanidad North of the Border." Unpublished manuscript. Paper presented at the *Crossing Borders Conference,* University of California, San Diego, March 5, 2004.

Charterjee, Partha. 1986. *Nationalist Thought and the Colonial World: A Derivative Discourse.* Minneapolis: University of Minnesota Press.

Chavez, Ernesto. 2002. *¡Mi Raza Primero! Nationalism, Identity, and Insurgency in the Chicano Movement in Los Angeles, 1966–1978.* Berkeley: University of California Press.

Gonsales, Patrisia. 2003. *The Mud People: Testimonios, Chronicles and Remembrances.* San Jose, CA: Chusma House Press.

Hernandez, Daniel. 1998. "Differences Cause Split in MEChA." *The Daily Californian* (November 30): 1.

Lee, Richard. 2002. "Bucking the System: The TimeSpace of Antisystemic Movements." Pp. 21–32 in *The Modern/Colonial Capitalist World-System in the 20th Century: Global Processes, Antisystemic Movements, and the Geopolitics of Knowledge,* ed. Ramón Grosfoguel and Ana Margarita Cervantes-Rodriguez. Westport, CT: Greenwood Press.

Macias, Reynaldo, ed. 1977. *Perspectivas in Chicano Studies: Papers Presented at the Third Annual Meeting of the NACSS, 1975.* Los Angeles: Chicano Studies Center.

Mariscal, Jorge. 2002. "Left Turns in the Chicano Movement, 1965–1975." *Monthly Review,* vol. 54, no. 3 (July/August): 59–68.

Martinez, Elizabeth Betita. 2002. "A View from New Mexico: Recollections of the Movimiento Left." *Monthly Review,* Vol. 54, no. 3 (July/August): 79–86.

Minoo Moallem. 1999. "Transnationalism, Feminism, and Fundamentalism." Pp. 320–348 in *Between Woman and Nation: Nationalisms, Transnational Feminisms, and the State,* ed. Caren Kaplan, Norma Alarcon, and Minno Moallem. Durham, NC: Duke University Press.

Muñoz, Carlos. 1989. *Youth, Identity and Power: The Chicano Movement.* London: Verso.

Pérez, Emma. 1999. *The Decolonial Imaginary: Writing Chicanas into History.* Bloomington: Indiana University Press.

Quijano, Anibal. 1997. "Colonialidad del poder, cultura y conocimiento en América Latina." *Anuario Mariateguiano* 9, 9: 113–121.

Rodríguez, Roberto. 1997. *The X in La Raza.* Albuquerque, NM: Roberto Rodríguez.

———. 1998. *Codex Tamuanchan: On Becoming Human.* Albuquerque, NM: Roberto Rodríguez.

Saldaña-Portillo, Josefina. 2001. "Who's the Indian in Aztlán: Re-Writing Mestizaje, Indianism, and Chicanismo from the Lacandón." Pp. 402–423 in *The Latin American Subaltern Studies Reader,* ed. Ileana Rodríguez. Durham, NC: Duke University Press.

Trouillot, Michel-Rolph. 1995. *Silencing the Past: Power and the Production of History.* Boston: Beacon Press.

Wallerstein, Immanuel. 1995. "The Inventions of TimeSpace Realities: Towards an Understanding of our Historical Systems." Pp. 135–148 in *Unthinking the Social Sciences: The Limits of Nineteenth-Century Paradigms,* ed. Immanual Wallerstein. New York: Polity Press.

Wright, Roland. 1992. *Stolen Continents: The Americas Through Indian Eyes Since 1492.* Boston: Houghton Mifflin.

PART V

Decolonizing Spiritualities

8

A Latin@ Jewish Disruption of the Holocaustic U.S.-Centric Constellation of Suffering

Toward a Polycentric Project of Spiritualities in a Transmodern Context of Voices

Santiago E. Slabodsky

I

Only a few years ago Juan Gelman, a well-known Latino Jewish poet and social activist, claimed, as a Latino American who has suffered from his people's annihilation: "I need to denounce [Jewish participation in]... genocide practices because I am a Jew as well" (Gelman 2001, 31). Is Gelman a Jew as well? Is he perhaps a Latino *as well*? Probably, Gelman is one of the intellectuals/activists who inherently would recognize himself as a border thinker because of not only a double racialization from which he is objectified by colonial power, but also by the borders created by the own subversion of the imperial project. On the one hand, his struggle for the oppressed in the Americas and Israel/Palestine is not welcome among Jews who have engaged in an only recent *Judeo-Christian neocolonial constellation of suffering* that justifies oppression through the reduction of the modern paradigm of suffering to the U.S.-centric interpretation, appropriation, and monopoly of the European Jewish Holocaust. On the other hand, Gelman's apparent deep self-identification with the subversive spirit of a European Jewish critical radicalism—leading to such diverse thinkers as Baruch Spinoza, Karl Marx, Rosa Luxemburg, or Walter Benjamin who are collectively one of the germs of the European countermodern thought crucial to opening a door for the subsequent decolonization of the Eurocentric coloniality of power—is seen with distrust by intellectual heirs of the above-mentioned thinkers, the Latin@ transmodern voices.

Gelman, as a Latino Jew, is not a border thinker because two communities recognize his affiliation, but because neither of the above groups is willing to fully consider him as representative. Nevertheless, his borders would be especially useful for a polycentric project of spiritualities in a transmodern context, because they allow the decolo-n/r-ization of one of the most successful components of the contemporary epistemology of knowledge: *the neocolonial constellation of suffering through and only through a U.S. interpretation of Jewish experience.* I will understand for the latter the post–1945/1967 attempt to reduce all the sufferings which are not *as tremendous as the Jewish* to necessary accidents/incidents in history and the incorporation of the Jews, as the model of a formerly oppressed people that was able to *reach a white and western status.*

In support of this epistemology, as Norman Finkelstein points out, hundred of museums for the Holocaust are built in the United States for the European Jewish genocide and enslavement, but, in the United States itself, there is no explosion of museums for their own—Native American genocide or Afro/Black American enslavement (Finkelstein 2000, 8); or, as Marc Ellis criticizes chairs and chairs for Holocaust studies have been opened in academia, but hardly, I may add to the words of my mentor, a Somalian or even an Armenian is appointed for them (Ellis 2002, 96–101); and finally the *Judeo-Christian crusade to "liberate" the peoples of the axis of evil* attempts to prevent almost in each occasion a new Adolph Hitler—helped nowadays by an Ayatollah Khomeini, rather than a new Francisco Pizarro, Jefferson Davis, or Joseph Stalin. Even the permanent "Satan of the back door," the interminable Fidel Castro, is free from accusation … this time.

On the one hand, the aim of my paper is to collaborate with a decolo-n/r-ization of this constellation of suffering through a Latin@ Jewish perspective. Namely, I will suggest that Spanish/Portuguese/Ladino-speaking Jews (let me divorce French-speaking Jews for the moment and take a few paragraphs before justifying this move through a reading of, paradoxically, peripheral-born

French Jews, Jacques Derrida and Emmanuel Levinas) are in a particular position to propose a parallel liberationist and multiborder constellation of experiences around suffering and struggle against suffering: I will argue that though Jews, as a nebulous collective, are part of the people who are welcomed—after seeing the disappearance of one-third of its members between 1933 and 1945 because of the pernicious inaction or criminal action of the western world—as the last white modern group, Latin@ Jews have confronted the coloniality of power from 1492 and suffered in practice, since then, until now, the consequences of the colonial and neocolonial narratives. On the other hand, a second goal will be to claim an internal reevaluation of essentialisms in both Christian voices that have engaged with a philo-Semitic ecumenical liberal deal that was crucial for the implementation of the above-mentioned constellation and transmodern thinkers who fail in recognizing the *exterior* character of their European Jewish intellectual forerunners.

Nevertheless, the aim of the work will not be reduced to a general critique of these three groups pointing out the consequences of the U.S.-centric abuse of Jewish suffering, but will propose a Latin@ Jewish possible exit for them. I will explore how there is an alternative to this abuse in the reflection of a Jewish Latin American thought that is in the process of migration to the north. Therefore, the increasing numbers of Latin@ rabbis with liberationist training in major U.S. cities (e.g., New York, Atlanta, and Miami), and the attempt of a Jewish Latin@ dialogue in centers such as Chicago's Alliance of Jews and Latinos will be sources of an alternative constellation of experiences around suffering/struggle in the United States that recalls Gelman's parallel constellation and removes the post–1945/1967 western/neocolonial understanding of the Judeo-Christian tradition. As the third of my aims, after the critic and the primary parallel construction, I will conclude reflecting on how this new Latin@ Jewish proposal might collaborate with the debate within the general transmodern movement.

II

Just as several transmodern stories begin, my reflection on praxis starts with a dialogical encounter with a particular *Other* who proudly thinks of him/herself as *The Totality* attempting to postulate that the *Alterity* is no more than the *Same*. It was a cold afternoon this past December (2003) only a few blocks away from the philo-American *Freie Universität Berlin* when, after riding four buses, we abandoned our noble intentions. Only a day before, presenting a paper on Jewish Liberationism under postcolonial lens in the setting of a conference informally affiliated with the annual meeting of the European globephobic group Kaos, we met Franz Eckerd. He, a young Austrian-born sociologist, or what Max Weber would depict as a *privatdozent,* promised us a visit to *4 Magdeburger Platz,* the house where Jewish heterodox *theologian* Walter

Benjamin dangerously learnt his most subversive weapons (i.e., how to read, write…
and quote). Nevertheless, after hours and more than a couple of precious euros
trying to find a probably nonexistent place in the twenty-first century old west
side of Berlin, we were exhausted and decided to enter a bohemian bar with him,
along with an Afro-Canadian philosopher and a German musician.

Soon after we sat down, Franz started to interrogate me about my thesis
of the day before:

> You intend to prove that Jews, from Baruch Spinoza to Theodore Adorno, from
> Rosa Luxemburg to Leon Trotsky, and from Franz Kafka to Paul Celam before
> the Holocaust, were subverting modernity through the secularization of tradi-
> tional Jewish eschatology, and, after the Holocaust, Jews, from Emmanuel Levinas
> to Jacques Derrida and from Henry Kissinger to Hans Morgenthau, have been
> co-opted by a colonial epistemology of knowledge that cleverly decided to rec-
> ognize, after more than one thousand five hundred years, Jewish suffering and
> *only* Jewish suffering as legitimate. The result of this co-option was a change in
> the center of Jewish thought. While before 1942 we can strategically assert that
> most of the Jews speaking to the world were *subverting modernity* through a
> secularization of the eschatological reading of the *political*, after 1945 the vast
> majority have become the object of the *reaffirmation of modernity* replacing the
> above-mentioned center for the *political* consequences of Jewish suffering. And
> you call this construction *the neocolonial constellation of suffering through an
> 'industrial' abuse of the Jewish experience.*

He referenced his notes and continued:

> In this way modern Western thought is able to recuperate from the abyss
> where the Holocaust arises to neocolonial thought and, most important,
> blocks the sufferings of non-*Jewish Others,* because they have not suffered
> *enough,* and proposes Jews as a model of those who have been able to overcome
> the limitation of being *Others.* In this way, Jews supposedly demonstrate that it
> is plausible to *overcome* the *exterior status,* and U.S. epistemology reserves the
> freedom to *liberate* other people because the perpetrators of genocides are al-
> ways non-Americans. In exchange for the service to the colonial power, Jews are
> promised security, even if *Others,* let us say Palestinians, South Africans or Nica-
> raguans, ought to suffer for it. (Ellis 1987, 56–59)

Once he finished, I tried to remember my own words. I found that he
understood my hypothesis better than I did, though I added that this was a critique that emerges from the interconnection of the pre-1945 elective affinity between *non-Jewish Jewish* thought and libertarian/liberationist proposals of Brazilian French Michael Lowy (1992, 6–13); the criticism to Jewish empowerment
and Jewish leadership alliances of American Marc Ellis (1997, 1–41) and (stateless)

German American Hannah Arendt (1999, 115–120); and the critique of Jewish Eurocentric Lithuanian French Emmanuel Levinas made by Mexican Argentinean Enrique Dussel (1973, 111–115). Nevertheless, I added, "My aim is to construct a Latin@ exit to the vicious circle of post–1945/1967 Jewish thought that reproduces the neocolonial epistemology of knowledge. My project," I told him, "is the recuperation of the Latin@ Jew as one among the *Other Jews* who would be able to incorporate an alternative constellation of experiences into a polycentric project within a transmodern context of voices."

The Afro-Canadian philosopher and the Austrian sociologist looked at each other and I knew that they were ready to deconstruct my work. I was expecting the classic critiques I received only one day before from poststructuralist and postmodern thinkers: that not all the Jews were revolutionary before 1945 and not all of them are co-opted after 1945, that Levinas is an interesting starting point because he replaces the ontology of the Being with a dialogic encounter with the Other, that postcolonialism is only destructive deconstruction without aim to offer an alternative to class struggle, that the Palestinian case hosts special characteristics because it is not proven that they are a *real political entity.* However, to my surprise, they did not call for a reformulation of my argument, but my location of knowledge: "Santiago, come on, a Latino exit? You are not precisely a Latino." While the sociologist pointed out that I was Jewish and Latin@s are Catholics, the philosopher (a proud doctoral student at one university of Quebec) remarked I was Argentinean, "almost a white European, perhaps [he seemed proud] even French, born in the south probably by accident after your ancestors embarked on the wrong ship." My first reaction was to answer the first with the different internal variety of the Catholic church that led to the association with other groups read through even the materialist interpretation of Antonio Gramsci (Portelli 1991), or the recent growth of Pentecostals analyzed by many others, and to invite the second to consider the reformulation of the idea of Latin America that would be read in the work of, among others, Walter Mignolo (2001).

However, soon after this first attempt I started to reflect on the success of the neocolonial epistemology of knowledge and its incorporation of the Jew into the neocolonial power knowledge. These two diverse, deep, and brilliant young radicals, sympathetic to pre-Holocaust Jewish libertarian radicalism were—in the same Berlin where fifty years before Jews were being industrially annihilated because they were the *antiwhite and western* group—now unable to identify a Jew with anything else than a *white and western* group (i.e., part of the industrial colonial project). Rephrasing and adding, the turning points are 1492 and 1942: while, as Jewish Australian literary critic John Docker remarks, in 1492 a Eurocentric neodiasporic world emerged from the expulsion of the Jews from Spain—in addition to the consequences related to the discovery of the Americas and the finalization of the *El-Andalus* project (Docker 2001, vi–2)—we suggest in 1942, the year of the Wannasse Conference that formally initiated the Final Solution for the Jewish Question and also the formal intervention of America into the Second

World War after Pearl Harbor—that another level, this time U.S.-centric, of the epistemology of knowledge entered the scene, one that incorporates into the constellation of suffering of Christendom, centered in the suffering of Jesus (Christ), the Judeo-Christian liberal reading of the suffering of the Holocaust and use it as a rejection of the Jewish diasporic narrative creating other diasporas such as the Palestinian (Said 1992).

In other words, this new level of construction declares the death of contaminated Europe, finishing the European work with the intention of avoiding the contamination military conquest brings (see readings of American foreign thought of Henry Kissinger) that differentiates, through his political realism, the contaminated character of Europe and the pure intentions of the United States (1991, 23–31). The Palestinian cause and Israel as the center for a Colombian paramilitary refugee or as a central trade partner of South Africa during the Apartheid emerges under a new lens of analysis through this perspective. Indeed, this thought is reinforced after we realize that these actions were under the umbrella of the new *stars* of defense or security public offices in both Republican (Henry Kissinger) and Democrat (William Cohen) administrations. *Stateless* insecure Jews become (please, forgive me for giving birth to a new term) *Statefull*, representatives of the guarantee of security. Rephrasing, for America the colonial plan remains, but as George Steiner would argue, with the incorporation of the Jew, the former (insecure) "scapegoat" (the *only* Other in Enrique Dussel interpretation of Levinas), now (security) "priest," the "concentric reading" changes (Steiner 1988, 154–157 and Ellis 1997, 82–108).

III

The above-mentioned new level of the epistemology of knowledge was especially attracted to the incorporation of the Jews into the project, as a reading of the production of two peripheral-born Jews who become part of the central thought in France suggests. Let us analyze the consequences of Levinas' conception of "the Other" and Derrida's self-understanding of himself as the "Last Jew."

Levinas, as a European Jew apparently trying to recuperate the European center, is paradoxically involved in the Americano-centric epistemology of knowledge because even French thought, perhaps as an exception following Alexis de Toqueville, saw in America a mix between the new experience and its heirs. Levinas, as Dussel suggests, reduces the conception of "the Other" in history to the experience of "the Jew" that fails to acknowledge that Jews were "an-Other" among "Other Others" in European history. In fact, Levinas even calls the interesting moments of other traditions as "Jewish moments," claiming for one of his borders (one that, as a Jew, I share with him) the extraordinary elements of other traditions (Levinas 1961 and Dussel 1973). In consequence, the "Exteriority" and "the Alterity" in Levinas, is reduced to the Jewish experience without comprehending the consequences of this theoretical move. First, Levinas divorces Jews from the experience of the "Other" sufferers helping the neocolonial epistemology to incorporate Jews into its project after a simple divorce of American thought from European history (a move where the already mentioned Jewish German–born Kissinger and Morgenthau are crucial in generating a real-politics in foreign policy that utilizes Wilson idealism as one realist weapon). Second, the *move* that recognizes a particular and exclusive category for Judaism reproduces the neocolonial Christian use of Jewish experience for its neocolonial benefits. Jews are once again presented as witness *objects* of truth after their suffering for the good of humanity. Traditionally in Christian thought (i.e., Augustine) the suffering of the Jews is to assert the coming of the Messiah and the freedom from sins (and, just by coincidence, to remember their deicide). However, after the Holocaust, for Henry Kissinger, Francis Fukuyama, and especially, Samuel Huntington, the suffering is to show how human beings should avoid nonwestern democratic tyranny (Huntington 1996). Paradoxically, while in the first case the reading led to sins of Christians against Jews, the second incorporates an orientalist justification of tyranny of Jews (recently admitted western people) over Palestinians as readings of literary critic Edward Said and liberation theologian Naim Attek would show (See Ateek 1988 and Said 1992).

The case of one of the most famous critiques of the above-mentioned thinkers is not beneficial either for the incorporation of the contemporary peripheral-born French school into our trend. Though sharing his own experiences in diverse writings, Derrida is unable to compete with Levinas in the exposition of his Jewish self-identification. In one of the few writings where the Algerian French literary critic writes on his experiences as a Jewish child during the Holocaust times, (http://bearcat.baylor.edu/search/tM%7B226%7Demoires+d%27aveugle.+English/tmemoires+daveugle+english/-5,-1,0,B/browse*Circonfession*), he proclaims an intimidating statement "I am the end of Judaism . . . I am the last Jew" (Derrida 1991, 178). According to Israeli scholar Gideon Orfat in his book *Derrida ha-Yehudi* (*The Jewish Derrida*), the literary critic understands that after deconstruction and the "*truth*" that emerges from it as well as the nullification of the demarcation among identities, Judaism is no longer a possibility (Orfat 2001, 9–11). As far as I am aware, there is no particular category for Judaism as Levinas proposes, but the links of Derrida's statement with his recounting of the Holocaust let us open the debate on the particular attraction of Derridian thought on the Otherness of Jewish people. Whether or not after the (post-Holocaust) deconstruction there is no more Judaism, we are able to link him with another Jew, critical theorist Theodor Adorno, who asserts that, after the Holocaust, poetry is no longer a possibility (Adorno 2000, 42–47). Nevertheless, while Adorno claims for the impossibility of one discipline that canalizes the expression of (to be fair with both philosophical schools) feelings and knowledge, Derrida denies a complete tradition through which it is possible to think the political conception of identities.

It is possible that Derrida understood better and before us that the Jewish model that hosts a special elective affinity with libertarian and liberationist thought, has been nullified in his adopted land (France) and the Center (the United States). However, once again, Derrida is forgetting his own origins and the possibility to think the political on the colonial difference negating the survival of this Jewish identity in peripheral locations where the above-mentioned elective affinity is still alive. Once again, the proposal of deconstruction is unable to understand the emergence of a countercolonial project that resists the new racialization of Jews as white and western, and proclaims its solidarity with other oppressed people in the Americas, South Africa, and Israel/Palestine. This struggle that will be our next step translates the countercapitalist aim of pre-1945 Jewish thinkers for a counterimperial aim after 1945. However, in both cases, it presents its countermodern aim that transcends the only internal critique of postmodern literary criticism and philosophy.

The contemporary post-Holocaust French school, perhaps in opposition to the school of Frankfurt, should be excepted as a subaltern Latin@ Jew. Levinas' impossibility to understand the Otherness beyond Jewish experience and Derrida's inability to see Judaism beyond the death of a Euro-American center, lead to the exaltation of the new neocolonial epistemology because it creates a vicious cycle that connects the Jew as the only Other, American-centric reading of the Holocaust as the saviors of Jews, to the death of Jewish struggle (or Judaism itself in the case of Derrida) for *Others* liberation. Currently, only sixty years later, every thinker who tries to deconstruct this constellation is banned from the discussion by the accusation of being anti-Semitic (as it was in the 80's Christian Enrique Dussel, among other liberationists, and is today Muslim Tariq Ramadan who was denied entry to the United States from pressure of Jewish official representatives) or self-heating Jews (i.e., Marc Ellis or Noam Chomsky).[1] In other words, the new taboo of the epistemology of knowledge is to defy the new spirituality of suffering based on the Judeo-Christian ecumenical deal because it offers the oppressor the chance to see him/herself as the oppressed. The Empire is not seeing itself as conquistador, but sufferer ... and perhaps its own liberator from its own suffering through the oppression of *Others*.

Nevertheless, to the surprise of academic environments, this project would not (I extend my apologies for most of my conversation partners) be labeled as conservative. The discussion around Mel Gibson's *The Passion of the Christ* is a witness to the liberal character of the above-mentioned project. The movie is not (only) a slow and bloody film (with a funny, but I should recognize medieval neat Aramaic rarely spoke by Jesus' historical contemporaries). It is part of an attempt to reject this twentieth-century Judeo-Christian model returning to a purely Christian-centric prototype: only Christians are able to understand the suffering because it was experienced by their Messiah for them. Jews—the sinners and deicides—are participants only as those responsible for his/their (unlikely her on singular or plural) suffering. This thought recovers the pre-1945 position of theologians such as Martin Niemoller who, in addition to his harsh anti-Nazism, treated Jews as an *eschatological reserve* in order to justify his also anti-Semitism. Nevertheless, both images of *the Jew* (both responsible for and receiving suffering) lead to colonialism. The first oppress Jews, and the second abuse the Jewish suffering of the first period in order to oppress *Others*.

Both projects, the conservative and the liberal, agree in understanding themselves as sufferers in a time of empowerment. Nevertheless, the liberal, with the incorporation of the Jews, a former *Other*, become even more powerful. From this transmodern perspective both projects completely ignore the ultimate sufferers, but only the liberal aims to co-opt part of them. Rephrasing, both projects take a *preferential option* for the oppressors, but only the liberal divide the oppressed.

IV

As an alternative to the conservative and liberal mutual understanding, a transmodern radical Jewish reading will disrupt this coexistence that leads to a doctrine of National/International Security decolonizing the constellation of suffering with the incorporation of a parallel conjunct of experiences.

The confrontation of Spanish/Ladino/Portuguese-speaking Jews with colonial powers was particularly active during the last five hundred years and six attempts of empires. Let us rethink the relationship of Jews with colonial powers in the Americas: in 1492 Spanish/Ladino-speaking Jews were expelled from the first modern empire and during the next centuries were persecuted through the Inquisition that set the first modern anti-Jewish/Semitic policy not only in Europe, but also in the southern part of the new world. It is impossible to understand the deconstruction of the main precursor of the self-centrality, Rene Descartes, made by a member of this community, Baruch Spinoza, without understanding the countermodern praxis and theoretical center of early modern Judaism (Sutcliffe 2003, 103–147). In 1642, Portuguese-speaking Jews, trying to escape from the Inquisition were rejected by the Dutch colonial power in North America, setting the first anti-Jewish policy of the northern part of the new world (Sacher 1993, 27). Indeed, in the twentieth century, the descendents of this group of dark-looking Jews, forced to convert to Christianity in the transcurse of the last four hundred years and live in, among other locations, the south of the United States and north of Mexico, has been ignored by the white mainstream Jewish community. While accusing them of *looking like Latin@ Christians,* the institutional Jews do not realize that they *look like Anglo-Saxon Christians* (see personal relates on Kessel 2000, 17–38). Consequently, Latin@ Jews have been racialized by and have confronted Spanish, Portuguese, Dutch, and British colonial epistemologies of knowledge.

The above-mentioned reality is not reduced to the northern part of the continent. During this last century Latin@ Jewish confrontation was particularly bloody in the South. In 1919 during the *Semana Trágica,* the Americas saw its first neocolonial pogrom in Buenos Aires and in 1930, 1943, and 1966, according to specialized historians, saw anti-Semitism installed as an official policy in Argentina (Senkman 1989 and Lvovich 2003). During the period between 1974/76–1983 young Jewry in this last country, my homeland, engaged in a strong confrontation against the American-endorsed *Proceso de Reorganización Nacional,* as the cold numbers show us: while Jews represent only 0.8 percent of the population, according to the result of the current research, 12 percent of the total of the *desaparecidos* were born Jews. It means not only a 1,500 percent of overrepresentation, but also a final break between Judaism in the south and the north (Slabodsky 2003, 76–79).

While in the south Jews, along with other citizens, were being tortured in detention camps such as the Escuela de Mecanica de la Armada (ESMA) and threw down from helicopters to the Rio de la Plata, in the United States two European-born American Jews were especially functional during this period and, as a consequence, received the Nobel Prize of American Pax in the 1970s and 1980s. While Henry Kissinger, first as Assistant of National Security Affairs and later on as Secretary of State, was one of the most important supporters of the politics that lead to the Doctrine of National Security in Latin America, Elie Wiesel (paradoxically a human rights spokesman) became the most powerful voice of an official sector of Holocaust survivors and was appointed chair of the presidential commission of the above-mentioned reading of the Holocaust that blocked the suffering of Others. The Latin@ Jews have had neither voice in the Nobel Prizes nor voice in the link between American epistemology of knowledge and the white reading of the Holocaust. Ironically, the new reading was not only ignoring (as in Levinas) the *excluded Others,* such as Indo-Americans, Afro/Black Americans, Armenias, and women, but also one of the *Other Jews,* the Latin@.

V

Once we locate a *subaltern Jew,* the question I would like to explore is whether *he/she is speaking by him/herself.* The military dictatorships in the south are not only the final separation between north and south Judaism(s), but also are a crucial event in building a parallel constellation of spiritualities of suffering that disrupts the white constellation of the ecumenical deal that leads to the neocolonial epistemology. In an article published in 2001 that was already mentioned at the beginning of this article, Juan Gelman offers us an alternative Latin@ Jewish constellation of suffering to the liberal that links the Holocaust with colonization that includes, but it is not limited to, Israel/Palestine.

The reflections we will read were composed after he was detained for five hours by the Israeli airport security service because he mentioned, in a private conversation in Spanish to his wife, his solidarity with Palestinians:

> What I cannot understand is that the [Israeli] security agents have become a political police force that rivals Hitler's or Stalin's. Is Israel a Democracy? Would a democratic state subjugate millions of Palestinians to a siege under the oppression of the arms? And how is it possible that these siegers are the sons, grandchildren, and great-grandchildren, whom, as my mother and her brothers and father, a rabbi, suffered from the Czarist siege in the ghettos, and later on, such as my cousins, the internment in the Nazi concentration camp? And now, the descendents of these people build ghettos for the Palestinians, dynamite their houses, lay siege to the hungry, cut down olive trees, and raze crops? And what is the relationship of the Jews to this state of Israel?
>
> This State of Israel has nothing to do with Jewish tradition ... I know that these opinions will be seen as anti-Semitic by those who do not want to hear, see or speak as the three monkeys of India. This tactic reminds me of the pretension of the last military dictatorship in Argentina that named every denunciation of their crimes as an "anti-Argentine campaign." I need to denounce the genocidal practices of the State of Israel because I am a Jew too. (Gelman 2001, 31)

After reading Gelman's reflection, the primary question needs to be formulated once again: Is Gelman solely a Jew or is he solely a Latin@? Neither of the options would do justice to his words and struggle because his identities are both impossible to divorce from his thought and collaborate in the creation of a transmodern perspective for the two identities. In other words, his parallel decolonization of the only Holocaust-Israel constellation of suffering is neither *white Jewish* nor *Christian Latin@*. In Gelman, the Jewish experience of the Holocaust and Israel is mediated by Czarist, Stalinist, and especially, Argentine and Palestinian oppressions. This parallel construction is a product of a border thinker because it not only transcends—as Walter Mignolo energetically taught me when I was one of his students—area studies, but also offers a radical alternative to the reading of Jewish suffering that oppress, among others, Latin@ thought. Indeed, this perspective is originally Latin@ American, but is emerging as a Latin@ opportunity in the United States because of two related phenomena: Latin@ Rabbis (indeed, I refer to women and men), and new Latin@ Jewish conversations.

In the last twenty years, a growing number of Jewish rabbis trained in the *Seminario Rabínico Latinoamericano,* a center that was called by its founder "the only Jewish institution in the world that practices a real Jewish Liberation Theology" (Marshall Meyer in Freund 1994, 30), have been hired by American congregations in large population centers (i.e., New York, Miami, and

Atlanta) and smaller cities (i.e., Roanoke, VA). These rabbis are between 35 and 50 years old, the same age that the son and daughter-in-law of Juan Gelman would be today if state terrorism had not *disappeared* the couple with their unborn child. They belong not only to a people who had been annihilated sixty years ago in Europe, but also to a generation that a military dictatorship tried to *cut off* around thirty years ago in Latin America. During the summer of 2003, doing fieldwork at the seminary, my second home during my college years, and wondering about the increasing number of South American rabbis who are appointed by American congregations, a reputed administrator of the *Seminario* who has lived through the dictatorship years at the movement, attempted to answer my inquiry: "the phenomena is hard to define because of the variety of appointments and the diversity of our rabbis. Nevertheless, one element should be pointed out is that these congregations, in general, are not liberal but moderate or, I may say, for our progressive standards, conservative. Please, do not ask me to explain it. Why do they want our rabbis?" He ironically smiled and concluded: "...it is a mystery of the universe."

Let me begin to understand the "mysteries of the universe" in my humble article delineating a hypothesis. In his *Ethics of the Jewish Power* Irving Greenberg, an official voice of liberal institutional Judaism, alerts Jews that after the Holocaust, they should not be more than 10 percent "better" than others in their political behavior because this ethical inflexibility would lead to a second Holocaust (Greenberg 1988, 8–9). In opposition to Greenberg, one of the most important thinkers of the contemporary ecumenical deal, the conservative Jewish institutions in the United States are emulating the behavior of conservative Christians attacking the liberal consensus that proclaims that Jews are representatives of the central *Being*. While Mel Gibson tries to divorce Jewish suffering from the Christian constellation, conservative Jews (despite having a diverse group of institutions that train rabbis in the United States) are appointing rabbis who were born, raised, and trained as Others in order to defy the new liberal axiom that proclaims that Jews are not Others, but white and western.

It is true that, *a priori*, this phenomenon is not new in modern Judaism; for example, the conservative struggle against Reformism by orthodox forces in nineteenth-century Central Europe and *Hasidism* by *Mitnagdim* thinkers in eighteenth-century East Europe also reinforced Jewish Otherness in opposition to what they understood as assimilations or syncretistic tendencies. However, this time the phenomenon is novel because Jews, for the first time, are in power. Whether the analysis is plausible, the question that arises is the following: Are conservative institutions inviting Latin@ Jews who were raised as Others to lead their institutions in America in order to confront the liberal constellation of suffering which reduces differences? In other words, are conservatives opening the door to radicalism because they see in it an opportunity for recuperating the Otherness that liberalism requires aborting? Rephrasing, are Mel Gibson's Jews the new alliance for a transmodern radical Jewish project?

During the last ten years Jews and Latin@s have been attractive targets for Washington. This was true for politicians of both traditional parties, but especially for the self-called liberals that have seen the candidatures of individuals of both communities as a channel through which they could gain political support from minorities. Though originally I was trained, along with my rabbinical studies, as a political sociologist, my task is not to analyze the advantages and disadvantages of this political move, but the possibilities of a parallel construction of identities through a conversation of two groups that are seen by Washington as necessary in order to identify its parties as sensitive to minorities. *A priori* the differences between communities are more remarkable than the similarities. In the words of the Alliance of Latinos and Jews in the city of Chicago, Illinois: "Jews and Latinos have not shared common neighborhoods." Founded in 1994, the Alliance attempts to construct fraternal relationships between the communities. Its mission statement could be read as a product of multicultural and typical liberal thought: "[Our mission is] Building new and enhancing existing relations between the Jewish and Latino communities by focusing on issues of common concern: business and economic development, policy/ civic, and social and cultural affairs" (ALJ 2004).

Nevertheless some of its practices result in the construction of a parallel constellation of the idea of suffering and liberation that could be useful for thinking through transmodern approaches. Only a few months ago, celebrating the Jewish Passover, a religious holiday which remembrances the historical and ethical exodus from slavery, which has been a center in Latin American and Black liberation theologians since the late 1960s and early 1970s, the Alliance replaced the traditional religious service and meal which is mostly conducted in Hebrew and vernacular language adding a Ladin@ (*Sefaradi*-speaking) inspired service. After reading a copy of the material used at the meeting that kindly was offered to me by e-mail I was able to understand the radical possibility that acts like the above mentioned would mean.

Let me explain myself: Jews and Latin@s, as a *community,* replace Hebrew and English (perhaps two current imperial languages) for a medieval derivation of Spanish that is a remembrance of not only a historical period when the three monotheistic religions lived together in premodern Spain under the *el-andalus* project, but also the suffering of peripheral Jews in ancient (XII century B.C.E) and modern (1492) times that has inspired, as Jewish political theorizing Michael Walzer would argue, the paradigm of revolution and liberation (Walzer 1986). In other words, through a mutual common construction Jews (mostly descendent of central and east European immigrants) are rediscovering their sense of Exteriority through the help of (non-Jewish) Latin@s who understand, not only because of the language, but also because of the practical experiences, better than American Jews the experience of being Others and having their own hopes of liberation that the Jewish Passover offers.

VI

In April 2004 two events (a radical interreligious dialogue and the Twenty-eighth Conference of the Political Economy of the World-System) were hosted by the department of Ethnic Studies at University of California–Berkeley and a first version of this paper was presented then. During each meeting a central theoretical problem was provocatively presented by brilliant thinkers. While during the first Boaventura de Sousa Santos and Marc Ellis, after a magnificent presentation of the father of the transmodern thought and the philosophy of liberation Enrique Dussel, requested for a reformulation of the conception of Exteriority in order to incorporate exterior Europeans into it, namely Iberians and Jews, during the second Aisha Beliso, with the helpful intervention clarifying terminology of Anibal Quijano, alerted the audience to a possible recolonization that transmodern thought was practicing. In both cases the most categorical answer emerged from the always lucid, provocative (and controversial) voice of Walter Mignolo. Duke's scholar, while answering the first question accepted the exterior character of people who speak and write in some exterior languages but reenforced the idea of the oppression that, what I would call *others Others,* suffered above the *Exterior Interiority.* However, in the second case, Mignolo rejected the question arguing that this methodological debate would force us to loose our center. Namely, In Walter's words, "we will forget why we are decolonizing."

Is a decolonization of the neocolonial constellation of suffering through a Latin@ Jewish reading collaborating in the discussion of the above-mentioned theoretical problems? The main concern of this article was to formulate a triple critique. First, I tried to jeopardize the consensus in Jewish thought that lost its Otherness while incorporating Jews into the white and western canon. Second, I critiqued the philo-Semitic Christian voices which gave birth to an only recent *Judeo-Christian tradition* and have used Jewish suffering for Western world political interests. Third, I remembered to transmodern voices that this school has not been able to fully engage with the particular exterior character of its Jewish European forerunners. My aim is to think the first problem (the limits of exteriority) through the third critique (transmodernism and European Libertarian Judaism) and the second problem (the recolonization) through the first and second critiques (to Jews and Christians of the ecumenical deal).

First, even though the main problem of this article has been the decolonization of liberal thought I have reinforced the elective affinity between exterior European libertarian Jewish thought and Latin@ transmodern proposal. If we were to accept that there are different levels in the oppression of people who were Exterior European or Exterior non-European, we would start to divide forces among the exterior traditions. Indeed, the idea of thinking the different oppressions in different levels has been a practice among the neocolonial ecumenical deal believers who acknowledged that the only possibility to practice their oppression is by dividing the Others and accepting only the suffering of part of them justified by the *levels* of suffering (here is where the Holocaust Americanocentric reading takes places). A transmodern Jewish proposal needs to reevaluate the concept of exteriority understanding, simply, that we are able to utilize Spinoza's critique of Rene Descartes, Luxemburg's formulation of imperialism, Fromm's understanding of the individual fears, Arendt's link of Totalitarianism, anti-Semitism, and Colonialism, and Kafka's ironic understanding of modern bureaucratic society, without the risk of loosing the exterior character of our proposal.

Second, if my first answer might be read as moderate, the second would be labeled as radical even beyond Mignolo's always provocative answers. If we understand the agenciality of the neocolonial epistemology of knowledge, we should accept the need to counterarrest it through an active parallel construction. I am intending to return neither to a Leninist romantic vision of Vanguard nor to a structuralist adoption of the Gramscian (in-)organic intellectual. Nevertheless, if our aim is to confront Jews and Christians who are autoracialized as white and western in order to oppress Others, we need to recover our nonwhite category with which we were racialized a counterarrest the coloniality of power from the subversion of the own categories that lead our suffering. Some of us might call the plan recolonization. I would prefer to understand it, following libertarian Jewish European thought, as the decolonization of the theological conception of liberation and the final fusion of libertarian and liberationist voices within a comprehensive polycentric transmodern project of spiritualities.

Note

1. This paper was written before the decision of the U.S. immigration authorities to revoke Prof. Tariq Ramadan's visa. Nevertheless, the central (French and American) Jewish participation in not only the accusation of anti-Semitism, but also the practical influence to have his visa revoked, is just one element that ratifies the thesis presented in relation to central Jewry. Unfortunately, it was not just an anecdotic element for Prof. Tariq Ramadan and his family, as well as it is not for the hundreds of Muslims that are discriminated against each day at the U.S. embassies worldwide.

References

Adorno, Theodor. "Meditations in Metaphysics." In Michael Morgan, ed., *A Holocaust Reader*. Oxford: Oxford University Press, 2000, 42–47.

Alliance of Latinos and Jews, www.latinosandjews.org.

Arendt, Hannah. *Origenes del Totalitarismo*. Madrid: Taurus,1999.

Ateek, Naim. *Justice and Only Justice. A Palestinean Theology of Liberation*. Maryknoll, N.Y.: Orbis Books, 1988.

Benjamín, Walter. *Illuminations*. New York: Schoken Books, 1985.

——— *Reflections: Essays, Aphorisms, Autobiographical Writings*. New York: Schoken Books, 1986.

Derrida, Jaques. *Mémoires d'aveugle: l'autoportrait et autres ruines*. Paris: Ministère de la culture, de la communication, des grands travaux, et du bicentenaire, 1991.

Docker, John. *1492: The Poetics of Diaspora*. London and New York: Continuum, 2001, vi–2.

Dussel, Enrique. "El método analéctico y la Filosofía Latinoamericana." *In America Latina, Dependencia y Liberación*. Buenos Aires: Garcia Cambeiro, 1973, 108–131.

———. *Las Metáforas Teológicas de Marx*. Navarra: Editorial del Verbo Divino, 1993.

———. *Filosofía de la Liberación*. Bogota: Editorial Nueva America, 1996.

Ellis, Marc. *Toward a Jewish Liberation Theology*. Maryknoll, NY: Orbis Books l, 1987.

———. *Unholy Alliance. Religion and Atrocity in our Times*. Minneapolis, MN: Fortress Press, 1997.

———. *Out of the Ashes. The Search for Jewish Identity in the Twenty-First Century*. London and Sterling, VA: Pluto, 2002.

———. *Toward a Jewish Liberation Theology*. Waco, TX: Baylor University Press, 2004.

Finkelstein, Norman. *The Holocaust Industry. Reflections on the Exploitation of Jewish Suffering*. London, New York: Verso, 2000.

Freund, Richard. "'Somos Testigos—We Are Witnesses': The Jewish Theology of Liberation of Rabbi Marshall T Meyer." *Conservative Judaism*, n. 47, Fall, 1994.

Gelman, Juan. "Israel." *Pagina/12*, 12 March 2001, 31.

Greenberg, Irving. *The Ethics of Jewish Power*. New York: National Jewish Center for Learning and Leadership, 1988.

Huntington, Samuel. *The Clash of Civilizations and the Remaking of the World Order*. New York: Simon and Schuster, 1996.

Kessel, Barbara. *Suddenly Jewish*. Hanover, NH: Brandeis University Press, 2000.

Kissinger, Henry. *La Diplomacia*. Mexico D.F.: FCE, 1991.

Lander, Edgardo, ed. *La Colonialidad del Saber*. Buenos Aires: CLACSO, 2000.

Levinas, Emmanuel. *Totalité et infini; essai sur l'extériorite*. Paris: La Haye, M. Nijhoff, 1961.

Lowy, Michael. *Redemption and Utopia*. Palo Alto, CA: Stanford University Press, 1992.

Lvovich, Daniel. *Nacionalismo y Anti-Semitismo en la Argentina*. Buenos Aires: Javier Vergara Editor, 2003.

Mignolo, Walter. *Local Histories/Global Designs*. Princeton, NJ: Princeton University Press, 2000.

———. *Capitalismo y Geopolitica del Conocimiento*. Buenos Aires: Editorial del Signo/ Duke University, 2001.

Orfat, Gideon. *The Jewish Derrida*. Syracuse, NY: Syracuse University Press, 2001.

Sacher, Howard M. *A History of the Jews in America*. New York: Vintage Books, 1993.

Said, Edward. *The Question of Palestine*. New York: Vintage Books, 1992.

Senkman, Leandro. *El Anti-Semitismo en Argentina*. Buenos Aires: CEAL, 1989.

Slabodsky, Santiago. " Relocalizando Sinai en Los Andes. Especificidad Latinoamericana en un duelo Judio Post-Holocaustista," in *Majshavot* Year XL 1–4 (2003): 72–94.

Steiner, George. "The Long Life as a Metaphor: An approach to the Shoah," Berel Lang, ed., *Writing and the Holocaust*. London: Holmes and Meier, 1988.

Sutcliffe, Adam. *Judaism and Enlightenment*. Cambridge: Cambridge University Press, 2003.

Trossero, Enzo. *Los Marxistas y la Cuestion Judia*. Buenos Aires: Ed. Del Valle, 1996.

Walzer, Michael. *Exodus and Revolution*. Perseus Books, 1986.

Decolonizing Spiritualities

Spiritualities That Are Decolonizing and the Work of Decolonizing Our Understanding of These

Laura E. Pérez

Among the 5 percent of the U.S. population that does not consider itself religious or spiritual in any way, are scholars, artists, and other intellectuals. A group that considers itself among the best educated and culturally sophisticated.

Ninety-five percent are, however, not only religious, "believ[ing] in God or a universal life force" (Cimino and Lattin 1998:1), but in the 1990s, "one-third of [United States] Americans [reported that] they have had a profound spiritual experience, sudden or gradual, that has transformed their lives" (Ibid.:2). According to one survey of 113,000 Americans, 86 percent considered themselves Christian, Jews represented 2 percent, Muslims, Buddhists, Hindus, and New Agers had even fewer numbers (Ibid.). One sociologist (Peter Berger) "has said that [the United States of] America often appears as secular as Sweden at the top, but more like India in the profuse religious expression of the people."

The civil rights era's radical critiques of traditional religious institutions—Christian, Jewish, Muslim—have produced a small, but productive and very visible body of baby boomers and beyond who consider themselves spiritual, but not religious in the sense of being affiliated with traditional religious institutions. And this includes New Agers, and other spiritual do-it-yourselfers.

AnaMaría Díaz-Stevens and Anthony Stevens-Arroyo has written (*Recognizing the Latino Resurgence in U.S. Religion: The Emmaus Paradigm* (Boulder, CO: Westview Press, 1996) of the civil rights era U.S. Latina/o activism within the Catholic and different Protestant churches, at the level of criticizing Eurocentric language in prayer, liturgy, theology, and of course, in the use of English-only services; also, in terms of the histories of overt racism and anti-Mexican and anti–Puerto Rican sentiment on the part of Christian clergy and school teachers; and finally, in terms of such things as relegating Spanish-language services to the basement of churches at odd hours.

I have not yet seen research on the effect and civil rights presence of Latina/os in the Jewish religious communities of the United States. Stevens-Arroyo cites one source, based on a 1989–1990 survey reporting that 67 percent of Latina/os identified as Catholic; 26 percent Protestant; 6 percent as having no religion; and 1 percent refused to identify (Barry A. Kosmin, The National Survey of Religious Identification, 1989–1990. NY: City University of New York, March 1991). As to which Latina/os believe what, he cites a 1992 source reporting (Rodolfo O. De la Garza et al., Latino Voices: Mexican, Puerto Rican, and Cuban Perspectives, Boulder: Westview 1992) that 73.7 percent of Mexican Americans are Catholic; 65.1 Puerto Rican, 74.8 Cuban (21.2 Euroamerican). Fifteen percent of Mexican Americans are Protestants; 22.3 Puerto Rican, 14.4 Cuban (54.2 Euroamerican). Eleven point three percent of Mexican Americans are Other/No preference; 12.5 Puerto Rican, 10.9 percent Cuban (24.5 Euro-American).

My own research as a scholar of literature and visual and performance arts produced from the 1970s through the present, and focusing on the work of feminist and queer U.S. Latina/os, reveals the emergence of what I have argued elsewhere are decolonizing, hybrid spiritualities.

The panoply of spiritualities I am referring to as culturally hybrid is so in various ways. They have emerged in the large, pan-Latina/o communities of San Francisco and Los Angeles, and in San Antonio, Chicago, Miami, and New York, among other places. They are largely do-it-yourself mixtures of consciously non-Christian—that is, indigenous, African diasporic, so-called pagan feminist goddess spirituality, Buddhist, and Hindu—and salvaged Christian. When they are Jewish or Christian, they are infusing a non-Eurocentric theology and practice.

They are visible as well in the cults of people's saints, such as Don Pedrito Jaramillo of the Texas borderlands, and Juan Soldado, the safeguard of Mexican border crossers. In the practice of panindigenous prayer ceremonies of various types, including the *temescal* (sweat lodge), *danza* Azteca ("Aztec" dance), and developments such as Luis Valdez and Teatro Campesino's development of prayerful theatrical movement, *Los Veinte Pasos* (The Twenty Steps), based on orally and physically transmitted Mexica and Mayan teachings (Broyles-Gonzales 1994). They are like Sandra Cisneros and her BuddaLupe tattoo and writings, and Ana Castillo claiming descent from *curanderas* (healers) and offering *recetas* (remedies) of different sorts. They are writers like the late Gloria Anzaldúa and Cherríe Moraga and numerous visual artists seriously exploring the possible meaning of *tlamatinime* models of art and artist in our times, as socially responsible makers of heart or soul, and face.[1]

They are queer writers, visual, and performance artists interrogating the heteronormative, patriarchal, and Eurocentric nature of diverse religious traditions, including the Indigenous, the African diasporic, the Catholic, Jewish, and Protestant.

They are immigrant *mexicanos* and U.S. Chicanos visiting *santeros,* and they are Christians adding more so-called pagan deities to their home altars. They are Latina factory and farm-working mothers and *abuelas* (grandmothers) with Buddha, Christ, the Virgin Mary, Santa Bárbara-Changó, and pre-Colombian and European pagan goddesses on their *altares.*

Judging by Latina/os, the United States is not just "the World's Most Religiously Diverse Nation" (Diana Eck, *A New Religious America. How a "Christian Country" Has Become the World's Most Religiously Diverse Nation,* San Francisco: HarperCollins, 2001). More specifically than that, we are religiously hybrid, and we are so in politically decolonizing ways—reinserting the once-silent and so-called pagan Indian and African presence into what is picked and chosen from historically imposed Christian traditions.

Among artists and intellectuals, this cut and paste has taken them beyond Eurocentric Judeo-Christian religious beliefs and practices, in self-consciously decolonizing ways. It results as well, by the way, in the development of culturally hybrid, visual languages or aesthetics that are no longer based on those received from Europe, but I won't address that here, as I have elsewhere.[2]

Even more to the point, I would argue, this option for the spiritual is in itself decolonizing among once atheists, or agnostics, or the merely silenced by Eurocentric assumptions dismissive of spirituality and in particular of those of the "Third World," as ultimately naïve, irrational, or put plainly in the Eurocentric language of cultural evolutionism, culturally and historically backward.

Atheists have existed at least of course since the time of St. Augustine, as he argues against them in his fourth century *City of God.* Thus, I am not suggesting that atheism per se is Eurocentric. However, the atheism of our own time, I would suggest, is an unexamined legacy of post-Enlightenment and sociocultural racist Darwinism. I would argue further and more strongly that the dismissive concept of religion and spirituality as some sort of universally collapsible unity, and, therefore, as an opium of the masses *"en la última instancia,"* everywhere, and always, are a part of the very epistemological, culturally invisible, hegemonic ideological projections parading as rational, philosophical fact.

I see it as a part of our decolonizing epistemological work to question and dismiss the assumption that there exists a continuum of spiritual and religious development that begins with a historically or culturally remote so-called pagan shamanism of supposedly primitive pantheistic cultures, whether those are of the Americas, the Third World, or pre-Christian Europe.

Latin America's founding fathers accepted both the racial and cultural evolutionary discourses of Europe that resulted in immigration packages to supposedly improve our Indigenous and African "racial" stock; the press of the time joined in the anti-Asian yellow scare discourses of the first four decades of the twentieth century; they belittled the religion and practices of the Indigenous as mere superstition or deviltry; and the liberals and leftists among them joined in a general antireligious, and at best, anthropological, intellectual culture that accompanied the division of church and state.

But further, religiosity of any stripe among our *próceres* (national founders) and leaders of the Liberal and Left persuasions has been a *"cosa de viejas,"* (a woman's thing) and the so-called vague world of spirituality *"a cosa de indios y gentes incultas e incrédulas,"* a stance appropriate for Indians, the uneducated, and the credulous.

Thus, the history of the fates of Indigenous, institutionalized colonial, and New Age–like do-it-yourself *inventos* (inventions) has been a gendered and sexed one. And this is so among the U.S. Latina/o communities as well as among the colonizing cultures. This is a history that has reproduced, wittingly and unwittingly, a Eurocentric colonial logic that continues to *desprestigiar* (disparage and discredit) women, gay men, and the indigenous in favor of the image of a male or male-like Eurocentric specimen.

Thus, for women of color—writers and artists and other intellectuals—as members of historically oppressed minority groups in the United States, it has taken courage to consciously embrace spirituality in the face of Latina/o and politically progressive atheism, agnosticism, antireligiosity, or condescending and silencing disinterest.

Dominant cultures of the United States, Latin America, and the U.S. Latina/o communities assume that women or the queer, especially in communities of color, would, "of course," believe in spirituality. We have been exotified by Euro New Agers and other Euro seekers and spiritual tourists as "naturally" being more spiritual, for better or for worse. Thus, one of the risks for nonreligious artists and intellectuals to take up spirituality as a field of inquiry and struggle nonetheless runs the risk of reinforcing such stereotypes of cultural backwardness, quaintness, and naïveté.

And this it seems to me is the foundational contradiction of Latin Americans and U.S. Latina/os alike in all matters of art and scholarship if we remain within the binary mode of Eurocentric imperialist thought: to react against or to imitate, of which neither response, I might add, can ever result in more than tokenistic inclusions.

Progressive intellectuals and artists and other well-educated Latin Americans and U.S. Latina/os have largely accepted the rejection of both Judeo-Christian, Indigenous, and African diasporic spiritualities, in favor of abstract philosophical definitions of an increasingly atheistic/godless concept of humankind's spiritual nature, where instead, spirit is replaced by Eurocentric concepts of intellect, artistic sensibility, political sensibility, and in poststructuralist thought by the rigorously vague and detheified concepts of khora, excess, aporia, supplement, and other discursive loopholes.³ Whatever we may personally think of creation, deity or deities, and the spiritual nature of man, intellectually, Progressives have ended up with Western man colonizing even the spiritual imaginary through a so-called atheism that remains nonetheless in its negation, Eurocentric.

The hypocritical, genocidal, dominant cultural Christianities of the last five hundred years do not refer to universal truths about all forms of spiritual belief and practice. They do not even refer to all forms of Jewish and Christian belief.

The Western philosophical rejection of religiosity in the post-Enlightenment aftermath is a reaction of the western European and Euroamerican intelligentsia to the histories and cultures of their own so-called First World.

Orientalism with respect to Latin American cannot and has not produced reliable knowledges about the plural religious and spiritualities of this continent.⁴ It has dispatched the autochthonous and the African diasporic to the zone of timelessness, to the history of eternal returns, to the supposed *estancamiento and sangre gruesa* (stagnation and thick-bloodedness) of the black, Indigenous, Asian, and their mixed-blood, mixed-culture offspring, where like mules, our hybridity is assumed to be ultimately sterile, in terms of so-called progress and development. In terms of that discourse of capitalist global imperialism, I hope that this is so.

I would like to caution us therefore against hasty, unconsidered dismissals of Latina/os practicing within Jewish and Christian traditions, just as I believe it is a mistake to dismiss the New Age as merely another instance of colonizing cultural appropriation of the native, important as this preliminary observation has been.

The postmodern effect in large cities of the United States has made them meccas of pan-Latin/o and pan-TW and peripheral European migrations. This is creating *mestizajes* at the level of mixed ethnicities as we all know, but also at the level of mixed cultural spiritual beliefs and practices.

Our Latina/o hybridities today, for example, are the cultural—not hereditary—Jewish Puerto Rican feminist spirituality of a Rosario Morales. They are the Chicana initiated into Transcendental Meditation. The *cubana norteamericana* Zen Buddhist with some *santería* thrown in. They are the offspring of ex-Muslim, ex-Christian unions. They are, I say, increasingly complex, increasingly mixed, increasingly tolerant of difference, thereby; I would add, increasingly visionary with regard to egalitarian coexistence of cultural difference.

U.S. Latina/o artists, like mystics of various traditions, tell us that we are spirit. Part and parcel of a, or the, creator being(s), and that without awareness of this aspect of embodied existence we are in essence *manqué*—disabled as fully operating human beings.

U.S. Latina/o feminist and queer artists are, among others, leading the way in observing in the larger U.S. Latina/o communities, the decolonizing power of culturally non-Western belief systems and their practices, and of

mixtures with colonizing religions that dispute theories of syncretism that ultimately posit the incoherence of a terribly fragmented cultural detritus from the
colonized cultures. Not so. They suggest instead that the struggle for psychic wholeness against the psychological colonization that Frantz Fanon spoke so penetrat-
ing of, and that W.E.B. DuBois wrote of as double consciousness, and that Anzaldúa
described as the hellish rendering of the Coatlicue State, that this struggle for
psychic wholeness includes a reclamation of culturally different, healing notions
of spirituality than those imposed through the legacy of colonial invasion, destruction, substitution, and unequal syncretisms.[5]

If it is well known that a Western, imperialist Christianity helped to impose
a colonizing self-loathing in the native and their mixed offspring, then it is known,
though less so, that it is decolonizing for us to explore the issue of spirituality and
its many different cultural understandings *for ourselves* and our communities.

At the very least, we must be cognizant that spirituality matters profoundly to real people, and that as we have begun to see on the world stage, it
matters profoundly in its political effects. It is intellectually tautological to
define the spirit and the spiritual that are specific to the European and
Euroamerican understanding as universal. And it is not disinterested blindness
to dismiss those that have indeed survived five hundred years of cultural genocide into the present in forms that are not outside the flow and current of
history, of course, and thus in changed forms.

Far from being an opium that allows for a mercifully deadening escape from
the pain of European and Euroamerican imperialist exploitation and depredation,
Indigenous, African-diasporic, and decolonizing hybrid spiritualities in our own
time have nourished, strengthened, and given social courage to our peoples, assuring us in the face of racist discourses of our intrinsic worth, teaching us spiritual
and material technologies to heal the body and the spirit, showing the difference
between the paths of wisdom and mere knowledge/power accumulations, and
most of all, reminding us beyond the Westernizing credos of self-enrichment at
increasingly any cost, that we are responsible for each other and the planet.

Notes

1. "*Tlamatinime*" is a Nahuatl ("Aztec") word describing the Nahua sage and decoder of
the glyphs, but also, arguably, that of the glyphmakers themselves. Contemporary Chicana/o
artists have reappropriated this word to describe their own socially significant, spiritually responsible artmaking activities. For more in-depth discussion of this phenomenon, see Pérez 1998.

2. See my forthcoming *Altarities: Chicana Art, Politics, and Spirituality* (Durham, NC:
Duke University Press), as well as Pérez 2002 and 1998.

3. See Julia Kristeva and Jacques Derrida regarding linguistic and conceptual (or cultural) excesses through the concept of c/khora. (Derrida 1993; Kristeva 1984).

4. I am referring to Edward Said's development of this term in his 1979 book of the same title.

5. Fanon 1952; Anzaldúa 1987; DuBois 1903.

PART VI

Latinization and Decolonization

Sociopolitical Logics and Conflicting Interpretations of "Latinization" in the United States

James Cohen[1]

Is U.S. society becoming "Latinized"? Commentators are more and more frequently evoking this notion, or similar ones, in various ways, but for reasons that all begin with the hard demographic fact that people of Latin American or Hispano-Caribbean origin are increasingly numerous within U.S. borders. Obviously, however, the changes now taking place in U.S. society under the impact of Latin@s cannot be fully understood and interpreted in the quantitative language of demographics. The challenge, in adopting a notion such as "Latinization," is to make of it an instrument that can help to refine our readings of possible futures rather than stylize and reify them.[2]

We may begin with the observation, which has been articulated and substantiated in various ways, that the United States is now undergoing a deep, multiform and gradual metamorphosis its social, political and cultural space. The question of the content and the deeper and longer-term significance of this phenomenon is an affair of both the present and the future. Since

"Latinization" will be what social actors make of it, the examination of the phenomenon requires us to adopt the perspective of the *longue durée*. There is no other choice than to engage in prospective thinking, mobilizing whatever rigor the social and human sciences can muster while also having the modesty to recognize that we do not know exactly what the society of tomorrow will look like.

To investigate and attempt to define the content and significance of U.S. Latinization, there is no choice but to work in a pluri- and transdisciplinary spirit, keeping in mind that C. Wright Mills's "sociological imagination" (1959) extends to ethnology, political science, economics, demography, linguistics, cultural studies and the literary disciplines, gender studies, etc., and invites all these approaches to combine their strengths in flexible and innovative ways in order to shed new light on the processes of incorporation of immigrant populations into U.S. society, and their cultural and linguistic practices, without neglecting manifestations of racism, xenophobia, and ethnicized nationalism, when these contribute to the shape that Latinization is concretely taking.

While Latinization is without a doubt a contested terrain, some confusion continues to reign in public debate regarding the significance of Latin@s' growing presence in U.S. society. Historian Kevin Starr writes: "Latinization of the United States is so profound that no one really sees it" (quoted by G. Rodríguez 2004). Latinization by no means announces itself as a unified and perfectly coherent process.

There is no need here to rehearse the elementary facts and figures about the demographic side of Latinization, which many U.S.-based researchers now take for granted (Mike Davis's essay *Magical Urbanism*, 2001, is as good an introduction as any to this aspect of the subject; see also the reports of the Tomás Rivera Center and the Pew Hispanic Center, as well as the basic data available from the U.S. Bureau of the Census). Above and beyond the rapid demographic growth of the Latin@ population, what cannot help striking us is its sheer diversity, according to many different parameters: national origin, region of settlement, generation, socioeconomic condition, levels of educational attainment, relationship to the Spanish and English languages, etc.

What is not always clearly understood about Latinization, especially (though not exclusively) when observed from afar, is that fully 60 percent of U.S. Latin@s are U.S. natives and are engaged in multigenerational processes of incorporation that make it just as important to observe them as *citizens* as to place them in a particular "ethnic group" or "diaspora." This is by no means to deny the growing importance of transnational social relations in the lives of many immigrants (see section 4 below).

The diversity of sociological profiles among U.S. Latin@s makes it particularly questionable to refer to them, as is often done in an automatic and untheorized way, as forming a "community." The example of such a broad and diverse ethnoracial category shows precisely how much the very notion of "community," in reference to ethnoracial categories, is in need of critical examination.

It would seem preferable to reserve this term for situations where observation reveals modes of sustained and dense interpersonal exchanges that amount to the collective functioning of a community. For example, the Puerto Ricans of East Harlem and the Dominicans grouped together in Washington Heights form communities in many ways, but it would be an exaggeration to speak of Latin@s as forming a "community" across the entire New York metropolitan area—even though there may be contexts in which this is true. "Mexicans" constitute such a huge and varied group in the United States that the notion of community does not seem pertinent, but when one examines the forms of organization that prevail among specific groups of Mexicans, the emigrant or-ganizations of indigenous peoples from Oaxaca, for example (Bacon 2002), the notion of community becomes more concrete.

The notion of "community" is also invoked in broader, more national, "eth-nic" and/or political contexts. The nationally or regionally based Latin@ lobbying organizations, whose chosen mission is to formulate social and political demands in programmatically coherent ways, have a modus operandi that involves organiz-ing the "community" in the ethnic sense. But it cannot honestly be claimed, as professional Hispanic conservatives do, that over the past 30 years Latin@ organi-zations have functioned in an ethnically sectarian and ingrown way that would somehow severely impede their full incorporation into U.S. citizenship. Some of the more radical forms of nationalism rife in the late 60s and early 70s may have fit the profile that conservatives are fond of denouncing, but it was never the prevail-ing model and is certainly not today. When Latin@s invoke ethnic community, the thrust is rarely sectarian and much more frequently oriented toward the affir-mation of citizenship rights and citizenship status. In mainstream Latin@ politics, programmatic demands are articulated in such a way as to fit into the broader pattern of citizens' demands formulated in the nation as a whole, even while mani-festing certain distinctive characteristics. Samuel Huntington has predictably ig-nored this phenomenon, since he prefers or feigns to see as "representative" of all Latin@s the most extreme and isolated exponents of Chicano nationalism. At bottom Huntington is driven by the need to define Latin@s as fundamentally foreign to U.S. "culture" and thus outside the bounds of U.S. "identity" as he sees it (Huntington 2004).

Latinization in the Sociocultural Sense

In some of its guises, Latinization is an altogether banal process, hardly sugges-tive of epoch-making change. For example, it can take the everyday form of appropriation, by Spanish-language media, of the same marketing techniques and discourses that characterize mainstream U.S. society, only laced with ele-ments of Latin American or Caribbean cultural imagery for added effective-ness in targeted "ethnic" markets (see Dávila 2001).

Latinization as usually referred to in journalistic commentary also takes the form of an introduction into Anglophone commercial and mass media culture, including the musical and film industries, of greater numbers of Latin@ performers and/or selected forms of expression defined in one way or another as "Latin" (C. Rodríguez, ed., 1998). There is also a banalization of the presence of Latin@s in great numbers in certain areas of public life such as professional sports, baseball in particular.

Can one speak of a changing cultural substratum of U.S. society under the impact of Latin@s? This is no doubt true, but rather than looking in the commercial and media realms for signs of this, one would do better to turn toward the concrete analysis of the different immigrant groups, the different socioeconomic strata, the variations by generation—in short, become sensitive to the immensely varied sociological profiles of those falling demographically into the Latin@ category. The large numbers among Latin@s of first-generation immigrants, and among them many wage workers, clearly leaves a strong mark on today's patterns of Latinization. If one social category among Latin@s could be taken as "emblematic" or "representative" of the group as a whole, it would no doubt be wage workers; it is clear enough that the difficulties of socioeconomic incorporation, faced disproportionately by Latin@s, are the lot of most Latin@s—in other words, not just first-generation immigrants, but second, third and fourth-generation U.S. Latin@s who in no small number have undergone problems of marginalization and educational deprivation. Nonetheless, some would argue (see section 1b, below) that the emerging Latin@ middle classes are the main driving force behind Latinization. Discussion on this point is open, and as we shall see, the question of "class" that is raised thereby is also posed as a question of "culture."

It has been shown by a growing number of commentators that elements of popular Latino culture are indeed having a lasting effect on life in U.S. cities (Davis 2001), on urban music of many varieties and other art forms (Flores 2000; Habell-Pallán and Romero 2002), not to mention in ways of thinking as well as about such common social themes as education, health, sexuality, family, etc. (See Súarez-Orozco and Páez, eds. 2002). All of these statements are no doubt true, but in the future they need to be specified and fleshed out, without falling into the Huntingtonian culturalist trap of fetishizing and hardening the lines of difference before they have had a chance to work through their dialectic openly and democratically within the broader U.S. society.

Huntington is right on one point, and one only: a deep process of cultural and linguistic Latinization is taking place in U.S. society, and the immigration of many Mexicans, Central Americans and South Americans has much to do with it. Fortunately, however, there are few signs of the open ethnocultural strife he attempts to conjure up (even while denying he is doing so). If plausible long-term future scenarios are what interest us, it is more plausible to argue that sociocultural Latinization has the strong potential to be a relatively smooth and harmonious process, as such processes go, given that, as anthropologists François Laplantine and Alexis Nouss have observed, *métissage* always takes place in history against a background of anti-*métissage* (1997: 9). There are not only significant reasons to think that U.S. Latinization could prove to be one of the smoother processes of ethnoracial and cultural blending in history, but there are also powerful reasons to hope so, and to resist the harder scenarios, given that the alternative they promise is prolonged ethnonational conflict over resources, power, and cultural hegemony in U.S. society, with increased opportunities for rampant authoritarianism to progress.

The sociopolitical implications of Latinization are just as important as its sociocultural ones, the two being intimately linked in ways which in themselves require more exploration. In the remainder of this paper, the sociopolitical pole will take precedence in the analysis, which does not exclude attention to cultural themes, nor imply the slightest disdain for them.

Sociopolitical Latinization

The changes now taking place in U.S. society under the impact of Latin@s are orienting U.S. society toward important choices with implications for the entire society. In ways that only a few specialists of varying perspectives are now focusing on, the coming years will be a time in which U.S. society will be called upon to choose: 1) what sort of relationship it wants to entertain with its own immigrants, foreigners, ethnoracial minorities, etc., given that the latter are less and less in the minority; 2) what sort of relationship this society wants to entertain more generally with its own ethnoracial, cultural and linguistic differences; 3) how socioeconomic inequalities and inequalities of opportunity should be treated, given that they have steadily widened over the past few decades and maintain, as much as in the past, though in new contexts, strong ethnoracial connotations; 4) last but not least, important choices will have to be made regarding the types of relations the United States seeks to maintain with the countries of its southern periphery, and which are increasingly "interpenetrated" with U.S. society itself.

In short, Latinization is posing—and to some extent precipitating or radicalizing—choices that affect the heart of the established social and political system, the essence of U.S. citizenship, and imply at least a partial questioning of their bases. In France and certain other European countries, such questions are posed in a much more encompassing and intellectually coherent way than in the United States. What is at stake are these countries' "models of integration" or "public philosophies" of citizenship and difference; that is, the social thought and philosophical objectives that inform the elaboration of norms and rules, in all areas concerning citizenship and the democratic management of ethnoracial, cultural, religious and linguistic differences as well as the distribution of opportunities for socioeconomic welfare, education and social mobility (see Favell, 1998, for one example).

In the United States, where for various historical reasons it is not customary to formulate the terms of a "model of integration" understood in this way, public responses to these questions describe much less a "model" than a patchwork or jumble of public policies and corresponding legitimations. Certain stubborn, ongoing controversies illustrate this point: 1) the never-ending ideological, philosophical, political and judicial trench warfare over affirmative action; 2) the permanent and bitter controversy over bilingual education for the children of immigrants, and more generally the question of linguistic pluralism; 3) the controversy that has arisen since the 1980s over electoral districting for local and federal (congressional) elections and the mode of assuring representation for ethnoracial minorities; 4) theoretical and political debates over the significance of "multiculturalism," in a context where much lip service is paid to the notion, but very little public policy is presented as an expression of it; 5) the ongoing sociopolitical controversy over the regulation of migratory flows, security in border areas, the status (regulated or deregulated) of immigrant workers.

These rampant or open conflicts reflect the habitual state of a political system in which, in the absence of a "model of integration" to which different actors refer, there has reigned a form of "trench warfare" over the past 40 years. What also characterizes the situation in the United States is a state of permanent *malentendu* (mutual incomprehension): different actors do not speak the same language and it is not clear from where the impulse for a more coherent discourse and set of practices might come. At the state and federal levels, the public policies that give shape to citizenship form a whole that was never designed or wished for, in its concrete form, by anyone. For example, a policy orientation such as affirmative action as a method for combating ethnoracial discrimination was never discussed in any theoretical or philosophical way until it had already been adopted. As John Skrentny (1996) shows, it was conceived in a bureaucratic and pragmatic manner by one group of Justice Department legal specialists behind closed doors, on the basis of a legislative mandate much more general and abstract in scope.

Latinization: The Main Currents of Political Thought

Given the low degree of coherence in public policies regarding immigration, ethnoracial minorities, "minority languages", and more generally the scarcity of long-term visions regarding citizenship and social relations, close observation of day-to-day U.S. political life obscures the stakes of Latinization as much as it sheds light on them. It is difficult to understand the virtualities and contradictions of the U.S. political system by simply examining the cleavages at given moments between Democrats and Republicans. A handful of social scientists and politically motivated intellectuals, having observed the deep antinomies of the system, have attempted in recent years to resist and overcome them by defining new conceptual and political strategies with a higher quotient of strategic thinking and philosophical vision.

Among these researchers and intellectuals, however, one finds many of the same polarizations and mutual misunderstandings as within the general population. It is nonetheless worthwhile to sketch out a conceptual map of the currents present, beginning with those which appear to have the greatest chances, in coming years, of conditioning the ways in which the question of the incorporation of Latin@s into U.S. society is posed in theory and in practice.

1. Mainstream Latino Reformism

Latino reformism, or "ethnic Keynesianism," Agustín Lao-Montes' expression (Lao-Montes 2000), in an important subset of a much broader nebulous that corresponds, broadly, to the voters and sympathizers of the Democratic Party, given that neither this party nor its main adversary have the vocation to be spaces of ongoing programmatic elaboration. It is not difficult to tease out of the programs elaborated by the main Latin@ lobbying organizations (National Council of La Raza, Mexican American Legal Defense and Education Fund, National Association of Latino Elected Officials, etc.), as well as the Latin@ media in both English and Spanish, an "average" or "mean" political thought whose main characteristics are as follows:

- Political demands are in general articulated in "republican" (small r) or "universal" terms rather than in ethnic and particularist ones, even if the appeal to ethnic solidarity is part of their repertoire of modes of expression.
- Demands are formulated in the framework of a pragmatic reformist program in which the state is called upon to play a greater role as service provider, particularly in the areas of education and health care.
- While resembling classic liberal politics (in the U.S. sense of the term) in many ways, this current has certain specificities: 1) it invests much energy in the defense of the civil and social rights of immigrants; 2) without defending affirmative action unconditionally, it opposes as a matter of basic principle all forms of ethnoracial discrimination; 3) it articulates with more conviction than other liberal currents a moderate form of multiculturalism, taking into account the presence of the Spanish language and the diversity of forms of cultural expression that may in one way or another be referred to as "Latin@" or "Hispanic."

This current takes for granted that the United States remains a country of abundant immigration and must guarantee to today's immigrants, as to yesterday's, those basic rights that will allow them to become incorporated economically and politically. Without actively encouraging illegal immigration, this current seeks to protect the rights of all immigrants, taking into account the fact that those who cross the frontier, even illegally, do so as a matter of economic necessity.

In the linguistic and cultural domain, this current calls for a harmonious form of integration that amounts neither to total assimilation, nor to an affirmation of particularize at any price. Latin@ reformists call for the right of all citizens to learn English under the best possible conditions, while defending the right of those who do not master English to express themselves and have basic services administered in their native tongue, in conformity with existing constitutional norms.

"Bilingual education" programs, in recent years abolished in certain states, maintained in others and increasingly discouraged by the federal government, are seen by this current as one pedagogically sound method among others for assuring the transition toward the mastery of English, provided that sufficient resources are allocated to their development. The members of this current oppose the relentless hounding of bilingual education programs by their militant adversaries but are not, today, in any position to propose an encompassing alternative policy. There is, indeed, no consensus within the current regarding a long-term vision of U.S. society: some harbor the ideal of a future bilingual (English-Spanish) society, while others are more openly "assimilationist" in linguistic terms.

The Vision of the Mestizo *Melting Pot*

Gregory Rodríguez, journalist and researcher with the New American Foundation, gives the Latin@ reformist project a slightly conservative twist while articulating with greater force than others a moderate form of multiculturalism. Rodríguez foresees, in coming years, the emergence of a "racial and cultural synthesis that will fundamentally transform the attitudes of the nation" (G. Rodríguez 2004: 126). He casts this transformation in a broadly optimistic light, since it represents in his view a cultural enrichment for the nation while taking place in full respect of democratic institutions.

More controversially, Rodríguez strikes an optimistic pose regarding the socioeconomic incorporation of Latin@s (it should be pointed out that he refers almost always to Mexican Americans, but that most of his observations are also applicable to Latin@s in general). He holds that the abundant and continuous migratory flows from south to north deform the perception of many observers regarding the social mobility of Latin@s; if immigrants, who represent about 40 percent of all Latin@s in the United States, are left out of the equation, it comes to light that Latin@s already established in the United States for two generations or more are engaged in a contradictory but broadly successful process of incorporation. Although there are many Latin@s for whom socioeconomic incorporation remains very problematic after two or three generations, Rodríguez prefers to place greater emphasis on the Latin@ middle class, whose emergence contributes, in his words, to a "normaliz[ing] of the image of the Latino in the mainstream imagination" (G. Rodríguez 2004:129).

Taking clear distance from the nationalist and/or leftist militants of the 1960s and 1970s, and in particular from the internal colonialism thesis, Rodríguez presents Mexican immigration (and by extension, other Latin@ immigrations) as resulting from a largely voluntary process. Rodríguez does not go to extreme lengths, like professional Hispanic conservatives, to deny the racist and xenophobic treatment visited on Latin@s at certain periods in U.S. history, but it is important in his view to reject any approach to politics that plays on the notion of victimhood.

There is no implication in Rodríguez's work that Latin@s should deny their origins, since they are "asserting their ethnicity more confidently than ever" (2004: 129). He refuses the sort of multiculturalism that "promotes the coexistence of separate but equal cultures" (p. 130) and proposes, instead, a "new paradigm"—which he defines as representing a significant step "beyond" multiculturalism, that of "*mestizaje*" and "hybridity." By this, he means that Mexican Americans represent, historically, a "continual synthesis, a blending of Spanish and indigenous cultures" (p. 130). They have "always been more fluid and comfortable with hybridity" and are thus in a position to encourage the rest of U.S. society to accustom itself to culture mixture and intercultural contact. The "ambiguous" place that they occupy in the "racial scale," as a racially heterogeneous group, constitutes in this respect an advantage, since it places Latin@s in a good position to invent "their own vision of the *melting pot*": "instead of adding one more color to the multicultural rainbow, Mexican Americans are helping to forge a new unifying vision" (p. 126). They add new ingredients to the melting pot by imparting a more "Latin" tonality to society as a whole. At the same time, Latin@s tend to erase the borders between themselves and others: Rodríguez stresses that by 2050, 40 percent of all Latin@s will have a multiple-ethnic heritage. He further observes that few Latin@s support ethnic institutions while many join nonethnic civic associations.

There is no impulse on the part of Latin@s to impose an identity on the rest of society, but rather to "inject [a] *mestizo* vision into American culture" (p. 133). "Mexican Americans have become numerous and confident enough to simply claim their brownness—their *mestizaje*. By bringing their ancient understanding of racial and cultural synthesis to the nation, they are "transforming the melting pot into a more inclusive cauldron that mixes races as well as ethnicities" (p. 138).

In the linguistic domain, Rodríguez places himself among the "assimilators," stressing that by the third generation fully two-thirds of Latino children speak only English. "While Spanish persists as a second language for many

Mexican Americans in heavily Latin@ regions of the country, it clearly does not slow acquisition of nation's primary language" (p. 135). Rodríguez minimizes the importance of Spanish-language media, which in his opinion appeal only to first-generation immigrants.

Rodríguez seeks above all to present the integration of Latin@s as a process that is moving along successfully and needs above all to be normalized rather than overdramatized. This normalization is, in his view, best guaranteed by the growth of a Latin@ middle class as well as the emergence of "an unprecedented array of political and pop cultural figures" (p. 129). Yet the debate, of course, remains open about how large and how consolidated the middle sectors really are. Rodolfo Torres and Victor Valle, who belong to the critical current to be examined below (section 4), admit that "Latinos are becoming more socially mobile" (Valle and Torres 2000: 177) but reproach Rodríguez for exaggerating the magnitude of the phenomenon by overestimating, for example, the significance of income figures by household, an aggregate that may encompass the incomes of several adults—immigrants in particular—living in a single dwelling without necessarily constituting a family unit.

2. Ethnocentric Nationalism and Contradictions among Conservatives

Even the moderate multiculturalism, highly respectful of existing institutions, as illustrated by an author such as Gregory Rodríguez, would be defined as excessive by those perturbed by any significant manifestations of cultural pluralism within U.S. borders—a defining characteristic of the thought of Samuel Huntington, whose recent work (2004) has gone further than ever in attempting to provide an intellectual veneer to xenophobic and ethnocentric currents in U.S. society by stigmatizing the growing presence of Latin@s and attributing to them a project of cultural and political "*reconquista.*"

It is worth asking, however, whether the xenophobic currents into whose hands Huntington willingly plays are strong enough to prevail politically, even in today's ultraconservative political climate. The current of interest in Congress for strong measures to restrict the inflow of Mexican and other Latin@ immigrants is not as strong as one might imagine when reading Huntington or listening to certain AM radio talk shows. It is true that the 1990s saw a qualitative leap in the militarization of the border (see Andreas 2000; Palafox 2001), yet only a handful of members of the House of Representatives are ready to propose active measures to "seal off the border," as if such a thing were possible. The anti-immigration restrictionists are prevented from realizing their maximum program, not only because organizations defending immigrants' rights exist and have significant support among Latin@s, but also because Latin@s' votes are beginning to count and are valued as dearly by Republican candidates as by Democrats; and because the conservative coalition in power includes many powerful interests that prosper thanks to abundant immigration, legal and illegal. Some of the most conservative Republicans in socioeconomic or foreign policy terms are nonetheless all in favor of embracing "diversity"; one of their main aims is to form a conservative coalition as broad as possible, which means eschewing racializing distinctions within their ranks.

Latin@s were estimated in 2000 to have voted almost 2/3 in favor of Democrats, 1/3 in favor of Republican candidates, though this figure varied widely by region. Republicans have every reason to want to capture a greater portion of the Latin@ vote. If they do not wish to limit their support among Latin@s to a minority of confirmed conservatives, they will have to accept that Latin@ voters as a whole are not inclined to accept policies that generate greater insecurity for immigrants or that pay more lip service than direct attention to problems of public education.

3. The "Civic Nation" Rehabilitated?

Among the specialists of migrations and ethnoracial minorities, and among historians of U.S. society and politics, there exists a constellation of researchers who show a greater interest than others in articulating a coherent national "model of integration" or "public philosophy" defining the terms of national citizenship with respect to ethnoracial and cultural difference. They call for the rehabilitation of a civic model of citizenship, which they consider to be the most essential element in the democratic heritage of the nation (see, for example, Smith 1997; Hollinger 1995; Gerstle 2001). The proclaimed objective of these authors is to forge a vision of citizenship—and public action—that reconciles ethnoracial and cultural diversity with a sense of national belonging, on the basis of a recognition of the equality of all citizens before the law, independently—insofar as possible—of their "communities of descent" (Hollinger 1995).

This current has produced some original rereadings of U.S. history in the light of a central contradiction that can be traced over the decades since the founding of the U.S. republic: the one which pits a "civic" and inclusive conception of the nation against a "racial" (or "ethnoracial") and exclusive one. "Throughout its history," writes historian Gary Gerstle, "American civic nationalism has contended with another potent ideological inheritance, a racial nationalism that conceives of America in ethnoracial terms, as a people held together by common blood and skin color and by an inherited fitness for self-government" (Gerstle 2001: 4).

In itself, the pointing out of this ongoing antinomy contributes nothing original to the theory of national formations, because analogous contradictions have often been pointed out in many countries, but the analysis of how civic and ethnoracial nationalism have played out in U.S. history facilitates an interesting and coherent *political* reading of the past and present. One observation that emerges from these authors' work is that the civil rights movement of the 1950s–1960s represented the apogee of the civic-national perspective in the twentieth century, because this movement, founded in large part on the principle of equality of all citizens before the law, gave rise to laws (the Civil Rights Act of 1964; the Voting Rights Act of 1965 and all their ramifications) that represented a significant concretization of this principle. At this point in history began a "minority rights revolution" (Skrentny 2002) as the civil rights movement gave rise to demands by various other categories of excluded citizens for the recognition of their elementary rights, including a right to be recognized as forming a particular group.

Paradoxically, however, according to this reading, at the same moment there began a movement in the opposition direction; that is, the emergence of a range of currents that rejected any vision involving a civic reunification of the nation: certain ethnonational movements (Black Power, Chicano or Puerto Rican Power, etc.) and certain multiculturalist currents which tended to justify these movements as expressions of an irreducible diversity that carried more weight than the idea of national unity. Although multiculturalists and ethnonationalists of different stripes constitute a small minority, they succeeded, in the view of Gary Gerstle, in "shatter[ing] a broad consensus on the virtue of the American nation, the beneficence of its civic ideals, and the imperative of fighting community where it reared its head" (Gerstle 2001: 327). Their ideas resulted in an "emphatic" rejection of melting pot metaphors and polices of assimilation in favor of celebrating the diverse cultures of America's many racial and ethnic groups, and in a vision of the U.S. nation as "inescapably exclusionary and repressive" (Gerstle 2001: 347).

Although they all support a rehabilitation of the "civic nation," the authors within this current are not all in agreement regarding the measures to be adopted in order to inaugurate a new, more coherent model of integration. At least two sensibilities can be detected: one stresses the necessity of forging at new civic patriotism as a value in itself, without necessarily questioning the foundations of the social and economic system in place (see Gerstle 2001); the other could be characterized as a version of "social democracy," for it stresses the importance of the treatment of socioeconomic equalities as an indispensable element in any strategy for civic-national reconstruction (see Hollinger 1995).

With the internal diversity that characterizes it, the civic-national current seeks among other goals to set general guidelines for the implementation of a renewed civic-national model of citizenship. The democratic rights it seeks to defend are, by preference, those of individuals and not groups, be they defined as ethnoracial or ethnocultural. On the highly controversial subject of affirmative action, the current affirms the need to promote a more "color blind" policy to fight discrimination; it is thus, on the whole, most unenthusiastic about the general principle of "group preferences," except insofar as it operates as a "temporary expedient" for the express purpose of overcoming the particularly radical form of discrimination against African Americans (see Hollinger 1996). (It is of course politically impossible to oppose all forms of affirmative action completely and head-on, since African Americans and Latin@s still support it in great numbers.) On the subject of multiculturalism, there reigns, within this current, a consensus on two points: 1) a rejection of the visions—referred to as "radical multiculturalism"—that construct cultures as separate entities rather than emphasizing the search for a "common ground" of citizenship; 2) strong suspicions with regard to another constellation of multiculturalists referred to as "diasporic" (or "hybridic" in the pejorative vocabulary of Gary Gerstle 2001: 350–351), who are accused of scorning the national framework itself, due to an obsession with transnational social relations, *mestizo* or "hybrid" or "border" identities. (We refer here to the fourth current, to be examined below).

Civic nationalists understand, however, that the critique of national borders is not just an obsession of a certain multicultural left, since transnational capitalism and its elites are more and more accomplished in making an instrumental and selective usage of these same borders (see Gerstle 2001: 356; Hollinger 1995: 149).

It would seem that these authors have a serious blind spot when it comes to the "Latinization" of U.S. society, in particular regarding the status of the Spanish language. Spanish appears to them to be just one more immigrant language like the others; that is, due to be buried one of these decades in the "graveyard of languages" (Jacoby 2004: 24) that is the U.S. melting pot—or at least would be due, if only Latin@ immigration were to descend to much lower levels—a big "if"! Spanish thus has no particular place in the public sphere of a nation defined, implicitly if not in law, as Anglophone. The civic nationalists have little or nothing to say about emerging Spanish-language public spaces, including several important daily newspapers and two large cable networks, which already play a significant role in socializing many Hispanophone Americans into U.S. citizenship and into a sense of belonging to the U.S. nation. The position of the civic nationalists is, of course, nowhere near the unabashed ethnocentrism of a Samuel Huntington; but they fail to make it clear why the civic nation they wish to (re)construct could not be one in which bilingualism is promoted and widely practiced.

These authors, while defending the principle of "equal opportunity, in which no one suffers on account of race, religion, gender or creed" (Gerstle 2001: 367), also remain strangely indifferent to the transnational dimension, which others—see below—consider indispensable for rethinking both the role of the Latin@s in the United States and the future of citizenship in the Americas.

4. U.S. Society as "Borderland" and Transnational Social Fields: The Emerging Critical Paradigm

This broad and varied current, made up largely of "progressive" or left-wing intellectuals, many of whom are of Latin@ origin, holds that the incorporation of Latin@s into U.S. society is, at least in part, a process of cultural and linguistic *mestizaje*, and worthy of celebration as such, but its members refuse, unlike the mainstream Latin@ reformists examined above, such as Gregory Rodríguez, to idealize *mestizaje* by presenting it as a process that is by definition harmonious.

Such an idealization runs the risk, in their view, of obscuring the persistence of class inequalities, ethnoracial divisions of labor and xenophobic currents in U.S. society.

This current develops a critical reflection on borders—geographic, political, cultural, linguistic—and stresses the growing lack of correspondence in today's world between national spaces, cultural spaces, and spaces of citizenship rights (see, for example, several contributions to Darder and Torres, eds., 1998). According to a metaphor which serves as a central reference for this current, U.S. society as a whole is becoming one large borderland. The contact and mixture of languages—for example, the phenomenon of Spanglish in its different manifestations—represent for this current another powerful metaphor for what social relations in the United States are becoming (see Morales 2002).

The current accords great importance to transborder, transnational, or "translocal" or "diasporic" social relations, although the latter term is sometimes extended in an uncontrolled way to all sorts of disparate phenomena. In one way or another, the current stresses the compression of time and space in the lives of those migrants, more and more numerous, who maintain networks of contact with their country of origin and contribute to the emergence of "transnational social fields" (see Basch, Glick Schiller, and Szanton Blanc 1994, for some seminal insights on this question).

The civic nationalists suspect this current of being too rooted in the literary disciplines and in cultural creation to be able to understand clearly what is at stake in the rehabilitation of national citizenship. Among the founding texts of this current, one indeed finds several remarkable literary works that invite readers to reflect on hybrid, mixed, or syncretic identities (see, among others, Anzaldúa 1987; Gómez-Peña 1993). These authors underline the contradictions—explosive or rampant, and often unexpected—of processes of *métissage* that are taking place under conditions of inequality and too often of patterned ethnoracial hierarchies from which colonial heritages are not absent (Lao-Montes 2000; Grosfoguel 2003). Within the current one finds university researchers who have contributed powerfully to the enrichment of ethnic studies, or American studies, and more generally to sociology, ethnology and cultural studies (see, for example, Oboler 1995; Saldívar 1997; Aparicio and Chávez-Silverman, eds. 1997; Flores 2000; Lao-Montes and Dávila, eds. 2000).

Politically, this current takes its distance from—without fully repudiating—the heritage of the generation of Chicano or Puerto Rican militant nationalists of the 1960s–1970s, of which its older members are a product. They insistently call into question the nation-state as the exclusive framework of political socialization and citizenship rights, calling forth from their imagination new forms of citizenship which would no longer be limited to the U.S. framework but would deploy themselves in the broader space of the Americas. One representative example would be María de los Angeles Torres's call for a "transnational political identity or citizenship" that would "better accommodate the rights of individuals who for a myriad of reasons cross the frontiers of multiple nation-states and whose lives are affected by decisions made by more than one state" (M. Torres 2003: 382). Susanne Jonas (2001) goes into further detail about what such transnational citizenship mechanisms might look like and why they are indispensable for promoting a more humane and democratic hemisphere. She is fully aware of how far against the grain such thinking goes in today's post-9/11 security environment.

As for defining the future stakes of citizenship within U.S. boundaries, it is my assessment that this current is far from having reached its potential, except in a few path-breaking analyses of urban social movements (see A. Torres and Velásquez, eds. 1998; R. Torres and Katsiaficas, eds. 1999; Valle and R. Torres 2000; Lao-Montes 2000; M. Torres 2001). For example, Victor Valle and Rodolfo Torres (2000), who study as sociologists and ethnologists the forms of cultural *mestizaje* in Los Angeles—a city that is today nearly 50 percent Latin@—innovate by combining their analysis of these longer-term cultural processes with research on their implications for a more active and participatory form of citizenship. They explore, in particular, the conditions for the emergence of a broad, pluri- and trans-ethnic social movement with a strong Latin@—and in part Spanish-speaking—component, capable of successfully challenging the prevailing social model, characterized as a hierarchical system of "racial relations" that perpetuates socioeconomic inequalities and also determines the conditions for exercizing urban political power.

However pioneering some of this work may be, the current as a whole seems to involve itself rather little in political debates of national interest. And yet there is much to be gleaned about the public activities of Latin@ groups—citizens and noncitizens—from the press, in English and in Spanish. It is true enough that some political scientists have trained a keen eye on the social and political struggles in certain urban areas. However, there has yet to emerge from critical thinking in these quarters any clear ideas about how the "empowerment" of Latin@s can contribute to the revitalizing of democracy more broadly. It is safe to say that such thinking has taken place in a more implicit than explicit vein to date. By contrast, the institutional forms and everyday practices of national politics are at the heart of the mainstream Latin@ reformist project, as embodied, for example, by the major Hispanic/Latin@ lobbying organizations. One could, indeed, imagine interesting and productive dialogues between the pragmatic reformers and those who, from a critical margin, prefer to channel their energy into honing the vision and the principles of a more egalitarian society, one more at ease with its historically given forms of cultural difference.

Stakes of the Future

The currents we have briefly reviewed can sometimes combine, as should be clear from the above, though not all are compatible. For example, the broad Latin@ reformist current has within it some components that lean toward a more civic-national posture, while others are clearly seeking to articulate a moderate, centrist form of multiculturalism. The social and economic content of this moderate multicultural vision may also vary: the Gregory Rodríguez School is clearly seeking affinities with U.S. conservatives even as it tries to legitimate in a conservative mode the multicultural theme. The Patrick Buchanan form of hard ethnic nationalism, reinforced by the recent anti-Hispanic posturing of Samuel Huntington, is in a category of its own, with at least one foot outside the democratic consensus insofar as it calls for more rigid and ethnicized distinctions among categories of citizens, and an even more tightly policed border than is now the case. The civic-nationalists, as we have seen, are trying to establish a mainstream democratic position in favor of a more "color-blind" and "universal" model based in the rehabilitation of the nation-state. They are not fundamentally hostile to all manifestations of cultural diversity, but they are, for the time being, on a very different wavelength from those, such as the critical "border thinkers," who foresee a bilingual future and call for more "translocal" ways of conceiving citizenship. This latter current, however, is only beginning to descend into the public arena with ideas about how to improve U.S. democracy and enrich its form of citizenship.

The work of these activists and/or researchers, in its most academic forms, is very far from exhausting the rich social-science literature in recent years on migratory flows, incorporation processes and the treatment of cultural differences. What can be said is that these currents' work structure and orient, more than most, public debates on the future of citizenship and the role of Latin@s in U.S. society.

The stakes of this nascent debate are of fundamental importance, not only for the future of U.S. society but also, as is eminently clear, its relation with the rest of the Americas. In the most optimistic hypothesis, the choices with which U.S. society are confronted in the coming years could lead it to define a new "politics of civilization" (Edgar Morin); that is, to respond to "the aspiration for more community, fraternity and freedom," in order to "improve relations between human beings, from inter-personal relations all the way up to planetary-scale relations" (Morin and Naïr 1997: 137–138). In other words, certain key decisions with which U.S. society will be confronted in the coming years will determine whether the border separating the United States from the countries of its southern periphery should be treated, even more than is now the case, as a "wall of separation," or whether U.S. society should be encouraged to reinvent itself as a zone of (multi)cultural and linguistic contact and as a laboratory for new national and transnational forms of democratic solidarity.

Notes

1. This paper is a product of several years' observation of the dynamics of Latinization by a U.S. native living in Europe. The author would be most interested in readers' comments and suggestions, which can be sent to the following address: jim.cohen@libertysurf.fr.

2. I have purposely left aside here any consideration of notions of Latinization or Latinity (*Latinidad*) associated with the idea of continuity from ancient Rome to the present day, via those countries which define themselves as "Latin": Italy, France, Spain, Portugal, Rumania, and the countries of Latin America belong to such organizations as the "Unión Latina"/ "Union Latine" (Paris).

References

Andreas, Peter (2000). *Border Games: Policing the U.S.-Mexico Divide*. Ithaca, N.Y., Cornell University Press.

Anzaldúa, Gloria (1987). *Borderlands/La Frontera: The New Mestiza*. San Francisco, Spinsters/Aunt Lute.

Aparicio, Frances and Susana Chávez-Silverman, eds. (1997). *Tropicalizations: Transcultural Representations of Latinidad*. Hanover, N.H. and London, Dartmouth University Press.

Bacon, David (2002). "International Solidarity, Oaxacan Style: Cross-Border Organizing at the Grassroots." Published on line by LabourNet Germany.

Basch, Linda, Glick Schiller, and Cristina Szanton Blanc (1994). *Nations Unbound: Transnational Projects, Postcolonial Predicaments, and Deterritorialized Nation-States*. Amsterdam, Gordon and Breach.

Darder, Antonia, and Rodolfo D. Torres, eds. (1998). *The Latino Studies Reader: Culture, Economy, and Society*. Malden, Mass., Blackwell.

Dávila, Arlene (2001). *Latinos, Inc.: The Marketing and Making of a People*. Berkeley, University of California Press.

Davis, Mike (2001, revised and expanded edition). *Magical Urbanism: Latinos Reinvent the U.S. City*. London and New York, Verso.

Favell, Adrian (1998). *Philosophies of Integration: Immigration and the Idea of Citizenship in France and Britain*. New York, Macmillan.

Flores, Juan (2000). *From Bomba to Hip-Hop: Puerto Rican Culture and Latino Identity*. New York, Columbia University Press.

Gerstle, Gary (2001). *American Crucible: Race and Nation in the Twentieth Century*. Princeton, N.J., Princeton University Press.

Gómez-Peña, Guillermo (1993). *Warrior for Gringostroika: Essays, Performance Texts, and Poetry*. Saint Paul, Minn., Graywolf Press.

Gracia, Jorge J. E., and Pablo De Greiff, eds. (2000). *Hispanics/Latinos in the United States: Ethnicity, Race and Rights*. New York, Routledge.

Grosfoguel, Ramón (2003). *Colonial Subjects: Puerto Ricans in a Global Perspective*. Berkeley, University of California Press.

Habell-Pallán, Michelle, and Mary Romero (2002). *Latino/a Popular Culture*. New York and London, New York University Press.

Hollinger, David (1995). *Post-Ethnic America: Beyond Multiculturalism*. New York, Basic Books.

—— (1996). "Group Preferences, Cultural Diversity and Social Democracy: Notes Toward a Theory of Affirmative Action." *Representations* 55, summer 1996, pp. 31–40.

Huntington, Samuel P. (2004). "The Hispanic Challenge." *Foreign Policy*, March–April 2004. Article incorporated into *Who Are We? The Challenges to America's National Identity*. New York, Simon and Schuster, 2004, chapter 9, pp. 221–256.

Jacoby, Tamar (2004). "The New Immigrants: A Progress Report." In Tamar Jacoby, ed., *Reinventing the Melting Pot: The New Immigrants and What It Means To Be American*. New York, Basic Books, pp. 17–29.

Jonas, Susanne (2001). "Reconceptualizing Citizenship in the Americas: Cross-Border Perspectives." In Norma Klahn et al., eds., *Las Nuevas Fronteras del Siglo XXI*. Mexico, La Jornada, UNAM, University of California–Santa Cruz, UAM.

Lao-Montes, Agustín, and Arlene Dávila, eds. (2000). *Mambo Montage: The Latinization of New York*. New York, Columbia University Press.

Lao-Montes, Agustín (2000). "Niuyol: Urban Regime, Latino Social Movements, Ideologies of Latinidad." In Agustín Lao-Montes, and Arlene Dávila, eds., *Mambo Montage: The Latinization of New York*. New York, Columbia University Press, pp. 119–157.

Laplantine, François, and Alexis Nouss (1997). *Le métissage*. Paris, Flammarion.

Mills, C. Wright (1959). *The Sociological Imagination*. New York, Oxford University Press.

Morales, Ed (2002). *Living in Spanglish: The Search for Latino Identity in America*. New York, Saint Martin's Press.

Morin, Edgar, and Sami Naïr (1997). *Une politique de civilisation*. Paris, Arléa.

Oboler, Suzanne (1995). *Ethnic Labels, Latinos Lives: Identity and the Politics of (Re)presentation in the United States*. Minneapolis, University of Minnesota Press.

Palafox, José (2001). *New World Border*. Documentary film, Peek Media, 28 minutes.

Rodríguez, Clara E., ed. (1998). *Latin Looks: Images of Latinas and Latinos in the U.S. Media*. Boulder and Oxford, Westview Press.

Rodríguez, Gregory (2004). "Mexican-Americans and the Mestizo Melting Pot." In Tamar Jacoby, ed., *Reinventing the Melting Pot: The New Immigrants and What It Means to be American*. New York, Basic Books, pp. 125–138.

Saldívar, José David (1997). *Border Matters: Remapping American Cultural Studies*. Berkeley, University of California Press.

Skrentny, John David (1996). *The Ironies of Affirmative Action: Politics, Culture, and Justice in America*. Chicago, University of Chicago Press.

—— (2002). *The Minority Rights Revolution*. Cambridge, MA: Belknap Press of Harvard University Press.

Smith, Rogers (1997). *Civic Ideals: Conflicting Visions of Citizenship in US History*. New Haven, Yale University Press.

Súarez-Orozco, Marcelo M., and Páez Mariela, eds. (2002). *Latinos Remaking America*. David Rockefeller Center for Latin American Studies, Harvard University, and University of California Press.

Torres, Andrés, and José E. Velásquez, eds. (1998). *The Puerto Rican Movement: Voices from the Diaspora*. Philadelphia, Temple University Press.

Torres, María de los Angeles (2001). *In the Land of Mirrors: Cuban Exile Politics in the United States*. Ann Arbor, University of Michigan Press.

—— (2003). "Transnational Political and Cultural Identities: Crossing Theoretical Borders." In Francisco H. Vázquez, and Rodolfo D. Torres, eds. *Latino/a Thought: Culture, Politics and Society*. Lanham, MD, Rowman & Littlefield, pp. 370–385.

Torres, Rodolfo, and George Katsiaficas, eds. (1999). *Latino Social Movements: Historical and Theoretical Perspectives*. New York and London, Routledge.

Valle, Victor M., and Rodolfo D. Torres (2000). *Latino Metropolis*. Minneapolis, University of Minnesota Press.

11

Decolonization from within the Americas

Latin@ Immigrant Responses to the U.S. National Security Regime, and the Challenges of Reframing the Immigration Debate

Susanne Jonas

Within the context of the post-1996, post-9/11 national security regime imposed by the U.S. government on immigrants and noncitizens generally, this article summarizes strategies of Latin@ immigrant communities for immigrant rights. Since 9/11/01, state policies and practices toward these migrants have become exceptionally repressive (beyond their generally colonizing, racialized nature), often conflating those immigrants with "terrorists." In this post-9/11 era, Latin@ immigrant communities have been challenged to move beyond their initially defensive stance, to undertake more proactive responses for legalization and citizenship—a process which will remain on the long-range agenda, given the structural realities in the Americas in an age of globalization.

Beyond the challenge for immigrant grassroots/community and advocacy organizations to fight against national security policies and for legalization and citizenship—a topic which we have more fully addressed elsewhere (Jonas and Tactaquin, 2004)—this article also formulates a challenge to the community of public intellectuals in Latin@ Studies: the battle for hegemony in defining the terrain and terms of the debate over Latin@ immigration. The challenge here is to reframe that debate from one that is dominated by "national security" concerns to one that reflects migrant interests. I shall argue that, although the national security regime and new nativist/racist attacks by anti-immigrant think tanks and even academics such as Samuel Huntington (2004a, 2004b) have forced their critics into a defensive posture for the time being, immigrant rights advocates should (and eventually will) be able to reshape that debate. My intention is to reflect upon this debate within the United States from the standpoint of its objective context in the hemisphere and worldwide. These reflections are designed to contribute to developing Latin@ Studies as an enterprise that grows out of a tradition of engaged research, with a goal of "changing the Americas from within the United States" (Bonilla 1998).

Anti-Immigrant Attacks, Patriot Act(s), and Latin@ Immigrant Responses

It is common knowledge that the sea change in U.S. immigration policy began well before 9/11/01, with the trio of anti-immigrant laws of 1996: the Illegal Immigrant Reform and Immigrant Responsibility Act, the Welfare Reform Act, and the Anti-Terrorism and Effective Death Penalty Act (the antiterrorist bill that gratuitously introduced punitive provisions against immigrants—Legal Permanent Residents as well as undocumented—none of whom had anything to do with the terrorist bombing in Oklahoma City). Taken together, the three laws stripped immigrants, legal and undocumented alike, of virtually all of the (limited) due process rights and (very limited) entitlements that previously existed; replaced appeals procedures with unchecked arbitrariness as the norm ("court stripping"); and imposed a harsh, punitive anti-immigrant regime.

From the end of the 1990s through mid-2001, there was a brief political opening in many quarters (including not only labor and business, but also in Congress and even the Supreme Court) to "fix" some excesses of the 1996 laws. Meanwhile, during the summer of 2001, President Bush was engaged in a dialogue with Mexican President Vicente Fox on the terms of a new guest-worker program, in which the Mexicans made a serious effort to attach provisions for "earned legalization," i.e., a path by which guest workers could earn the right to legalization. The Bush administration did not accept these legalization provisions, but many Democrats, to compensate for having been caught off guard by the Bush-Fox entente, felt pressured to go one step further, proposing to extend earned legalization to Latin@ immigrants—not only Mexicans, but others who had lived and worked in the United States for many years.

In the aftermath of 9/11/01, however, all such moves were abruptly halted, and immigrants once again—with a vengeance—became (and have remained) targets of repressive legislation and practices. Most widely publicized initially were the overt, unapologetic racial profiling measures and hate crimes directed against Arab Americans and South Asians. But the national security regime imposed by the Patriot Act and accompanying measures after 9/11 have also made U.S. state policies and practices toward Latin@ migrants far more draconian—in effect, criminalizing and punishing those immigrants/noncitizens, and in many respects treating them as if they were "terrorists." In the name of "national security," many thousands of migrants have been subjected to arbitrary roundups, preventive detention, and deportation, with no recourse to legal counsel or court appeals.

Furthermore, unlike many other provisions of the 2001 Patriot Act restricting civil liberties, the provisions affecting immigrants were not even slated for review under a 2005 "sunset clause," but were *deliberately designed* to remain permanent. Immigration law has been overused by the Department of Justice under Attorney General John Ashcroft, because it does not guarantee the due process rights available under criminal law. Finally, the proposed (still contested) CLEAR Act (Clear Law Enforcement for Criminal Alien Removal Act) would give state and local police forces legal authority to enforce federal immigration laws—in essence to be deputized as immigration agents. This proposal has been so controversial as to generate opposition from police forces around the country, and it will be debated in Congress after the 2004 elections. (For far greater detail on all of the above, see Jonas and Tactaquin 2004.)

Within the context of these domestic preemptive strikes against them, immigrant communities and rights organizations began to move beyond purely defensive struggles against exclusion by/from the dominant society. Once they recovered from the initial shock and organized defensively at the community level during the first year after 9/11, over time, they began to develop proactive coalitional strategies. Examples of these strategies at the national level include the fall 2003 Immigrant Workers Freedom Ride, organized largely by major labor unions with significant immigrant membership (especially the Hotel and Restaurant Employees Union), and subsequently, a series of activities for the summer of 2004 directed toward the 2004 elections. Similarly, in February and May 2004, broad coalitions of immigrant organizations came together in Latino Immigrant Summits in Washington, with extensive agendas for immigrant rights and legalization. These activities will doubtless continue beyond the 2004 elections.

However weak their prospects appear as of mid-2004 and for the immediate future, I argue that *proactive, decolonizing immigrant rights strategies for legalization and citizenship will not disappear, but will remain on the agenda within the United States and throughout the hemisphere.* This argument is based on several complex and interrelated factors.

A first set of factors stems from political action within the United States. As mentioned above, there are increased organizing initiatives by Latin@ immigrant communities and rights organizations ("agency" from within colonized communities). At another level of agency, the Latin@ vote is becoming increasingly important in U.S. electoral politics, and it frequently prioritizes immigrant rights issues—although this is not always the case and cannot be taken for granted. For many Latin@ voters, especially the more recently naturalized voters, once the concept of "earned legalization" gained a high profile (from Mexican demands) during the 2001 Bush-Fox discussions, this concept has become a goalpost of what to fight for. Since 9/11, earned legalization has been vilified as "amnesty" and treated as a tainted concept or dirty term—something like "socialism" during the height of the Cold War—nevertheless, this genie is out of the bottle, and cannot be shoved back inside.

A second set of factors is related to long-range structural considerations in the Americas that are breaking down borders in the hemisphere. To mention the most prominent of these:

1. the well-documented, permanent, and ongoing need for (addiction to) low-wage Latin American migrant labor in the United States, even during periods of political immigrant bashing. The centrality of low-wage immigrant labor in the United States, particularly in the neoliberal economy of the early twenty-first century, is evidenced by new "guest-worker" proposals in late 2003 and early 2004, from both Democrats and Republicans—even while anti-immigrant measures are proliferating. These include the bipartisan "AgJobs" bill (covering agricultural workers only), the Bush guest-worker initiative, and a more progressive bill sponsored by Senator Kennedy and House Democrats, which, unlike the Bush initiative, includes a path toward earned legalization;
2. the essential role of migrant remittances in sustaining the economies of the home ("sending") countries in Latin America (see Central American example below); and
3. new free trade agreements—beyond the North American Free Trade Agreement (NAFTA), the planned Central American Free Trade Agreement (CAFTA), and the Free Trade Area of the Americas (FTAA). All of these are following the neoliberal NAFTA model, and (like NAFTA and other free trade agreements around the world), will certainly increase migration after opening up borders to capital.

A third set of factors grows out of recent international (global) immigrant rights agendas and agreements—not yet widely accepted, in most cases, but as a focus of organizing. The most important of these are the long-standing United Nations Convention on Refugee Rights (1951), and the more recent U.N. International Convention for the Protection of Rights for All Migrant Workers and Members of their Families—rights that workers carry across borders (which was written in 1990 but only entered into effect on July 1, 2003, and faces a long uphill battle for implementation). In May 2003, the International Commission on Human Security issued a report calling for a new paradigm of *human security* of migrants ("human security" serving as a framework to counter "national security"). In 2004, the International Labor Organization took up the theme of treatment of migrant workers, and the new Global Commission on International Migration began to function. For the most part (aside from the Convention on Refugee Rights), these international frameworks have not been ratified or implemented by migrant-receiving countries, but they are already gaining increased attention, they serve as goals for migrant rights organizing, and eventually they could establish higher standards for the treatment of migrants (Jonas and Tactaquin 2004, relying heavily on Tactaquin's work with Migrant Rights International).

For all of these reasons, Latin@ immigrant advocacy organizations within the United States have begun to coordinate with migrant rights organizations across borders in their home countries in Latin America and the Caribbean, hemisphere-wide. NAFTA and its planned future clones have raised the obvious demands that cross-border mobility for capital be matched by mobility and rights for labor. In addition, and as a result of pressure from migrant rights organizations, issues of cross-border and labor rights for migrants are beginning to be addressed by para-state institutions such as the Inter-American Human Rights Court of the Organization of American States. A key to the potential power of proactive, decolonizing rights strategies "from within" U.S. Latin@ immigrant communities lies in *their transnational ties throughout the region of the Americas*—i.e., their increasing coordination with counterpart communities and organizations in the countries of origin. In other words, we are seeing the gradual emergence of transregional civil society networks for migrant rights within the hemisphere.

Transregional Central American Advocacy Networks and Perspectives

To illustrate the above points, I shall draw briefly upon examples of these dynamics from the transregional political advocacy networks of Central Americans (primarily Salvadorans and Guatemalans). I have worked with these organizations in California for over a decade, and more recent fieldwork includes Guatemalan and Salvadoran communities, both in the United States and in the sending countries, with Mexico as the country of transit. The migrant networks from these Central American countries have a particular dynamic because their leaders and activists emerged in large measure from struggles to break out of political exclusion and repression and achieve democracy in the home countries during the insurrectionary civil wars of the 1980s. Many of them, at least in the cohort of the 1980s, came to the United States with strong commitments to achieving full political, social/economic rights, and sought asylum on political grounds.

The objective situation of these refugees and immigrants today is specific to the circumstances under which they began coming to the United States. This is in large part an in-limbo population, neither legal nor illegal, because of its particular history during the 1980s and the 1990 *ABC v. Thornburgh* settlement.[1] During the 1990s and into the 2000s, the migrant streams continued, more for economic than political reasons; Salvadorans and Guatemalans came to constitute the second largest Latin@ population in California. As their circumstances changed, the Salvadoran and Guatemalan organizations in the United States were able to transform themselves from the 1980s networks of solidarity with the insurrectionary and mass movements and for human rights in Central America to immigrant rights networks during the 1990s and into the early 2000s (see Hamilton and Chinchilla 200; Jonas 1996). Even without having been legalized or naturalized, these Central Americans have been living and working in the United States, many of them for 15–20 years. They have become the central economic players in rebuilding Central America economically after the wars of the 1980s and subsequent natural disasters (Hurricane Mitch of late 1998, affecting particularly Honduras and Nicaragua, and the Salvadoran earthquakes of 2001). Without their remittances, the home-country economies would not be solvent, even to the very minimal extent that they are today.

Since the mid-1990s, Central American immigrant rights organizations have worked in their communities to defend/protect their rights—e.g., through informational campaigns and legal advice. In the Spring of 2003, these organizations made an important leap forward, with a February 21–23, 2003, meeting in Houston, sponsored by the Chicago-based Enlaces America, at which time the Coalition of Guatemalan Immigrants Residing in the United States (CONGUATE) joined forces with the much stronger and more established Salvadoran American National Network (SANN). According to the conclusions from the Houston meeting, even when the possibilities for immigrant rights legislation in Congress were virtually blocked, there was a real opportunity for these organizations to greatly increase their social base in their communities. Subsequent meetings included networks of other nationalities and eventually evolved into the Latin@ "Summits" of 2004. They could enrich existing immigrant rights agendas (developed over decades mainly by Mexican American organizations) from their uniquely Central American perspective—"uniquely" Central American, because of their political struggles against exclusion and for democracy during the 1980s, experiences which could guide their organizing within a repressive (post-1996, post-9/11) context in the United States.

While focusing on legalization/ rights struggles waged by Central American activists in the United States, I also locate them as players or actors on a regional stage that is undergoing a series of structural transformations. The new free trade proposals (CAFTA with the United States and Plan Puebla Panama, Mexico's "NAFTA" for Central America) will reshape the future of the region if/when they are implemented; this is the structural underpinning of the regional stage. At the level of "agency," the immigrant rights organizations in the United States are increasingly working together with coalitions in the sending countries, which have their own worldviews and "imaginarios." The Guatemalan coalition, National Forum for Migration in Guatemala (MENAMIG), has been particularly well structured and proactive. Hence, the analysis of immigrant rights/legalization struggles in the United States must also include perspectives from the Central American sending countries and Mexico, which share, but also go beyond, the legalization agendas defined by U.S.-based players.

A clear example of these transregional dynamics is RROCM (Regional Network of Civil Society Organizations for Migration). This network, whose demands focus on labor mobility and human rights for migrants, has made significant inroads as a network parallel to the regional association of governments, closely monitoring and pressuring governmental actions on migration—all of this through the "Puebla Process" (covering the United States, Canada, Mexico, Central America, and the Dominican Republic). The interactive, transregional actions of this coalition, in which the Mexican advocacy organization "Sin Fronteras" plays a central role, will likely be reproduced in other subregions of the Americas.

The multilayered, multidimensional stage described here (including the United States, Mexico, and Central America) presents a complex panorama that differs in some respects from the U.S.-Mexico bilateral relationship. Multiple actors, in different geographical locations, from diverse levels or strata—state actors, NGOs, and migrant communities themselves—are negotiating new relationships, at times, outside their own strictly "national" identifications. This regional stage is becoming increasingly interconnected and interactive, and the contacts among the different actors are multiple, overlapping, and increasingly dense. Tracing the process as it is happening now, we can see that initiatives are coming from different sectors/ locales at different moments in the process, and that the initiatives undertaken in one location can affect, even energize players in other locales. At the same time, however, state policies initiated by the United States (and Mexico, toward Central Americans) continue to affect multiple players in diverse locations, *in effect limiting their real options.*

This example demonstrates the importance of currently emerging practices and paradigms being generated by migration activists from the sending countries in the Americas. *Their worldviews are not permeated by considerations of "national security,"* as is the case so pervasively in the United States. From my own experiences in Central America and Mexico, I learned the importance of these cross-border coalitions and contacts for immigrant rights advocates, including public intellectuals in the United States (see below), in order to avoid unintentional assumptions of the colonial society in which we are located. Particularly since 9/11, it has been easier to see those embedded assumptions in the United States with much greater clarity from *outside* the United States, and to understand/imagine alternatives, such as the transregional, interactive process described above.

Implications for U.S. Citizens, and the Ongoing Problem of Second-Class Citizenship

Viewing the United States as the northern/colonial zone of the Americas, it can be seen that the fate of immigrants and their transnational organizing efforts is key to the future of democracy in the United States. This is, of course, is an argument that all U.S. citizens should be concerned about the attacks against immigrants/noncitizens (and should have been concerned since Proposition 187 in California and the 1996 immigrant-bashing laws in Congress [Jonas 1999]). However, this has become much clearer in the wake of 9/11/01, and the various wars and preemptive strikes abroad and domestically. Since then, we have seen that the growth of an entire national security state apparatus, embodied in the Patriot Act, poses serious threats to democracy in the colonizing society itself and to its citizens. In 2003, there were proposals for extending and expanding the Patriot Act to a "Patriot Act II," which included provisions to arbitrarily strip "suspect" citizens of their citizenship and numerous other provisions far more invasive than those of Patriot I. Because that proposal, when leaked from within the Department of Justice, aroused widespread opposition, the Bush administration switched to a "stealth" course, attaching pieces of Patriot II to other legislation (Martin, 2003), or passing them separately, under another name—as is the case with the CLEAR Act. (This is only one of many examples cited in Jonas and Tactaquin 2004). In short, there are obvious issues of self-interest to U.S. citizens, in protecting their own civil liberties.

But beyond self-interest, the treatment of immigrants/noncitizens affects the quality of democracy for all citizens of the United States. For one thing, the anti-immigrant discussion has brought such proposals as the repeal of the Fourteenth Amendment of the Constitution, in order to deny citizenship to children of undocumented immigrants who are born in the United States. Although this very extreme proposal has not yet succeeded, the fact that it continues to resurface (and even went "mainstream," in the 1996 platform of the Republican Party) constitutes an evident threat to the U.S. Constitution and to democracy in the United States. (For significantly expanded development of these arguments, see Donnelly 2001, and Jonas and Tactaquin 2004.)

More broadly, I argue, it is not a healthy situation for the fabric of U.S. society (or the entire hemisphere) to have a rapidly and ever-increasing mass of undocumented/in-limbo migrants whose labor (with or without legal papers) is essential to sustaining the U.S. economy, but who are prohibited from participating in U.S. public life. Many of these migrants have been here for 15–20 years, they have children born here (hence, citizens); they are supporting both the U.S. economy and their home-country economies, but they are being denied any path to legalization. (This situation would be perpetuated if the 2004 Bush initiative on guest workers from Mexico were enacted.) A more democratic process would be to incorporate these migrants by giving them a path toward legalization and naturalization.

There are historical parallels. It was impossible to consider South Africa a democracy (even for its white citizens) so long as it was an apartheid regime. Similarly, looking at the United States today, it is no longer possible to pursue racist, colonizing strategies or repressive/punitive strategies against Third World immigrants and noncitizens without damaging the quality of democracy for citizens of the colonial power. *In short, I argue, the challenge of reframing the issues of immigrant rights in the shadow of the national security state is one that should be of concern to all U.S. citizens—and additionally, one that will remain on our twenty-first-century public policy agenda throughout the Americas.*

A final problem must be mentioned because it complicates and compounds the above issues of citizenship for migrants from Third World countries and peoples of color in the United States. Even if a path toward legalization and eventual citizenship were to be established for a significant number of Latin@ (and other Third World) migrants within the United States, they will face the problem that the African American community has faced since the end of the Civil War: the problem of *second-class citizenship, as a result of racialization, which leads to living under second-class socioeconomic and psychosocial conditions.* Precedents for this kind of second-class citizenship also exist in the history of Latin@ American populations within the United States: for Mexican Americans in the Southwest (since the Mexican-American War of 1946–1948), and for Puerto Ricans (since the Spanish-American War of 1898). This issue of exclusion by means of racialized, second-class citizenship, which has plagued Western societies for centuries, since the French Revolution (Wallerstein 2003), has been and will continue to be explored by many writers and activists.

Reframing the Immigration Debate: The Intellectual Challenge in a National Security Era

Outside the realm of state policy, but within the ambience created by the national security state, racializing cultural anti-immigrant discourses are being reproduced by public intellectuals. This comes as no surprise from self-defined restrictionist, anti-immigrant think tanks in Washington, such as the Center for Immigration Studies and organizations such as the Federation for American Immigration Reform (FAIR). However, it took a new turn in 2004, when Samuel Huntington, Harvard's premier political scientist, and a very public intellectual, published a new book, *Who Are We?* The book's most polemical chapter in *Foreign Policy* (March–April 2004) suggested that Mexican migrants pose a "threat" to the unity of U.S. society. His most publicized argument to prove the "threat" is that many still speak their native Spanish (without specifying that this is largely at home, even while learning English and speaking it at work). This eminent professor appears to be promoting the (uniquely U.S.-based) logic that it is somehow better to speak only one language than to speak two languages.

Elsewhere (Chapters 8 and 10 of the book), he attacks dual citizenship (as "foreign to the American Constitution," implying "dual loyalties," rather than exclusive loyalty to the United States), as well as hometown associations, asserting (213) that "remittances flowing out of America do not speak English." The idea that the immigrant practice of sending remittances to families and communities in their home countries is a sign of dangerous "dual loyalties," which somehow detracts from becoming fully "Americanized," is ludicrous, and totally obscures the reality that, without these remittances, U.S. taxpayers would have to support the Mexican economy. He also argues that home-country governments (Mexico and others) use diasporas to serve their own interests (rather than U.S. interests)—e.g., through hometown associations and the "matricula consular" (identity card) issued by consulates to undocumented immigrants.

My reflections here are not designed to answer Huntington, but rather, to comment upon the nature of the contest for hegemony in the immigration debate—a broader debate, because other authors had previously taken up similar themes (see below), and because Huntington's attack was so virulent as to stimulate a wave of responses. Seen from the viewpoint of the United States alone, the national security stance is on the offensive in 2004, at the level of both state and civil society; hence, in this era of Patriot Act(s), it is not surprising that Huntington writes "as a patriot" and focuses obsessively on Mexican immigrants' insufficient patriotism/exclusive loyalty to the United States (xvi). In the name of preserving the "Anglo-Protestant" culture as "America's core culture" against the threats of "identity politics" and diversity associated with immigrants, Huntington exhibits the worst form of identity politics: U.S. nativism.

There has been a broad variety of critiques and responses to Huntington's restrictionism. In the subsequent issue of *Foreign Policy* (May–June 2004) and in other prominent publications, a number of eminent migration scholars have used data-based studies to refute his position—e.g., it is *not* the case that Mexican/Latin@ immigrants are refusing to learn English or are dividing the country culturally or are insufficiently patriotic (and so on). In short, the debate has taken place on the terrain of (primarily cultural) assimilationism. Some of the scholars answering Huntington build on the pioneering work of Richard Alba and Victor Nee (2003, and previous articles) in reconceptualizing assimilation, from the older and generally coercive state-imposed meaning to a view of assimilation as a natural social process that occurs differently for different migrant groups—and in which migrants change the culture of our society even as they are adapting to its "mainstream" culture. And yet within this discussion, some critics have exhibited a notable degree of defensiveness. One such critic (Daniel Griswold in *Foreign Policy*, May–June 2004) even attacks bilingual education, multiculturalism, and welfare in his response to Huntington. This defensive edge can be seen when some of Huntington's critics focus mainly and simplistically on the "unity" of U.S. society, without giving equal priority (or any priority) to immigrant rights. Hence, it is important to emphasize the distinction between assimilation and immigrant *incorporation* with political rights—the latter being a proactive and rights-centered (not defensive) stance, as I argue below.

Various examples of defensive assimilationism are also sprinkled throughout Tamar Jacoby's edited book, *Re-Inventing the Melting Pot* (2004). Aside from a few openly anti-immigrant articles and some that openly or implicitly support immigrant rights, many authors in this collection present arguments that are not restrictionist, but are based on old-style assimilationist premises. Elsewhere (*Los Angeles Times,* 3/3/04), Jacoby herself, who is based at the conservative Manhattan Institute, credited President Bush as a "champion" for immigrants, and his 2004 guest-worker initiative as "radical" (although it opposes legalization); she and 13 other self-defined conservatives, including Newt Gingrich, also defended the Bush proposal in hostile territory ("A Conservative Manifesto for Solving Border Woes," *Arizona Republic,* 8/15/04). This support for low-wage labor without a path to legalization is an example of the current among some antirestrictionists not to be concerned about immigrant *rights* or about the broader dangers to U.S. society of the model of immigration without political rights (see Donnelly 2001). What is too often lost in this discussion is the distinction between assimilation and political incorporation through legalization and citizenship.

A combination of both restrictionism and assimilationism had previously emerged in a major two-part essay in the *New York Review of Books* ("Who Should Get In?" November 29 and December 20, 2001) by Harvard professor and author Christopher Jencks, known since the 1960s as an eminent liberal and an expert on racial inequality in education. Jencks made surprisingly anti-(Mexican) immigrant arguments, based largely on those of Cuban American Harvard economist George Borjas, about the negative economic impact of migrants on wages for U.S. workers, and ended up blaming the victims rather than making the case for higher immigrant labor standards. Jencks also entered onto cultural territory, criticizing the Mexican migrant because "he" speaks Spanish and because "*he* clings to his national identity, sends money back to his parents, goes home for holidays, tries to buy property in Mexico for his retirement…, and retains his Mexican citizenship."—as if to suggest some pernicious "dual loyalty."

Given the xenophobic mood within the United States, perhaps it is not surprising that restrictionists and defensive assimilationists have dominated the debate *in the United States*—among intellectuals as well as ordinary citizens. Since 9/11, assimilationists of various stripes have been on the front lines in answering the most extreme U.S. restrictionists, who represent undocumented (or all) immigrants of color as if they were equivalent to (or as dangerous as) terrorists. *Stepping beyond U.S. borders and adopting a regional framework,* however (see Jonas 1999), a very different logic emerges. From the standpoint of Latin America and other immigrant-sending areas of the Third World, the U.S. national security regime has sparked sharp criticism and resistance at many levels—from social protests and governmental pressures, to the media and intellectual journals, to the steadfast refusal of individuals to stop migrating.

A regional perspective makes clearer the reality that structurally, in this era of neoliberal globalization (and in the Americas, regional globalization), the very policies of the colonial power are stimulating migration. This is the major lesson of NAFTA, which is now being extended to new entities—CAFTA and FTAA. In short, the borders have been opened up not simply by poor workers migrating from Latin America, as is presented to us in the U.S. media, but by capital, seeking new investments abroad in the hemisphere, and by the governments (United States and Latin America) promoting a development strategy based on those investments. The Americas are being integrated *by capital.* The United States is no longer simply a national sovereign state; it is the northern zone of the Americas. So long as neoliberalism, bringing job cutbacks and grossly underpaid jobs, is the name of the development game, and armed resistance in the countries of origin is no longer an option (as some thought it to be, during the 1960s–1980s), migration is a natural response by many Latin Americans. Even more important is the total dependence on low-wage immigrant labor on the part of corporate capital in the United States, which actively recruits such laborers. For these reasons, as has been demonstrated by a plethora of migration scholars such as Douglas Massey, Nestor Rodríguez, Jacqueline Hagan, and Wayne Cornelius—and is also shown by U.S. government statistics—the massive U.S. government efforts to prevent migration from Latin America through punitive border crackdowns have been only partially effective.

Viewing the United States as the northern zone of the Americas, incorporation of Latin@ migrants through legalization is a much more realistic and stabilizing approach overall than the exclusionary, nativist, racializing rejections. From this hemispheric perspective, it is much easier to see that the Huntington attack is itself a *defensive* attempt to preserve the "Anglo-Protestant" culture, and that the *"core culture" of the United States, as part of the Americas, is not "Anglo-Protestant" but extremely diverse.* Moreover, cultural and racial/ethnic diversity are compounded by diversity of gender/sexuality: the stereotypical views about migrants, based largely on the outdated view of "most" migrants as single males, or males accompanied by female spouses, has been refuted by the numbers. In other ways as well, feminist scholars (Pierrette Hondagneu-Sotelo, Patricia Pessar, Denise Segura, Patricia Zavella, to name only a few) have shown how gendered perspectives are transforming the entire migration paradigm.

Finally, although I cannot develop the theme in this article, I do want to point to the last decade's reformulations about citizenship as an important element in the intellectual challenge of developing proactive, nondefensive analyses of migration. The traditional, legal meanings of citizenship (incorporation into the dominant receiving society—e.g., through legalization and naturalization) must be brought together with new, nontraditional literatures that additionally address *transformative* meanings (transformation of the incorporating society) and participatory citizenship beyond state borders (rights and entitlements that accrue to all human beings by virtue of being human beings, and therefore are rights that people carry with them when they cross borders).[2] Virtually all of these nontraditional approaches emphasize participatory democracy and the "politics of difference," and serve as important additions to the traditional legal incorporative/ inclusionary notions of citizenship—i.e., political rights for migrant workers, and a path toward legalization and citizenship. In any case, these theoretical/ epistemological reformulations could prove essential as part of the intellectual endeavor of moving from defensive to hegemonic grounds.

Of course, it is not easy to get from the defensive to a hegemonic stance. As Edward Said and Daniel Barenboim (2002, 155) put it so eloquently in speaking about migration and music:

> The humanistic mission has to be able to maintain difference but without the domination and bellicosity that normally accompany affirmations of identity. And that's very, very hard to do. *We are going against every conceivable current that exists.* [emphasis added]

For the purposes of this article, the key is that transnational/ transregional civil society immigrant rights advocacy organizations working together across borders in the Americas (such as RROCM, described above) have begun to blaze a trail that intellectuals in the United States and Latin America can and should follow. Most important, public intellectuals in the United States must begin to develop cross-border ties, in order to strengthen their (our) own hand in the battle for hegemony in the immigration debate, to combat the national security discourse, and to reframe that debate in a serious way *inside the United States.*[3] This is one way we can begin to fulfill the promise of Latin@ Studies as an engaged discipline, one that contributes to the broader social goal of decolonizing the Americas from within the United States.

Notes

1. *American Baptist Church v. Thornburgh* was a class action lawsuit filed against the attorney general, in protest against the massive denial of asylum petitions by Salvadorans (97%) and Guatemalans (98%) fleeing the civil wars in their countries. The lawsuit was settled in December 1990, when the Department of Justice agreed to re-hear the petitions of each of the several hundred thousand Guatemalans and Salvadorans on a case-by-case basis. Given the very limited resources in the INS for immigration *services* as opposed to enforcement during the 1990s and early 2000s, most of the plaintiffs have remained in limbo for many years; they have not been legalized, but they cannot be deported, and they are permitted to work legally in the United States.

2. In addition to literatures on cross-border citizenship and transformative/cultural citizenship, there are other nontraditional approaches that emphasize participatory democracy and the "politics of difference," which have been extensively developed by feminist and indigenous theorists, and some postcolonial theorists focusing on *de-racialization* of citizenship.

3. This would not be the first time that Latin American ideas have made a major impact in the U.S.; one example that comes to mind is dependency theory, during the late 1960s and throughout the 1970s, which, for all its defects and weaknesses, did put modernization theorists who were shaping U.S. Latin America policy on the defensive, and eventually vanquished modernization theory, at least for a time (before modernization theory took its revenge, in the form of neoliberalism). More globally, several core concepts of dependency theory fed into and have been preserved in world-systems theory.

References

Alba, Richard, and Victor Nee. 2003. *Remaking the American Mainstream: Assimilation and Contemporary Immigration.* Cambridge: Harvard University Press.

Bonilla, Frank. 1998. "Changing the Americas from within the United States." In *Borderless Borders: U.S. Latinos, Latin Americans, and the Paradox of Interdependence,* eds. Frank Bonilla et al. Philadelphia: Temple University Press.

Donnelly, Paul. 2001. "The End of Ellis Island: Bush Abandons the American Immigrant Ideal while Democrats Dither." *The American Prospect Online* (April 5).

Hamilton, Nora, and Norma Chinchilla. 2001. *Seeking Community in a Global City: Guatemalans and Salvadorans in Los Angeles.* Philadelphia: Temple University Press.

Huntington, Samuel. 2004a. *Who Are We? The Challenges to America's National Identity.* New York: Simon and Schuster.

———. 2004b. "The Hispanic Challenge." *Foreign Policy* (March–April)—and responses in *Foreign Policy* (May–June).

Jacoby, Tamar (ed.). 2004. *Re-Inventing the Melting Pot.* New York: BasicBooks.

Jencks, Christopher. 2001. "Who Should Get In?" *New York Review of Books* (November 29 and December 20).

Jonas, Susanne. 1999. "Rethinking Immigration Policy and Citizenship in the Americas." In *Immigration: A Civil Rights Issue for the Americas,* eds. Susanne Jonas and Suzie Dod Thomas. Wilmington, DE: Scholarly Resources.

———. 1996. "Transnational Realities and Anti-Immigrant State Policies: Issues Raised by the Experiences of Central American Immigrants and Refugees in a Tri-National Region." In *Latin America in the World Economy,* eds. Roberto Korzeniewicz and William Smith. Westport, CT: Greenwood.

Jonas, Susanne, and Catherine Tactaquin. 2004. "Latino Immigrant Rights in the Shadow of the National Security State: Responses to Domestic Pre-emptive Strikes." *Social Justice* (Spring–Summer).

Martin, David. 2003. "With a Whisper, not a Bang: Bush Signs Parts of Patriot Act II into Law—Stealthily." *San Antonio Current* (December 24).

Said, Edward, and Daniel Barenboim. 2002. *Parallels and Paradoxes: Explorations in Music and Society.* New York: Pantheon.

Wallerstein, Immanuel. 2003. "Citizens All? Citizens Some! The Making of the Citizen." *Comparative Studies in Society and History* (October).

Latin@ Century, Pacific Century

Twenty-First-Century Possibilities in World-Systems Perspective

Thomas Ehrlich Reifer

At noon on one day coming, human strength will fill the streets,
Of every city on our planet, hear the sound of angry feet,
With business freezed up in the harbour, the kings will pull upon their hair
And the banks will shudder to a halt, and the artists will be there.
Cause it won't take long, it won't take too long at all,
It won't take long, and you may say,
"I don't think I can be a part of that," and it makes me want to say,
"Don't you want to see yourself that strong?"
Division between the peoples will disappear that honoured day
And though oceans lie between us, lifted candles light the way,
Half will join their hands by moonlight, the rest under a rising sun . . .
And beware you sagging diplomats for you will not hear one gun
And though our homes be torn and ransacked we will not be undone
For as we let ourselves be bought, we're going to let ourselves be free
And if you think we stand alone, look again and you will see
—FR Ferron, "It Won't Take Long," *Shadows on a Dime,* 1994

Immanuel Wallerstein and others (see this volume) have brilliantly explored the changing political identity of Latin@s, in ways that illuminate the central role of racial, ethnic and national oppression in the world-system, and the complexity of capturing this over time. This chapter focuses on analyzing the situation of Latin@s today in the context of racial, ethnic and class formation over roughly the last century, focusing particularly on their growing importance in the Southern California logistics sector. This global city-region is at the heart of the flexible just-in-time (JIT) production and distribution systems of the Pacific Rim, the key nexus of the contemporary world market. The critical role of Latin@ labor in this strategic nexus may provide opportunities for new alliances in the United States and across transnational borders, aimed at achieving a true decolonization of the global system, based on greater fraternity, liberty and equality.

Latin@ Demographic Growth

As of 2002, approximately one of every eight persons living in the United States was of Latin@ origin, and every two of these foreign born. U.S. Latin@s today compose a population of over 37 million. They are predominantly of Mexican origin (some 66.9%, followed by Central and South American with 14.3%). Latin@s are located predominately in the Southwest and are astonishingly urbanized, second only to Asians (though their rural presence may be substantially underestimated). As opposed to whites, over 22% of whom live in nonmetropolitan areas, Latin@s compose only about 8% of those in nonmetropolitan zones; just under half of all Latin@s live inside the central cities of metropolitan areas, and roughly the same number live right outside of them. Occupationally, Latin@s are most commonly concentrated in service and "precision" production, such as craft, repair, and transportation (U.S. Census, 2003; Davis, 2000).

Latin@s presence in the United States is set to increase from 2000 to 2050 by 188%, growing to some 103 million in a total U.S. population of some 420 million. In California alone, Latin@s—who already compose an estimated 500,000 factory and 1.5 million service workers—are slated to increase to some 48% of the population by 2040, with non-Latin@ whites numbering only 31%. Soon after 2050, whites will become a demographic minority in the United States, eclipsed by a majority population of persons of color, with Latin@s growing from some 13 to roughly 25% of the total U.S. population (U.S. Census, 2003; LAT, March 18, 2004, p. A18; Davis, 2000: 144).

The political participation of Latin@s is increasing tremendously today, as indicated by the surge in Latin@ voting in presidential elections. Latin@ voting registration and actual voting rose by 28 and 16%, respectively, in 1996, making this group an increasingly strategic electoral bloc (Davis, 2000: 130–135). Yet though there are roughly 18.4 million Latin@s of voting age, some 7 million are disenfranchised, without citizenship rights, a condition likely to persist for some time (Davis, 2000: 129). Nevertheless, this massive increase in the Latin@ population in the United States and the concomitant recomposition of most of the U.S. urban core into areas populated primarily by persons of color presages the future transformation of the United States and the global system, especially as these groups become more politically active.

Latin@ Century, Pacific Century: Latin@s and Logistics in the Pacific Rim

Today, Latin@s are an increasingly strategic group of workers, given both their rising numbers and role in the transportation industry. The logistics sector—ports, railways, trucking and distribution centers (DCs)—long critical, is an increasingly strategic component of globalized flexible production and distribution networks. Historically, the struggles of workers in transport played a central role in setting the terrain for labor-capital relations and labor-market segmentation as a whole. Indeed, it was the violent defeat of more inclusive visions of labor organization—notably during the railroad strikes of the late nineteenth century—that helped split the U.S. labor movement. The movement divided into a more radical current, which was largely crushed, and one increasingly convinced "that broad, class-based strategies and industrial ambitions were too costly and self-defeating" (Forbath, 1991: 78).

Thus, old white immigrant craft workers embraced a business unionism eschewing all social legislation, especially universal forms (Mink, 1986). The recurrent defeats of inclusive radical unionism more open to racial, ethnic, and gender diversity decisively shaped the racial segmentation of U.S. labor, its various organization forms and related unequal systems of civil, political and social citizenship, stratified by race, class, gender and ethnicity. In the twentieth century, Cold War anticommunism ensured the recurrent defeat of this alternative inclusive vision of social movement unionism. U.S. military spending provided a welfare state for corporations, the rich, and middle strata, replete with veterans benefits and private welfare states tied to firms, which citizen-soldiers—as well as organized workers in the core of the industrial economy—were forced to accept in lieu of universal social benefits for the working class as a whole. Concomitant with this incorporation of labor as junior partners in U.S. hegemony was the ejection of left-led unions from the Congress of Industrial Organizations (CIO), the major industrial federation of U.S. labor that historically played a much more progressive role on issues of race, class and gender than its craft-based counterparts in the American Federation of Labor (AFL)

(Stepan-Norris and Zeitlin, 2003). These defeats of inclusive visions of labor ensured that the growing sections of the postwar U.S. working class—Latin@s, women, persons of color, immigrants and white-collar workers—were left largely unorganized, with the consequence that white workers and the middle strata were swept up in the rise of a broad-based New Right culminating in Reaganism (Davis, 1986).

Yet in recent decades, changes in global production have altered the terrain for labor in ways that may provide new strategic openings, most especially for the burgeoning Latin@ workforce. In the 1970s and 1980s, rising global trade and flexible production networks, developing in tandem with the ascent of the Pacific Rim, saw this region sweep past the North Atlantic as the principal U.S. trading partner (Davis, 1986: 251). In sharp contrast to the Fordist-based transatlantic economy, where increases in military spending and wages stimulated aggregate demand, the transpacific one is based on huge inflows of foreign capital recycled into the United States, which serves as a consumer of last resort (with Wal-Mart the single largest importer), as evidenced by massive U.S. trade and current account deficits (see Davis, 1986: ch. 6; Davis and Sawhney, 2002; *Journal of Commerce*, 4/29/02). Today, the logistics sector of the Pacific Rim is an increasingly important strategic site for global capital and labor, linking up overseas production from China, Mexico and other locations to the huge markets of Southern California, the Sunbelt and the entire United States.

This radical demographic transformation of U.S. workers—notably the growth of Latin@ labor—is today intersecting with the rise of a Pacific Rim–centered global production and trading regime. The centrality of workers of color and women, who now make up the majority of the U.S. working class, may provide a fertile social base for a new labor upsurge, in which Latin@s will undoubtedly play a lead role. For the enormous changes in the landscape of transnational corporate power today—in which large retail firms such as Wal-Mart with their massive logistics and flexible production networks hold increasing sway—are putting potential strategic power in the hands of Latin@ labor.

The ascendancy of Wal-Mart and other giant retailers is arguably predicated on flexible production and distribution networks of manufactured goods coming from the Pacific Rim into the United States. And the invisible heart of the new geography of power in the global economy are the global supply chains of the giant multinational discount retail firms such as Wal-Mart and the specialized logistics firms—sometimes called Third or Fourth Party Logistics firms or 3 and 4PLs—they use. Like global cities, these logistics firms represent the necessary infrastructure of the global economy. These firms are a critical component of producer services, and as Saskia Sassen (2001: 91) notes, "services are produced for organizations, whether private sector firms or governmental entities, rather than for final consumers." Yet while Sassen has brilliantly underscored other aspects of the technophysical infrastructure of the global economy, the central role of the logistics complex stressed here has seldom

been explored. This logistical infrastructure, though, is fundamental to current configurations of transnational production, trade and finance. Moreover, the growing power of giant retail firms such as Wal-Mart and the related drive to cut costs is putting a downward pressure on wages as a whole, in logistics, global production, and the retail and grocery sector (see Boarnet and Crane, 1999; Peoples 1998). The 2003–2004 West Coast lockout and strike of grocery workers demonstrated the stakes involved, as the planned expansion of big box grocers, most especially the imminent arrival of Wal-Mart supercenters into the Southern California region, is expected to radically depress the wages and benefits of these workers by over a billion dollars a year (see Boarnet and Crane, 1999). At the forefront of the attempt to hold the line against Wal-Mart's degradation of labor were the rank and file locked-out and striking workers, nearly two-thirds of them women, and over a third of whom were Latin@, Asian or black (Shaiken, 2003).

This increased importance of logistics and supply chain management comes from the role of flexible JIT production and distribution in connecting world supply and demand in the global market centered around the Pacific Rim. Individually, the Ports of L.A. and Long Beach are by far the biggest entryways for goods coming into the United States, largely from Asia. Together they are the third-largest container ports in the world, following only Singapore and Hong Kong. The predominance of U.S.-based multinationals, especially giant discount retailers such as Wal-Mart and Home Depot, is evident in import flows into the United States (*Journal of Commerce*, 4/29/02, 7/8/02). U.S. waterborne foreign trade using container ships in 2000 came to 142,332,000 metric tons, over 50% of which comes into the United States from the Far East and Southeast Asia. Nearly 50% of all waterborne foreign trade comes through West Coast ports, while the percentage from the Far East and Southeast Asia stands at nearly 80% (U.S. USDOT, 2002: 11). By 2002, West Coast ports were responsible for just over half of the U.S. container trade, and over 80% of trade with Asia (Mongelluzzo, 6/17/02).

Accompanying these commodities flows into the West Coast ports are the influx of goods via trucks from Mexico, coming via states such as California and most especially Texas, supplemented by railway shipments. Yet it is the contemporary dominance of the West Coast, especially Southern California, as a node for the flow of Asian commodities into the United States, that today makes workers in the logistics sector, most notably the growing Latin@ workforce, a potential Achilles heel of the giant U.S. retail firms and the global empires of production and trade of which they are an integral part; hence a strategic site for labor solidarity. The point has wider applicability as well of course. Without continuous distribution bringing commodities to consumers, global production and trade would freeze up, on rail, trucks and in the harbors. As labor struggles in logistics link together different industries, locales and workers in states and in the global economy, transport should be prioritized as a strategic site for global social movement unionism and transborder labor organizing.

Logistics, Latin@s and Labor: Present Possibilities in Comparative World-Historical Perspective

A brief review of the role of labor in the logistics sector of the United States is necessary to get a historical sense of the possibility for intranational and transnational solidarity among transportation workers, across lines of race, ethnicity and nationality, and the role Latin@ labor might play in such struggles today. This is important as the institutional structures of the past formed "track-laying vehicles," influencing not only the present but also future possibilities of working-class formation and solidarity within and across lines of race, ethnicity and gender.

In the late nineteenth century, U.S. rail workers, including immigrant and nonimmigrant Chinese, Latin@s, Irish, African Americans, laid the tracks necessary to effectively create a national economy (Saxton, 1971; Glenn, 2000). Rather than providing for new alliances, anti-Chinese sentiment, which predated job competition on the railroads by some two decades, became central to racialized and gendered processes of white male working-class formation in places like California at the turn of the century (Saxton, 1971). Rail workers, whose numbers were 1 million strong by 1900, played key roles in the labor struggles of this period, leading to the Great Rebellion of 1877 and the Deb's/ Pullman Rebellion of 1894. At a time when mass production had not yet led to massive concentrations of workforces, the railway working class alone had the numbers and the organic ability for national coordination needed to become a leading force in the workers struggle (Davis, 1986: 30; see also Stromquist, 1993). These dramatic outbreaks of class struggle in the Northeastern United States in 1877 followed closely on the heels of what W.E.B. Du Bois (1969) called the bargain of 1876–1877, wherein U.S. federal troops were withdrawn from the South. This dealt a telling blow to Black Reconstruction, setting back the possibility for true worker solidarity in the United States right up to the present. The failure of whites to seize the opportunity to ally with their black brethren during Reconstruction and thereafter helped ensure the defeat of railroad workers in 1877 and 1894 (see Du Bois, 1969).

U.S. propertied classes, armed with the power of the law, and backed up by state and privately funded violence, defeated similarly broad attempts at organizing workers in basic industry—including across divides of race, ethnicity, class and gender by the Knights of Labor—who also arose from class struggles on the railroad—and later the Wobblies. These defeats greatly contributed to the formation of the increasingly conservative AFL, based on old-stock immigrant workers, whose market bargaining power as skilled workers led them to form exclusivist male-dominated racist craft unions that eschewed social legislation

(Forbath, 1991; Mink, 1986). The violence of the propertied classes in defeating more progressive historical alternatives for labor ensured the path-dependent primacy of racist business unions led by old white immigrant skilled craft workers, led by the AFL, which emerged as the first continuous organization of U.S. workers to survive a prolonged recession. This posed a formidable obstacle to the organization of workers in basic industry, to which the AFL was largely opposed. The foundations were thus set for the AFL to become a junior partner in U.S. overseas expansion.

There was a close connection in this period between the struggle for the Open Shop at home and an Open Door for U.S. state-corporate expansion abroad. The drive to impose Taylorism and the Open Shop—through epic battles like Homestead in 1892—eliminated what Big Bill Haywood called "the managers brain under the workman's cap" which threatened management control over the production process (Montgomery, 1987; Misa, 1995). Late nineteenth-century Taylorism undermined the market bargaining power of skilled craft workers who once exercised great control over shop floor production. Though rarely mentioned, Taylor did much of his key work in the foundries of the late nineteenth century military-corporate complex, the naval shipyards producing battleships for the expansion of the U.S. formal and informal empires abroad (Misa, 1995; Smith, 1985). This early role of military-funded high technology—through Taylorism and then Fordism—in providing for the recomposition of the labor force, presaged the later centrality of technological developments emanating from the militarized state sector in the late twentieth-century shift to flexible production, namely the satellite-telecommunications-computer-information technology revolution.

Just as developments in the corporate sector were transferred to the military, so too did the military-led rationalization of industrial production make its' impact felt in the corporate sector. Here, the military-supported Taylorist and Fordist transformations of the labor process that undermined the bargaining power of labor ironically provided for its renewal on newly enlarged social foundations with the birth of industrial unionism and the CIO (Misa, 1995; Smith, 1985; Montgomery, 1987). This rising social power of labor was integral to the early reformist thrust of the New Deal. Similarly today the move to far-flung empires of flexible production and distribution through outsourcing, arms-length contracting and the like, while weakening labor, especially in the core, is also providing new strategic openings for workers. A review of the rise and demise of workers power in the twentieth century illustrates some of these possibilities (see also Arrighi, 1990; Silver, 2003).

During the first half of the twentieth century, the rising social power of U.S. labor was based on the militant organization of some 25 million second-generation ethnic immigrant workers in mass production industry (who with their 15 million parents constituted the majority of the working class), in alliance with select skilled craft labor (Davis, 1986: 55). Workers of color, including Latin@s and African Americans, recognizing the opportunities industrial unionism offered, became key allies in many organizing drives during this period (Stepan-Norris and Zeitlin, 2003). A key year in the upsurge was 1934, as a series of successful strikes in Toledo, Ohio, Minneapolis, Minnesota, and San Francisco rocked the nation, with the latter two—Teamsters and International Longshoremen's and Warehousemen's Union (ILWU)—playing decisive roles in establishing strong bases of class power among transport workers for half a century or more (Preis, 1964: ch. 4).

Minneapolis depended upon transport workers in rail and trucking to move goods. And yet, despite the strategic location of the city in networks of production and distribution, the area was a leading Open Shop city (Preis, 1964: 24). AFL Teamsters Local 574 spearheaded a series of strikes that developed into a virtual mini–civil war, with scores of workers and police killed. The work of 574, notably its legendary organizer Farrell Dobbs, became the basis for a successful 11 state over-the-road organizing campaign resulting in the first multistate regional unified contract in 1938, which directly or indirectly covered some 125,000 workers (Belzer, 2000: 24; La Botz, 1990: 83–102). During the San Francisco general strike of 1934, the Teamster's aided the Longshore workers, first by refusing to take or haul "freight to or from the docks" and later by joining in a solidarity strike; such models of cooperation, including through interracial alliances, opened the doors for the unionization of the trucking industry in Los Angeles and the West Coast as a whole (La Botz, 1990: 108, 109–111).

The transformation of the labor process through Taylorist and Fordist mass production and the partial homogenization of labor that went with this ushered in this rise of industrial unionism and the mass worker (Davis, 1986; Gordon, Edwards, and Reich, 1982; Fraser, 1991). Mass strikes, using innovative sit-down tactics, were integral in these gains of industrial unionism expressed in the rise of the CIO. Although workers of color and women were important in many of these drives, these fastest growing sectors of the workforce were significantly excluded from organized labor and/or discriminated against within their ranks during World War II and the Cold War (Davis, 1986: 74–101). During this period, unionization via bureaucratic fiat and massive injections of military demand stimulus took an increasingly lethal toll, becoming a substitute for mass organizing. Moreover, the postwar ejection of left-led unions from the CIO and labor's incorporation as a junior partner in U.S. overseas expansion during the Cold War spelled the defeat of possibilities for domestic and international labor solidarity, reinforcing sexism, racism, narrow nationalism and related forms of craft exclusivism and labor market segmentation within labor (Davis, 1986; Stepan-Norris and Zeitlin, 2003). Thus, even as the postwar networks of U.S. state and corporate power expanded exponentially overseas, at home U.S. labor began a slow and then rapid decline, leading it ultimately into a crisis from which it is still trying to recover.

Yet despite these massive defeats of labor unity that set definite limits on the postwar accord between labor and capital, organized labor in the United States nevertheless managed for a time to win impressive gains, as a focus on transport workers reveals. Trucking rose from a negligible role in the 1920s to employ over 7 million by 1961, becoming one of the two largest sectors of employment. Between 1948 and 1961, the share of intercity ton-mile movement captured by trucking doubled to 21%, while during this same period that of railroads declined from 65.24 to 43.21% (Sloane, 1991: 188–189). The Teamsters worked to raise and standardize wages across the country. They eventually negotiated the landmark National Master Freight Agreement (NMFA), achieving 60% unionization in trucking by 1980 and among the highest wages of all manufacturing workers (Belzer, 2000: 21–22, 26–27). Similarly, after a series of militant strikes on the West Coast, helped by a strong history of progressive left-wing unionism and rank-and-file democracy (one which continues today), the ILWU gained impressive benefits in exchange for greater managerial prerogative and control over the work process (Olney, 2003: 37).

This social power of labor expressed in the rising gains of the labor movement worldwide is today being undermined through flexible production and distribution systems that are critical aspects of contemporary globalization (see Sassen, 2001: 32–36). Increased capital mobility today intersects with the historic segmentation of workers so as to undermine labor's bargaining power in the United States and the advanced capitalist states by moving overseas, while employing cheap, largely unorganized women, persons of color and immigrants in the United States. The result has been the decline of the social power of organized labor in the core and the slow but rising influence of these growing sectors of the workforce in the United States and overseas (see Arrighi, 1990; Davis, 1986).

Fundamental to all of this is a revolution in the way goods are produced and distributed, shifting away from standardized mass production and consumption to more flexible forms of labor and batch production. These developments are today undermining the historic power of concentrated mass production workers. Just-in-time (JIT) production and delivery systems provide for external economies that cut down on overhead costs and are the basis for the organization revolution in the strategies and structures of global capitalism sweeping the world today. Crucial in this organizational revolution is control over and access to information necessary to control geographically dispersed far-flung production and logistics empires of flexible specialization (Bonacich, 2003: 42; Abernathy, Dunlop, Hammond, and Weil, 1999).

Though the global economy is centuries old, new here "is the increasing interpenetration of all economic processes at the international level with the system working as a unit, worldwide in real time" (Castells, 1989: 26). This system puts a premium on JIT production and distribution through dependent suppliers and their contingent workforces of flexible labor, all competing against each other for access to the markets monopolized by core firms (Cerna, Marshall, and Valdez, 2003: 38–41). A key aspect of this logistics revolution at the heart of contemporary globalization and offshore production networks is containerization. Such technical innovations make it possible to move goods interchangeably through a variety of transportation modes from production— road, rail, sea—to final destination with no unloading in between, in what is called intermodalism. Today, sped along by the deregulation of the transport sector and associated wave of competition and consolidation facilitating intermodalism, containers account for 60% of global trade, a figure expected to increase to 70% in 2010, with a single dockworker today able to carry a workload that it would have taken an army to do in the past (Coulter, 2002: 134). As for trucking during the period of deregulation, while the number of workers in this sector dramatically increased from 1,111,000 to 1,907,000 be- tween 1978 and 1996, an equally dramatic offensive against labor got underway. Unionized workers fell from some 60% to under 25% of drivers from 1980 to the present, with wages plummeting some 30% from 1977 to 1995, so that trucks are now what one author calls *Sweatshops on Wheels* (Belzer, 2000: 21).

While the Teamsters remain strong in small package transport firms such as United Parcel Service (UPS), West Coast port truckers saw the Teamsters union eliminated and replaced by thousands of nonunion immigrant Latin@ workers from Mexico and Central America. Whereas trucking firms used to pay for gas, pension and health insurance benefits, immigrant workers are to- day considered by employers and the National Labor Relations Board to be independent owner-operators, akin to contingent workers. Working in terrible conditions at bare minimum wages, these employees are legally barred from unionizing under antitrust law that makes much of their organizing illegal while granting limited antitrust immunity to large steamship firms (Early, 1998: 95–96; Bonacich, 2003: 45–46; Leyshon, 2000–2001). Despite these obstacles, these workers continue to stage massive demonstrations in an upsurge akin to the great wave of immigration and organizing that characterized a rapidly in- dustrializing U.S. economy in the late nineteenth and early twentieth centu- ries, whose penultimate expression was the rise of industrial unionism and the CIO (Early, 1998: 95–96; Davis, 2000: ch. 15; *Labor Notes*, 6/04).

Another integral part of the global logistics supply chain are distribution centers (DCs). With the rise of discount merchandising in retail, firms such as Wal-Mart sought to overcome the difficulties serving their primarily rural markets by inventing the DC in 1970 to buy goods in bulk, using information technology to track consumer purchases and transmit this to DCs and suppli- ers (Cerna, Marshall, and Valdez, 2003: 4). A key area for DCs is east of Los Angeles in Southern California's Inland Empire (Riverside and San Bernardino Counties, whose population came to some 3.2 million in 2000 and is pre- dicted to rise to over 6 million by 2025), centered around Ontario (Bonacich, 2003: 46; Davis, 2003). While nationally the workforce of the wholesale trade industry consists primarily of young white males between 18 and 40, in Southern California it appears to be staffed largely by young workers of color—especially Latin@s—with extensive use of temps (see Bonacich, 2003: 46; cf. Cerna, Marshall, and Valdez, 2003: 22).

As for the primarily white, black and Chicano West Coast Longshore workers—whose number fell from 28,000 to 10,500 from 1960 to the present—they are today faced with an offensive from employers, as evidenced in the lockout of the ILWU in the West Coast starting in September 2002. The Pacific Maritime Union (PMA)—the association of employers that negotiates contracts with longshore workers—and the West Coast Waterfront Coalition (WCWC)—an organization of the PMA's largest customers, notably giant retailing firms such as Wal-Mart, Home Depot and Payless shoes—were geared up for a confrontation and imposed the lockout after accusing the ILWU of a slowdown. The employer strategy was to get the WCWC (recently renamed the Waterfront Coalition) to demand "injunctive relief against the lockout and then press for severe economic and criminal sanctions against the ILWU under the provisions of the 80-day cooling off period" prescribed under Taft-Hartley. Instead President Bush enjoined the lockout and opened the ports, while refusing to move against the ILWU for violating the injunction, thus paving the way for a settlement. Longshore workers, less amenable to the rise of nonunion competitors as in trucking, maintain a strong bargaining position, yet one likely to be undermined unless workers throughout the cargo supply chain—an increasing number of them low-paid Latin@s—are organized (Olney, 2003).

Conclusion

Given the growing centrality of logistics in the Pacific triangle and global economy, transborder organizing among Latin@s and other workers here, despite serious obstacles, offers great potential. The possibilities can be seen in a variety of recent struggles, from the grocery lockout/strike to the wildcat action by Latin@ and African American port truckers (the former called troqueros), who left their massive trucks on the freeways to protest conditions, including rising gas prices, from April to May 2004, with concomitant delays for shippers reported throughout the Pacific Rim (see *Labor Notes*, 4/04, 6/04). Latin@ labor in the logistics sector of the Pacific Rim, the critical epicenter of the global market, may represent the Achilles heel of contemporary state-corporate globalization. Latin@ workers could be at the forefront in attempts to truly decolonize the global system by pressing forward with demands for universal equality and global citizenship. The argument put forward here is that the growing numbers of Latin@s in the United States and most especially in Southern California, places them at the strategic center of the world market at the heart of the contemporary world-system. For global corporate and military logistics is a crucial underpinning of the present structure of global power. The multiple forms of oppression Latin@s experience combined with their growing numbers and strategic location make it likely that they will be in the forefront of moves to forge broad interracial and transborder alliances aimed at transforming the global system in a more socially just and peaceful direction. As Latin America experiences continued socioeconomic disaster, what with the rise of rival lower-wage producers such as China, the newly emerging transnational workforce and reserve army of unemployed may be poised to reconstruct solidarity across borders, paving the way for a "second decolonization more radical than the first," as Ramón Grosfoguel has so eloquently argued.

References

Abernathy, Frederick H., John T. Dunlop, Janice H. Hammond, and David Weil, *A Stitch in Time*, New York: Oxford University Press, 1999.

Arrighi, Giovanni, "Marxist Century, American Century," *New Left Review*, Number 179, January/February, 1990, pp. 29–64.

Belzer, Michael H. *Sweatshops on Wheels*, New York: Oxford, 2000.

Boarnet, Marlon, and Randall Crane, *The Impact of Big Box Grocers on Southern California: Jobs, Wages & Municipal Finances*, September 1999.

Bonacich, Edna, "Pulling the Plug," *New Labor Forum* 12 (2), Summer 2003, pp. 41–48.

Castells, Manuel, *The Informational City*, Cambridge: Basil Blackwell, 1989.

Cerna, Anita, John Marshall, and Rebecca Valdez, *The Growing Role of Distribution Centers and Warehouses in the Retail Supply Chain*, Los Angeles: UCLA, 2003.

Coulter, Daniel Y., "Globalization of Maritime Commerce: The Rise of Hub Ports," in Sam J. Tangred, ed., *Globalization and Maritime Power*, Institute for National Strategic Studies, National Defense University Press, 2002, pp. 133–141.

Davis, Mike, *Prisoners of the American Dream*, New York: Verso, 1986.

——, *Magical Urbanism*, New York, London: Verso, 2000.

——, "Inland Empire," *The Nation*, April 7, 2003, pp. 15–18.

Davis, Mike, and Deepak Narang Sawhney, "*Sanbhashana*," in Deepak Narang Sawhney, ed., *Unmasking L.A.: Third World and the City*, New York: Palgrave, 2002, pp. 21–46.

Du Bois, W.E.B., *Black Reconstruction in America*, New York: Atheneum, 1969.

Early, Steve, "Membership-Based Organizing," in Gregory Mantsios, ed., *A New Labor Movement for the New Century*, New York: Monthly Review Press, 1998, pp. 82–103.

Forbath, William E., *Law and the Shaping of the American Labor Movement*, Cambridge, MA: Harvard University Press, 1991.

Fraser, Steven, *Labor Will Rule*, Ithaca, NY: Cornell University Press, 1991.

Glenn, Evelyn Nakano, *Unequal Freedom: How Race and Gender Shaped American Citizenship and Labor*, Cambridge, MA: Harvard University Press, 2002.

Gordon, David M., Richard Edwards, and Michael Reich, *Segmented Work, Divided Workers*, Cambridge: Cambridge University Press, 1982.

Labor Notes, various issues.

Leyshon, Hal, *Port Drivers Organizing*. Unpublished Manuscript, 2000–2001.

Mink, Gwendolyn, *Old Labor and New Immigrants in American Political Development: Union, Party, and State, 1875–1920*, Ithaca, NY: Cornell University Press, 1986.

Misa, Thomas, *A Nation of Steel*, Baltimore: Johns Hopkins, 1995.

Mongelluzzo, Bill, "Hasbro Bolts to S. California: Move Underscores Long Term Shift in Handling of Asian Imports," *Journal of Commerce*, 6/17/02, pp. 28–30.

Montgomery, David, *The Fall of the House of Labor*, Cambridge, UK: Cambridge University Press, 1987.

Olney, Peter, "On the Waterfront," *New Labor Forum* 12 (2), Summer 2003, pp. 33–40.

Peoples, James, "Deregulation and the Labor Market," *The Journal of Economic Perspectives*, Volume 12, #3, Summer 1998, pp. 111–130.

Preis, Art, *Labor's Giant Step*, New York: Pioneer Publishers, 1964.

Sassen, Saskia, *The Global City: New York, London, Tokyo*, Princeton, NJ: Princeton University Press, 1991, 2nd revised edition, 2001.

Saxton, Alexander, *The Indispensable Enemy: Labor and the Anti-Chinese Movement in California*, Berkeley: University of California Press, 1971.

Shaiken, Harley, "Grocery Strike Animates Unions," December 4, 2003, *Los Angeles Times*. *http://www.commondreams.org/views03/1204–05.htm*

Silver, Beverly J., *Forces of Labor: Workers' Movements and Globalization Since 1870*, New York: Cambridge University Press, 2003.

Sloane, Arthur A., *Hoffa*, Cambridge, MA: MIT University Press, 1991.

Smith, Merritt Roe, ed., *Military Enterprise and Technological Change: Perspectives on the American Experience*, Cambridge, MA: MIT University Press, 1985.

Stepan-Norris, Judith and Maurice Zeitlin, *Left Out: Reds and America's Industrial Unions*, New York: Cambridge University Press, 2003.

Stromquist, Shelton, *A Generation of Boomers*, University of Illinois Press, 1993.

U.S. Census Bureau, "The Hispanic Population of the United States: March 2002–June 2003." *http://www.census.gov/prod/2003pubs/p20–545.pdf.*

U.S. Department of Transportation, *Maritime Trade & Transportation*, '02. *http://www.bts.gov/products/maritime_trade_and_transportation/2002/pdf/entire.pdf.*

About the Editors and Contributors

James **Cohen,** a native of the United States, teaches political science at the University of Paris VIII (Saint-Denis, France) and at the Institute of Advanced Study of Latin America (IHEAL, Paris). He has recently published *Spanglish America: les enjeux de la latinisation des Etats-Unis* (Paris: Le Félin, 2005).

Enrique Dussel is Professor in the Philosophy Department at the Universidad Metropolitana de Mexico. He is one of the founders of philosophy of liberation in Latin America and has written more than 60 books. His most recent books are *Etica de la Liberacion en la Edad de la Globalizacion y la Exclusion* (Spain: Editorial Trotta) and *Hacia una Filosofia Politica* (Spain: Desclee).

James V. Fenelon is Associate Professor of Sociology at California State University. He is of Lakota/Dakota descent from the Standing Rock Sioux and the author of numerous articles on American Indians and indigenous peoples throughout the world-systems, including his work with Thomas D. Hall on globalization and indigenous peoples, and *Culturicide, Resistance, and Survival of the Lakota "Sioux Nation"* (Garland, 1998).

Lewis R. Gordon is Laura H. Carnell Professor of Philosophy at Temple University, where he is also director of the Institute for the Study of Race and Social Thought and the Center for Afro-Jewish Studies. He is President of the Caribbean Philosophical Association and author of several influential books, including the award-winning *Her Majesty's Other Children: Sketches of Racism from a Neocolonial Age* and the forthcoming *Disciplinary Decadence: Living Thought in Trying Times.*

Ramón Grosfoguel is Associate Professor in the Ethnic Studies Department at the University of California–Berkeley and Research Associate at the Maison des Science de l'Homme in Paris. He has published many articles on Caribbean migration to Western Europe and the United States and on the political economy of the world-system. His most recent book is *Colonial Subjects* (University of California Press, 2003).

Thomas D. Hall is Lester M. Jones Professor of Sociology at DePauw University. In addition to his work on indigenous peoples with James V. Fenelon, he is the author of *Rise and Demise: Comparing World-Systems* (with Christopher Chase-Dunn, Westview Press, 1997) and editor of *A World-Systems Reader: New*

Perspectives on Gender, Urbanism, Cultures, Indigenous Peoples, and Ecology (Rowman & Littlefield, 2000).

Roberto Hernández is a Graduate Fellow at the Institute for the Study of Social Change and doctoral candidate in the Ethnic Studies department at the University of California, Berkeley. He is currently completing a dissertation examining the multiple manifestations of violence on the U.S.-Mexico border in the context of nationalisms, coloniality, and the modern/colonial world-system.

Susanne Jonas is Professor and Associate Chair of Latin American and Latino Studies at the University of California–Santa Cruz and coordinator of the "Latinos in California" Research Cluster of UCSC's Chicano/Latino Research Center. She coedited *Immigration: A Civil Rights Issue for the Americas* (1999) and is working on a forthcoming book with Nestor Rodríguez about Guatemalan migrant communities in the United States.

Nelson Maldonado-Torres is Assistant Professor of Ethnic Studies at the University of California, Berkeley. His publications include, among others, "The Cry of the Self as a Call from the Other: The Paradoxical Loving Subjectivity of Frantz Fanon," *Listening: Journal of Religion and Culture* (Winter 2001) and "Postimperial Reflections on Crisis, Knowledge, and Utopia: Transgresstopic Critical Hermeneutics and the 'Death of European Man'" *Review* 25.3 (2002).

Walter D. Mignolo is William H. Wannamaker Professor at Duke University. Among his publications are *The Darker Side of the Renaissance: Literacy, Territoriality, and Colonization* (1995), *Local Histories/Global Designs: Coloniality, Subaltern Knowledge, and Border Thinking* (2000), and *The Idea of Latin America* (2005).

Agustín Lao-Montes is Assistant Professor in the Sociology Department at the University of Massachusetts at Amherst.

Laura E. Pérez is Associate Professor in the Department of Ethnic Studies at the University of California, Berkeley. She writes on U.S. Chicana/o, Latina/o and contemporary Latin American writing and visual and performance art. She is the author of *Altarities: Chicana Art, Politics, and Spirituality* (Duke University Press, 1996).

Thomas Ehrlich Reifer is Assistant Professor of Sociology and an affiliated faculty member in the Ethnic Studies Program at the University of San Diego. He is also Research Associate at the Institute for Research on World-Systems (IROWS) at the University of California–Riverside and the Fernand Braudel Center for the Study of Economies, Historical Systems, and Civilizations at Binghamton University. He edited *Globalization, Hegemony, and Power* (Paradigm, 2004).

José David Saldívar is Class of 1942 Professor in the Departments of Ethnic Studies and English at the University of California, Berkeley. He is the author of *Border Matters: Remapping American Cultural Studies* (1997) and *The Dialectics of Our America: Genealogy, Cultural Critique, and Literary History* (1991).

Santiago E. Slabodsky holds the Molly Spitzer Fellowship in Jewish Studies at the Centre for the Study of Religion at the University of Toronto, where he is completing his doctoral dissertation. He has studied and taught in Argentina, Israel, the United States, and Canada, and published in English, Spanish, and Hebrew.

Immanuel Wallerstein is Senior Research Scholar at Yale University and author, most recently, of *World-Systems Analysis: An Introduction* and *The Uncertainties of Knowledge.*

Political Economy of the World-System Annuals Series

Immanuel Wallerstein, Series Editor

I.   Kaplan, Barbara Hockey, ed., *Social Change in the Capitalist World Economy.* Political Economy of the World-System Annuals, 01. Beverly Hills/London: Sage Publications, 1978.

II.   Goldfrank, Walter L., ed., *The World-System of Capitalism: Past and Present.* Political Economy of the World-System Annuals, 02. Beverly Hills/London: Sage Publications, 1979.

III.   Hopkins, Terence K. & Immanuel Wallerstein, eds., *Processes of the World-System.* Political Economy of the World-System Annuals, 03. Beverly Hills/London: Sage Publications, 1980.

IV.   Rubinson, Richard, ed., *Dynamics of World Development.* Political Economy of the World-System Annuals, 04. Beverly Hills/London: Sage Publications, 1981.

V.   Friedman, Edward, ed., *Ascent and Decline in the World-System.* Political Economy of the World-System Annuals, 05. Beverly Hills/London/New Delhi: Sage Publications, 1982.

VI.   Bergesen, Albert, ed., *Crises in the World-System.* Political Economy of the World-System Annuals, 06. Beverly Hills/London/New Delhi: Sage Publications, 1983.

VII.   Bergquist, Charles, ed., *Labor in the Capitalist World-Economy.* Political Economy of the World-System Annuals, 07. Beverly Hills/London/New Delhi: Sage Publications, 1984.

VIII.   Evans, Peter, Dietrich Rueschemeyer & Evelyne Huber Stephens, eds., *States versus Markets in the World-System.* Political Economy of the World-System Annuals, 08. Beverly Hills/London/New Delhi: Sage Publications, 1985.

IX.   Tardanico, Richard, ed., *Crises in the Caribbean Basin.* Political Economy of the World-System Annuals, 09. Newbury Park/Beverly Hills/London/New Delhi: Sage Publications, 1987.

X.   Ramirez, Francisco O., ed., *Rethinking the Nineteenth Century: Contradictions and Movements.* Studies in the Political Economy of the World-System, 10. New York/Westport, CT/London: Greenwood Press, 1988.

XI.   Smith, Joan, Jane Collins, Terence K. Hopkins & Akbar Muhammad, eds., *Racism, Sexism, and the World-System.* Studies in the Political Economy of the World-System, 11. New York/Westport, CT/London: Greenwood Press, 1988.

XII.   (a) Boswell, Terry, ed., *Revolution in the World-System.* Studies in the Political Economy of the World-System, 12a. New York/Westport, CT/London: Greenwood Press, 1989.

XII. (b) Schaeffer, Robert K., ed., *War in the World-System*. Studies in the Political Economy of the World-System, 12b. New York/Westport, CT/London: Greenwood Press, 1989.

XIII. Martin, William G., ed., *Semiperipheral States in the World-Economy*. Studies in the Political Economy of the World-System, 13. New York/Westport, CT/London: Greenwood Press, 1990.

XIV. Kasaba, Resat, ed., *Cities in the World-System*. Studies in the Political Economy of the World-System, 14. New York/Westport, CT/London: Greenwood Press, 1991.

XV. Palat, Ravi Arvind, ed., *Pacific-Asia and the Future of the World-System*. Studies in the Political Economy of the World-System, 15. Westport, CT/London: Greenwood Press, 1993.

XVI. Gereffi, Gary & Miguel Korzeniewicz, eds., *Commodity Chains and Global Capitalism*. Studies in the Political Economy of the World-System, 16. Westport, CT: Greenwood Press, 1994.

XVII. McMichael, Philip, ed., *Food and Agrarian Orders in the World-Economy*. Studies in the Political Economy of the World-System, 17. Westport, CT: Greenwood Press, 1995.

XVIII. Smith, David A. & József Böröcz, eds., *A New World Order? Global Transformations in the Late Twentieth Century*. Studies in the Political Economy of the World-System, 18. Westport, CT: Greenwood Press, 1995.

XIX. Korzeniewicz, Roberto Patricio & William C. Smith, eds., *Latin America in the World-Economy*. Studies in the Political Economy of the World-System, 19. Westport, CT: Greenwood Press, 1996.

XX. Ciccantell, Paul S. & Stephen G. Bunker, eds., *Space and Transport in the World-System*. Studies in the Political Economy of the World-System, 20. Westport, CT: Greenwood Press, 1998.

XXI. Goldfrank, Walter L., David Goodman & Andrew Szasz, eds., *Ecology and the World-System*. Studies in the Political Economy of the World-System, 21. Westport, CT: Greenwood Press, 1999.

XXII. Derluguian, Georgi & Scott L. Greer, eds., *Questioning Geopolitics*. Studies in the Political Economy of the World-System, 22. Westport, CT: Greenwood Press, 2000.

XXIV. Grosfoguel, Ramón & Ana Margarita Cervantes-Rodriguez, eds., *The Modern/Colonial/Capitalist World-System in the Twentieth Century: Global Processes, Antisystemic Movements, and the Geopolitics of Knowledge*. Studies in the Political Economy of the World-System, 24. Westport, CT: Greenwood Press, 2002.

XXV. (a) Dunaway, Wilma A., ed., *Emerging Issues in the 21st Century World-System, Volume I: Crises and Resistance in the 21st Century World-System*. Studies in the Political Economy of the World-System, 25a. Westport, CT: Greenwood Press, 2003.

XXV. (b) Dunaway, Wilma A., ed., *Emerging Issues in the 21st Century World-System, Volume II: New Theoretical Directions for the 21st Century World-System*. Studies in the Political Economy of the World-System, 25b. Westport, CT: Greenwood Press, 2003.

XXVI. (a) Reifer, Thomas Ehrlich, ed., *Globalization, Hegemony & Power*. Political Economy of the World-System Annuals, 26a. Boulder, CO: Paradigm Publishers, 2004.

XXVI. (b) Friedman, Jonathan & Christopher Chase-Dunn, eds., *Hegemonic Decline: Present and Past*. Political Economy of the World-System Annuals, 26b. Boulder, CO: Paradigm Publishers, 2005.

XXVII. Tabak, Faruk, ed. *Allies as Rivals: The U.S., Europe, and Japan in a Changing World-System.* Political Economy of the World-System Annuals, 27. Boulder, CO: Paradigm Publishers, 2005.

XXVIII. Grosfoguel, Ramón, Nelson Maldonado-Torres, and José David Saldívar. eds., *Latin@s in the World-System: Decolonization Struggles in the Twenty-first Century U.S. Empire.* Political Economy of the World-System Annuals, 28. Boulder, CO: Paradigm Publishers, 2005.